LIVING GOD'S WORD

YEAR A

DAVID KNIGHT

LIVING GOD'S WORD

Reflections on the Weekly Gospels

YEAR **A**

ST. ANTHONY MESSENGER PRESS

Cincinnati, Ohio

Scripture citations are taken from the *New Revised Standard Version of the Bible*, copyright ©1989, by the Division of Christian Education of the National Council of the Churches of Christ in the USA. Used with permission. All rights reserved.

Excerpts from the English translation of the Introduction from the *Lectionary for Mass* ©1981, International Committee on English in the Liturgy, Inc., are used by permission. All rights reserved.

The excerpt from *The Education of an Archbishop* by Paul Wilkes, copyright ©1992, is used by permission of Orbis Books, Maryknoll, New York.

The excerpt from *The Documents of Vatican II*, Abbott-Gallagher, copyright ©1966, is reprinted with permission of America Press, Inc., 106 West 56th Street, New York, NY 10019. All rights reserved.

Cover design and illustrations by Karla Ann Sheppard
Book design by Mary Alfieri

ISBN 0-86716-306-2

Copyright ©1998, David Knight
All rights reserved.

Published by St. Anthony Messenger Press
Printed in the U.S.A.

Contents

Liturgical Calendar x

Introduction 1

Advent Season

First Sunday of Advent 8
Second Sunday of Advent 12
December 8 • Immaculate Conception 16
Third Sunday of Advent 18
Fourth Sunday of Advent 22

Christmas Season

Christmas 28
Sunday After Christmas (Holy Family) 32
January 1 • Solemnity of Mary, Mother of God 34
Epiphany 38

Ordinary Time (First Sunday of the Year Through Eighth Sunday of the Year)

First Sunday of the Year (Baptism of the Lord) 44
Second Sunday of the Year 48
Third Sunday of the Year 52
Fourth Sunday of the Year 56
Fifth Sunday of the Year 60
Sixth Sunday of the Year 64
Seventh Sunday of the Year 68
Eighth Sunday of the Year 72

Lent

Ash Wednesday and
Weekdays After Ash Wednesday 78
First Sunday of Lent 80
Second Sunday of Lent 84
Third Sunday of Lent. 88
Fourth Sunday of Lent. 92
Fifth Sunday of Lent 96
Passion (Palm) Sunday. 100

Easter Triduum and Easter

Easter Triduum
(Holy Thursday, Good Friday, Easter Vigil) 106
Easter Sunday 109
Second Sunday of Easter 113
Third Sunday of Easter 117
Fourth Sunday of Easter. 121
Fifth Sunday of Easter. 125
Sixth Sunday of Easter. 129
Ascension of the Lord 133
Seventh Sunday of Easter. 136
Pentecost 140

Ordinary Time (Ninth Sunday of the Year
Through Thirty-Fourth Sunday of the Year)

Ninth Sunday of the Year. 144
Tenth Sunday of the Year. 148
Eleventh Sunday of the Year 152
Twelfth Sunday of the Year 156
Thirteenth Sunday of the Year 160
Fourteenth Sunday of the Year. 164
Fifteenth Sunday of the Year 168
Sixteenth Sunday of the Year. 172
Seventeenth Sunday of the Year. 176
Eighteenth Sunday of the Year. 180

Nineteenth Sunday of the Year. 184
Twentieth Sunday of the Year. 188
Twenty-First Sunday of the Year 192
Twenty-Second Sunday of the Year 196
Twenty-Third Sunday of the Year. 200
Twenty-Fourth Sunday of the Year. 204
Twenty-Fifth Sunday of the Year 208
Twenty-Sixth Sunday of the Year. 212
Twenty-Seventh Sunday of the Year. 216
Twenty-Eighth Sunday of the Year. 220
Twenty-Ninth Sunday of the Year 224
Thirtieth Sunday of the Year 228
Thirty-First Sunday of the Year 232
Thirty-Second Sunday of the Year 236
Thirty-Third Sunday of the Year 240
Thirty-Fourth Sunday of the Year (Christ the King). . 244

Solemnities of the Lord During the Season of the Year

Trinity Sunday (Sunday After Pentecost) 250
Body and Blood of Christ (Corpus Christi) 253
Sacred Heart of Jesus
    (Friday of the Second Sunday After Pentecost) . . 255

Other Solemnities and Feasts Which Replace Sunday

February 2 • Presentation of the Lord. 258
June 24 • Birth of John the Baptist. 260
June 29 • Peter and Paul, Apostles 260
August 6 • Transfiguration of the Lord. 260
August 15 • Assumption of the Blessed Virgin 261
September 14 • Exaltation of the Cross 263
November 1 • All Saints. 264
November 2 • Commemoration of the
    Faithful Departed (All Souls). 266
November 9 • Dedication of the Lateran Basilica. . . 266

Feasts and Saints' Days

January 25 • Conversion of Paul, Apostle. 268

February 22 • Chair of Peter, Apostle. 268

March 19 • Joseph, Husband of Mary 268

March 25 • The Annunciation of the Lord 269

April 25 • Mark, Evangelist. 269

May 3 • Philip and James, Apostles 269

May 14 • Matthias, Apostle 269

May 31 • Visitation 270

June 11 • Barnabas, Apostle. 270

July 3 • Thomas, Apostle 270

July 22 • Mary Magdalene. 270

July 29 • Martha 271

August 10 • Lawrence, Deacon and Martyr 271

August 24 • Bartholomew, Apostle. 271

September 8 • Birth of Mary 271

September 15 • Our Lady of Sorrows. 272

September 21 • Matthew, Apostle and Evangelist. . . 272

September 29 • Michael, Gabriel and
     Raphael, Archangels 272

October 2 • Guardian Angels 272

October 18 • Luke, Evangelist 273

October 28 • Simon and Jude, Apostles 273

November 30 • Andrew, Apostle 273

December 12 • Our Lady of Guadalupe 273

LITURGICAL
CALENDAR

Liturgical Calendar

	1999 (A)	2000 (B)	2001(C)
1st Sunday of Advent	11/29/98	11/28/99	12/3/00
2nd Sunday of Advent	12/6/98	12/5/99	12/10/00
3rd Sunday of Advent	12/13/98	12/12/99	12/17/00
4th Sunday of Advent	12/20/98	12/19/99	12/24/00
Christmas	12/25/98	12/25/99	12/25/00
Holy Family	12/27/98	12/26/99	12/31/00
Octave of Christmas	1/1/99	1/1/00	1/1/01
Epiphany	1/3/99	1/2/00	1/7/01
Baptism of the Lord	1/10/99	1/9/00	1/8/01**
2nd Sunday of the Year	1/17/99	1/16/00	1/14/01
3rd Sunday of the Year	1/24/99	1/23/00	1/21/01
4th Sunday of the Year	1/31/99	1/30/00	1/28/01
5th Sunday of the Year	2/7/99	2/6/00	2/4/01
6th Sunday of the Year	2/14/99	2/13/00	2/11/01
7th Sunday of the Year	——	2/20/00	2/18/01
8th Sunday of the Year	——	2/27/00*	2/25/01
Ash Wednesday	2/17/99	3/8/00	2/28/01
First Sunday of Lent	2/21/99	3/12/00	3/4/01
Second Sunday of Lent	2/28/99	3/19/00	3/11/01
Third Sunday of Lent	3/7/99	3/26/00	3/18/01
Fourth Sunday of Lent	3/14/99	4/2/00	3/25/01
Fifth Sunday of Lent	3/21/99	4/9/00	4/1/01
Palm/Passion Sunday	3/28/99	4/16/00	4/8/01
Easter	4/4/99	4/23/00	4/15/01
Second Sunday of Easter	4/11/99	4/30/00	4/22/01
Third Sunday of Easter	4/18/99	5/7/00	4/29/01
Fourth Sunday of Easter	4/25/99	5/14/00	5/6/01
Fifth Sunday of Easter	5/2/99	5/21/00	5/13/01
Sixth Sunday of Easter	5/9/99	5/28/00	5/20/01
Ascension (Thursday)	5/13/99	6/1/00	5/24/01
Seventh Sunday of Easter	5/16/99	6/4/00	5/27/01
Pentecost	5/23/99	6/11/00	6/3/01

2002 (A)	2003 (B)	2004 (C)	2005 (A)	2006 (B)	2007 (C)
12/2/01	12/1/02	11/30/03	11/28/04	11/27/05	12/3/06
12/9/01	12/8/02	12/7/03	12/5/04	12/4/05	12/10/06
12/16/01	12/15/02	12/14/03	12/12/04	12/11/05	12/17/06
12/23/01	12/22/02	12/21/03	12/19/04	12/18/05	12/24/06
12/25/01	12/25/02	12/25/03	12/25/04	12/25/05	12/25/06
12/30/01	12/29/02	12/28/03	12/26/04	12/30/05	12/31/06
1/1/02	1/1/03	1/1/04	1/1/05	1/1/06	1/1/07
1/6/02	1/5/03	1/4/04	1/2/05	1/8/06	1/7/07
1/13/02	1/12/03	1/11/04	1/9/05	1/9/06**	1/8/07**
1/20/02	1/19/03	1/18/04	1/16/05	1/15/06	1/14/07
1/27/02	1/26/03	1/25/04	1/23/05	1/22/06	1/21/07
2/3/02	2/2/03	2/1/04	1/30/05	1/29/06	1/28/07
2/10/02	2/9/03	2/8/04	2/6/05	2/5/06	2/4/07
——	2/16/03	2/15/04	——	2/12/06	2/11/07
——	2/23/03	2/22/04	——	2/19/06	2/18/07
——	3/2/03	——	——	2/26/06	——
2/13/02	3/5/03	2/25/04	2/9/05	3/1/06	2/21/07
2/17/02	3/9/03	2/29/04	2/13/05	3/5/06	2/25/07
2/24/02	3/16/03	3/7/04	2/20/05	3/12/06	3/4/07
3/3/02	3/23/03	3/14/04	2/27/05	3/19/06	3/11/07
3/10/02	3/30/03	3/21/04	3/6/05	3/26/06	3/18/07
3/17/02	4/6/03	3/28/04	3/13/05	4/2/06	3/25/07
3/24/02	4/13/03	4/4/04	3/20/05	4/9/06	4/1/07
3/31/02	4/20/03	4/11/04	3/27/05	4/16/06	4/8/07
4/7/02	4/27/03	4/18/04	4/3/05	4/23/06	4/15/07
4/14/02	5/4/03	4/25/04	4/10/05	4/30/06	4/22/07
4/21/02	5/11/03	5/2/04	4/17/05	5/7/06	4/29/07
4/28/02	5/18/03	5/9/04	4/24/05	5/14/06	5/6/07
5/5/02	5/25/03	5/16/04	5/1/05	5/21/06	5/13/07
5/9/02	5/29/03	5/20/04	5/5/05	5/25/06	5/17/07
5/12/02	6/1/03	5/23/04	5/8/05	5/28/06	5/20/07
5/19/02	6/8/03	5/30/04	5/15/05	6/4/06	5/27/07

Feast of the Holy Family falls on Friday, December 30, 2005.
** Baptism of the Lord moves to Monday in these years.
* 9th Week of the Year precedes Ash Wednesday in 2000.

Liturgical Calendar

	1999 (A)	2000 (B)	2001(C)
Week of the Year	8th	10th	9th
Trinity Sunday	5/30/99	6/18/00	6/10/01
Week of the Year	9th	11th	10th
Body and Blood of Christ	6/6/99	6/25/00	6/17/01
Week of the Year	10th	12th	11th
Sacred Heart (Friday)	6/11/99	6/30/00	6/22/01
9th Sunday of the Year	——	3/5/00	——
10th Sunday of the Year	——	——	——
11th Sunday of the Year	6/13/99	——	——
12th Sunday of the Year	6/20/99	——	6/24/01
13th Sunday of the Year	6/27/99	7/2/00	7/1/01
14th Sunday of the Year	7/4/99	7/9/00	7/8/01
15th Sunday of the Year	7/11/99	7/16/00	7/15/01
16th Sunday of the Year	7/18/99	7/23/00	7/22/01
17th Sunday of the Year	7/25/99	7/30/00	7/29/01
18th Sunday of the Year	8/1/99	8/6/00	8/5/01
19th Sunday of the Year	8/8/99	8/13/00	8/12/01
20th Sunday of the Year	8/15/99	8/20/00	8/19/01
21st Sunday of the Year	8/22/99	8/27/00	8/26/01
22nd Sunday of the Year	8/29/99	9/3/00	9/2/01
23rd Sunday of the Year	9/5/99	9/10/00	9/9/01
24th Sunday of the Year	9/12/99	9/17/00	9/16/01
25th Sunday of the Year	9/19/99	9/24/00	9/23/01
26th Sunday of the Year	9/26/99	10/1/00	9/30/01
27th Sunday of the Year	10/3/99	10/8/00	10/7/01
28th Sunday of the Year	10/10/99	10/15/00	10/14/01
29th Sunday of the Year	10/17/99	10/22/00	10/21/01
30th Sunday of the Year	10/24/99	10/29/00	10/28/01
31st Sunday of the Year	10/31/99	11/5/00	11/4/01
32nd Sunday of the Year	11/7/99	11/12/00	11/11/01
33rd Sunday of the Year	11/14/99	11/19/00	11/18/01
Christ the King	11/21/99	11/26/00	11/25/01

2002 (A)	2003 (B)	2004 (C)	2005 (A)	2006 (B)	2007 (C)
7th	10th	9th	7th	9th	8th
5/26/02	6/15/03	6/6/04	5/22/05	6/11/06	6/3/07
8th	11th	10th	8th	10th	9th
6/2/02	6/22/03	6/13/04	5/29/05	6/18/06	6/10/07
9th	12th	11th	9th	11th	10th
6/7/02	6/27/03	6/18/04	6/3/05	6/23/06	6/15/07
——	——	——	——	——	——
6/9/02	——	——	6/5/05	——	——
6/16/02	——	——	6/12/05	——	6/17/07
6/23/02	——	6/20/04	6/19/05	6/25/06	6/24/07
6/30/02	6/29/03	6/27/04	6/26/05	7/2/06	7/1/07
7/7/02	7/6/03	7/4/04	7/3/05	7/9/06	7/8/07
7/14/02	7/13/03	7/11/04	7/10/05	7/16/06	7/15/07
7/21/02	7/20/03	7/18/04	7/17/05	7/23/06	7/22/07
7/28/02	7/27/03	7/25/04	7/24/05	7/30/06	7/29/07
8/4/02	8/3/03	8/1/04	7/31/05	8/6/06	8/5/07
8/11/02	8/10/03	8/8/04	8/7/05	8/13/06	8/12/07
8/18/02	8/17/03	8/15/04	8/14/05	8/20/06	8/19/07
8/25/02	8/24/03	8/22/04	8/21/05	8/27/06	8/26/07
9/1/02	8/31/03	8/29/04	8/28/05	9/3/06	9/2/07
9/8/02	9/7/03	9/5/04	9/4/05	9/10/06	9/9/07
9/15/02	9/14/03	9/12/04	9/11/05	9/17/06	9/16/07
9/22/02	9/21/03	9/19/04	9/18/05	9/24/06	9/23/07
9/29/02	9/28/03	9/26/04	9/25/05	10/1/06	9/30/07
10/6/02	10/5/03	10/3/04	10/2/05	10/8/06	10/7/07
10/13/02	10/12/03	10/10/04	10/9/05	10/15/06	10/14/07
10/20/02	10/19/03	10/17/04	10/16/05	10/22/06	10/21/07
10/27/02	10/26/03	10/24/04	10/23/05	10/29/06	10/28/07
11/3/02	11/2/03	10/31/04	10/30/05	11/5/06	11/4/07
11/10/02	11/9/03	11/7/04	11/6/05	11/12/06	11/11/07
11/17/02	11/16/03	11/14/04	11/13/05	11/19/06	11/18/07
11/24/02	11/23/03	11/21/04	11/20/05	11/26/06	11/25/07

Introduction

*"By means of sacred scripture, read during the
liturgy of the word and explained during the homily,
'God speaks to his people, revealing the mystery of
their redemption and salvation and offering them
spiritual nourishment. Through his word, Christ
himself is present in the assembly of his people.'
Thus the Church at Mass 'receives the bread of life
from the table of God's word and unceasingly offers
it to the faithful.'"[1]*

There is mystery to ponder in these lines from the
Introduction to the *Lectionary for Mass*. But, in
practice, listening to the readings at Sunday Mass can
be frustrating. We frequently do not understand them. And
the more we do understand, the more we would like time to
reflect on them and absorb them—time not provided during
Mass. We are left feeling incomplete.

This is not only frustrating; it is dangerous. If our only
exposure to Scripture is at Sunday Mass and if we do not
understand what we hear, we will conclude, as many
Catholics have, that we "just don't understand" the Bible.
The obvious answer to this—"How can you understand it if
you don't read it?"—is countered by, "I hear it on Sundays,
and I don't understand it." So the danger is that we will not
ever begin reading the Bible because our experience of it at
Sunday Mass has been uninspiring or even frustrating.

This book will not change all of that, but it can help.

Typically, the liturgy includes four biblical passages
on Sunday. A Gospel passage is the centerpiece; preceding
it are a reading from the Old Testament, a psalm prayed or
sung as a response and a passage from another of the New
Testament writings.

This book will tell you what the readings are so that each

week, if you desire, you can look them over ahead of time, see the context in which they are found, call someone you know to ask about anything you don't understand, and come to Mass on Sunday prepared to sit back, enjoy and absorb what you hear.

I have been publishing weekly reflections like these in my Sunday bulletin for ten years. I began writing them because I remembered telling someone the year I graduated from high school that I could not remember one homily that had been preached in my parish church my whole life long. (In those days they were called sermons.) My experience was that, even if what was said in church inspired me momentarily, I never thought about it again once Mass was over. As a result, any seed planted in my mind died before it had a chance to root itself in my heart through decisions. The fault was not in the preacher; it was in the fact that I never took time to think about what I had heard.

I began publishing in the parish bulletin the main thoughts of my homilies in the hope that someone might read and reflect on them. And the feedback from the people was very good. Several told me they were sticking the bulletin on their refrigerator door and using it for meditation all during the week, especially the reflections on the daily readings.

All the reflections in these pages are based on the Gospel of the particular Sunday or weekday. I frequently approach the Gospel asking what light it casts on a particular question. For example, I might ask for several weeks in a row what the Gospel for the Sunday tells us about Baptism or another sacrament. When I do this, my concern is to find what there is in the reading itself, in its true meaning and interpretation, that relates to the topic at hand. The reflections are homilies; that is, reflections on the Scripture readings themselves, not sermons that develop topics for their own sake. But I have found that to approach any passage of Scripture with a question drawn from one's present concerns or experience of life is a way to discover in the text rich veins of meaning previously unmined.

How to Use This Book

I suggest that you read the reflection on the Sunday Gospel first. Ask yourself what this Gospel or this reflection says to you, what meaning it has for you. Then ask yourself what you intend to do about it.

In the section entitled "Living This Week's Gospels," I offer for each week five suggested responses you can make to the Gospel. These are based on five words which summarize our identity as Christians. Every one of us is a Christian by belief in Jesus Christ as Savior. And every one of us is called to be a disciple, which means to lead a life characterized by reflection on the teaching and example of Jesus, the Master of the Way.

In addition, at Baptism each of us was anointed with chrism and consecrated by God to continue Jesus' work as Prophet, Priest and King. These three words give us our job description as Christians.

Each week therefore offers a suggestion about how to express and live out our belief in Jesus as Savior and as Teacher (being a Christian and a disciple); how to bear witness to him in action (being a prophet); how to minister to others and nurture them (sharing in his priesthood); and how to work for the extension of his reign over every area and activity of human life (being responsible stewards of his kingship). No one could possibly live out all of these suggestions all the time, but you might try each one for a day. Or pick one and work at it all week.

For each day of the week I have chosen one line from the day's Gospel and offered one question to stimulate reflection. The ideal, of course, would be to read the whole Gospel passage for yourself—or, if your schedule permits, go to daily Mass and get it live! But in today's busy world, you may have only time to read one line and to think about one question whenever you can during the day.

Finally, there is a prayer that you can say each day all week, asking for the grace to live by the values proposed in the Sunday reflection. Repeated prayer increases desire.

Drawing People Together

Christian discipleship is both personal and communal. We grow in grace together. We nourish our hearts while we nourish the hearts of others. And so you could use this book to draw closer to others in the communion of the Holy Spirit while you yourself draw closer to God.

Invite someone to read the reflections with you and talk about them. Ask such questions as, "What does this say to you? How do you feel about it? What do you think you could do in response to it?" If you do this with family or close friends, it will raise the level of your interaction and deepen your understanding of each other. If you invite acquaintances, you will turn them into friends.

The Sunday Readings

The Sunday readings are presented in a three-year cycle (Years A, B and C). Over the course of the three years we hear the main sections of all four Gospels: Matthew in Year A (this volume), Mark in Year B, Luke in Year C. (Matthew, Mark and Luke are called the *Synoptics*, "seen as a whole," because they follow the same basic outline of Jesus' life and death. John's Gospel, written later, reflects on the *meaning* of Jesus' life and death.) In Year B, instead of Mark's version of the multiplication of the loaves, the liturgy inserts John's, along with its following teaching about the Bread of Life.

The Old Testament readings for Sundays were chosen individually because they relate in some way to the theme of the Gospel. They are presented as isolated passages, not book by book. There is no sequence or pattern in the order in which the books from the Old Testament appear. What we should be alert to, therefore, is the unity between the Old and New Testament readings, which becomes visible to us when we see how events or themes in both of them are related to each other.

The selections from other New Testament writings (Acts, the Letters and the Book of Revelation) are read "semicontinuously," that is, the main passages from one letter or book are presented sequentially. Because the readings from each book are presented as a block, it is possible to study each one as a whole during the period when selections from it are being read at Mass.

The Sunday and weekday liturgies together expose us to 128 of the 150 Psalms. The verses we use as responsorial chants are chosen to be responses to the readings they follow.

The Weekday Readings

The weekday readings are not geared to match the Sunday readings at all; they are a completely independent selection. Instead of an ABC cycle, there is a two-year cycle for the weekday readings (Year I and Year II). Only the first reading changes; the weekday Gospels are the same every year. To help us easily remember what year we are in, an odd-numbered year (like 1997, 1999) will always be Year I; Year II will always be a number divisible by two (1998, 2000).

During the Season of the Year or Ordinary Time, the weekday Gospels begin with the first one to be written, Mark (Weeks 1-9), and go straight through selected passages from Matthew (Weeks 10-21) and Luke (Weeks 22-34). Daily participation in the Eucharist gives us a tour of these three Gospels (the Synoptics) every year.

About half the selections for the first reading on weekdays come from the Old Testament. There is no precise order in the way the books are presented—Old and New Testament readings are interspersed during the year with no obvious guiding pattern—but, with a few exceptions all the readings from each book will be given consecutively. We can therefore study each book in turn while selections from it are read at Mass. In a given year, the Old Testament books are presented approximately in the order in which they were written. All of the Old Testament books except Obadiah and Judith and all of the New Testament books are represented in the readings.

During special seasons (Advent, Christmas, Lent and Easter) the themes of the season determine the choice of readings.

Special feasts and saints' days also have their own readings, which replace the weekday and sometimes the Sunday readings. Reflections for these special feasts are in a section of their own.

A liturgical calendar or church bulletin will aid tremendously in helping to match the date with the corresponding reflection. (See page x.)

"A Fountain of Renewal"

The introduction to the Roman *Lectionary for Mass* begins:

> The Church loves sacred scripture and is anxious to deepen its understanding of the truth and to nourish its own life by studying these sacred writings. The Second Vatican Council likened the bible to a fountain of renewal within the community of God's people and directed that in the revision of liturgical celebrations there should be "more abundant, varied and appropriate reading from sacred scripture." The council further directed that at Mass "the treasures of the bible should be opened up more lavishly so that richer fare might be provided for the faithful at the table of God's word. In this way a more representative portion of sacred scripture will be read to the people over a set cycle of years."[2]

That is the motive and prayer behind the writing of this book.

Notes

[1] Introduction, #1, *Lectionary for Mass*, copyright © 1970 by International Commission on English in the Liturgy. Used with permission.

[2] Ibid.

ADVENT
SEASON

First Sunday of Advent

To Be Human Is to Be Aware

Isaiah 2:1-5; Romans 13:11-14; Matthew 24:37-44

Awareness should characterize of human life; not just awareness of what we can see and hear around us, but also awareness of what we know through thinking. We know, for example, with absolute certainty that we were born and we are going to die. This makes us aware that *life* for us means the same thing as *time*. What we do with our time is what we do with our lives. Whatever we give our time to, we are giving our lives to. And whatever we were given life for, that is what we have time for. It is all we have time for! To live in a fully human way, we need to be aware of this. To be caught up simply in "eating and drinking, marrying and giving in marriage," working and surviving, is to lose sight of the limits of life; it is to lose the picture.

The Gospel tells us something we could not know except by faith, unless God told us: The real focus of time is on Jesus Christ's coming in glory. The purpose of human life is to prepare and to be prepared for the coming of Jesus Christ. As Christians, we have been given to know with more than human knowledge that our goal is something more than human existence. The goal of human life is to grow into the fullness of Christ as members of his Body (see Ephesians 1:23; 4:13; Colossians 1:15, 19, 24). We need to remain aware, then, that we are here to spend our time on something more than human life.

Isaiah describes how God helps us do this: "In days to come / the mountain of the LORD's house / shall be established as the highest of the mountains...all the nations shall stream to it. / Many peoples shall come and say, "Come, let us go up to the mountain of the LORD, / to the house of the God of Jacob; / that he may teach us his ways and that we may walk in his paths."

The Church was established to be "the light of the world, a city built on a hill," to give light to everyone who comes to be instructed in God's ways and to walk in the divine path (see Matthew 5:14-16). For from the Church "shall go forth instruction, and the word of the LORD." The Church—and that means us, all of us as a community and each one of us as a member of that community—is commissioned by Jesus to be the light of Christ, to preserve the light of Christ, and to provide the light of Christ to the world. If we lose our awareness of this and get caught up in "eating and drinking, marrying and giving in marriage"—that is, with the immediate preoccupations of work and study, family and social life, professional and civic involvement—without relating these to the coming of Jesus Christ and the real goal of human existence, then we lose the light. Like the bridesmaids who fell asleep waiting for the bridegroom, we let our lamps go out. We fail in faith and in awareness (see Matthew 25:1-13).

Saint Paul writes to the Romans and to us, "[Y]ou know what time it is, how it is now the moment for you to wake from sleep.... [N]ight is far gone, the day is near. Let us then lay aside the works of darkness and put on the armor of light." We know what human life is all about. We know its purpose and where it is heading. We know we were created to find our fulfillment in Christ and to let Christ come to fulfillment in us. We fulfill our destiny and let Christ fulfill his destiny of uniting and reconstituting all things in himself, under his headship, through our surrender to his instruction, by keeping awake and aware so that we can "walk in the light of the Lord."

In Christ, God has broken into history, intervened in human events and given a new direction and goal to human life. In us—through what we say and do, through the choices which shape us as persons, through the enlightened awareness which guides them and through the instruction he gives us through his Church—Christ continues to prepare the world for his coming. A fully human life includes awareness of this.

Reflecting on This Week's Gospels

First Week of Advent

Pray daily: O God, my heart desires the warmth of your love, and my mind is searching for the light of your Word. Increase my longing for Jesus. Amen.

Monday: Matthew 8:5-11. Jesus was amazed and said to those following him, "Truly I tell you, in no one in Israel have I found such faith." Who is Jesus for you? How do you relate to him?

Tuesday: Luke 10:21-24. Jesus said, "I thank you, Father, Lord of heaven and earth, because you have hidden these things from the wise and intelligent and have revealed them to infants." What is the difference between *knowing about* Jesus and *knowing* Jesus? What has been your experience of God's action in your life?

Wednesday: Matthew 15:29-37. Jesus summoned his disciples and said, "I have compassion for the crowd.... I do not want to send them away hungry." What hunger in you does Jesus want to satisfy? How has he done it in the past? How do you suspect that he wants to do it now?

Thursday: Matthew 7:21, 24-27. "Everyone then who hears these words of mine and acts on them will be like a wise man who built his house on rock." Can you say that your life is built on the words of Jesus? How do you use Scripture in your life?

Friday: Matthew 9:27-31. When he entered the house the blind men came to him. "And Jesus said to them, 'Do you believe that I am able to do this [heal you]?'" Do you really believe that Jesus can heal whatever is wrong in your life? What do you really trust to save you from your fears?

Saturday: Matthew 9:35—10:1, 6-8. "Jesus went about all the cities and villages, teaching in their synagogues, and proclaiming the good news of the kingdom, and curing every disease and every sickness." Have you experienced parts of Jesus' ministry (teaching, proclaiming and curing) in the Church? Have you experienced them as the action of Jesus in your life?

Living This Week's Gospels

As Christian: This week put your watch on a different hand or change the position of your clock to remind you that time has a new meaning.

As Disciple: Read the opening lines of each of the four Gospels, asking why the author chose to begin that way.

As Prophet: Reflect on your use of time. How does your daily schedule bear witness to the value Jesus Christ has given to time?

As Priest: Spend some time each day, even a few moments, ministering to other people.

As King: This week change one thing, no matter how small, at home or at work to make the world different because you were there.

Second Sunday of Advent

Human Acts Reveal Grace

Isaiah 11:1-10; Romans 15:4-9; Matthew 3:1-12

Isaiah presents a promise of divine goodness expressed in human acts, a vision of joy that gives hope. A human Messiah will come, "a shoot...from the stump of Jesse." The "spirit of the LORD" will be visible in him through behavior which reveals what today we call the gifts of the Holy Spirit: wisdom, understanding, knowledge, counsel, piety, fortitude and fear of the Lord. Divine power will be evident in the fruit of the Messiah's mission: The wolf shall live with the lamb; "[t]hey will not hurt or destroy...for the earth will be full of the knowledge of the LORD, as the waters cover the sea." Grace will be visible.

John the Baptizer holds out the same hope and gives the same message, but his emphasis is different. He focuses on what we should do to let the grace and power of God appear in our lives: "Repent, for the kingdom of heaven has come near.... Bear fruit worthy of repentance.... [E]very tree...that does not bear good fruit is cut down...." John calls people to express their response in human actions by being baptized and confessing their sins. He expresses his own faith by dressing in camel skins and living on locusts and wild honey.

What John shows us is Jesus impacting our lives like a meteor smacking into a planet. "The Messiah is here! The Reign of God is at hand! Wake up! Change! Get moving! Do something about it!" John believes in our ability to choose and respond, in the importance of our making human choices and acting on them. John presents Jesus Christ as the one who comes to bring us to life, to spark us into action. Jesus' coming stimulates and activates our human powers.

But all is not human action here. John boldly announces the action of God: "I baptize you with water for repentance, but one who is more powerful than I is coming after me....

He will baptize you with the Holy Spirit and fire." The "fruitful tree" is not the person who performs good acts, but the one who performs divine acts. Like the fruit of Mary's womb, the fruit of our lives must be divine—the fruit of the Holy Spirit acting within us, acting through our human actions.

Jesus is God made man: fully human and fully divine. We who are the Body of Christ on earth are called to be fully human and fully divine in everything we do—by letting God, who dwells within us and anoints us with divine grace, be reflected in everything we do. We live the life of grace; we grow in grace by letting it express itself in and through our human actions. We grow in faith by letting our faith in Christ's teachings reveal itself in our life-style. We grow in hope by letting hope in Christ's promises guide our choices. We grow in love by letting our love for God take flesh in all our words and actions.

Saint Paul teaches that the source of our unity as a community is common effort and encouragement of each other to live out what we believe. We will neither always agree on what we should do nor succeed in doing it; but if we have patience and encourage one another, we will be able to live in harmony "in accordance with Christ Jesus." To accept our humanness means accepting ourselves as imperfect and incomplete yet intended to grow toward perfection. Jesus, the shoot growing up from the "stump of Jesse," represents God's power acting in human events; this gives us hope (see Romans 14:1—15:13).

Paul's practical advice is to read Scripture. "For whatever was written in former days was written for our instruction, so that by steadfastness and by the encouragement of the scriptures we might have hope." In Scripture God expresses to us divine truth in human words. By making human efforts to understand God's human words, we grow in union with God. Then God's grace will be visible in us.

Reflecting on This Week's Gospels

Second Week of Advent

> *Pray daily: Lord, you came to share completely in our human condition except for sin. Give me a desire to share completely in your divine life. Draw me to study your mind and heart. Amen.*

Monday: Luke 5:17-26. " 'But so that you [the scribes and Pharisees] may know that the Son of Man has authority on earth to forgive sins,' Jesus said to the man who was paralyzed, 'I say to you, stand up and take your bed and go to your home.' " Which visible, human acts reveal the power of grace in you?

Tuesday: Matthew 18:12-14. "If a shepherd has a hundred sheep, and one of them has gone astray, does he not leave the ninety-nine on the mountains and go in search of the one that went astray?" Do you know any Christian who feels alienated from the Christian community? What can you do to show that person God's love, concern and invitation?

Wednesday: Matthew 11:28-30. "For my yoke is easy, and my burden is light." Is it a crushing burden to try to live on God's level in all we do? What makes it light?

Thursday: Matthew 11:11-15. "Truly I tell you, among those born of women no one has arisen greater than John the Baptist; yet the least in the kingdom of heaven is greater than he." What have we received from God that is greater than anything we could receive from our greatest efforts at prayer and fasting?

Friday: Matthew 11:16-19. "[T]he Son of Man came eating and drinking, and they say, 'Look, a glutton and a drunkard....'" Is any pleasure that God created bad in itself? What is the Christian reason for abstaining from food, drink or anything else?

Saturday: Matthew 17:10-13. "I tell you that Elijah has already come, and they did not recognize him...." What things are happening in the Church that you might not recognize as God's divine action?

Living This Week's Gospels

As Christian: When the water is added to the wine at Mass, ask God to join your humanity to Jesus' divinity, totally and intimately.

As Disciple: Put a copy of the Bible in some visible place at home or at work to remind you to live out in daily life what you believe.

As Prophet: Each day this week make one choice that is a conscious, deliberate response to something Jesus said or did.

As Priest: Make a list of principles drawn from Jesus' teaching that really are a unifying rule of life in your family or circle of friends.

As King: Ask what fruit you have borne for the Kingdom of God in your professional, social and family life.

December 8 • Immaculate Conception

A Sign of God's Mercy

Genesis 3:9-15, 20; Ephesians; 1:3-6, 11-12; Luke 1:26-38

Mary's Immaculate Conception is a key to understanding God's mercy to us. To have mercy is not just to help someone; it is to come to the aid of another out of a sense of relationship. To give aid to panhandlers on the street, for example, while seeing them as winos or simply as "them" rather than as "us" is not mercy; it is condescension—especially if we write them off as hopeless wrecks from whom nothing can really be expected.

If a recovering alcoholic who used to beg on the street—someone who has "been there"—offers help to one who is still there, that is very different. That is to have mercy; it comes from a sense of relationship.

If God had saved us purely from above, without involving human nature in the work of redemption at all, that actually would have shown contempt for human nature. It would have been God's admission that the humanity he created was hopelessly flawed and could only be saved as inert matter, by the unassisted action of God alone. And this was, as a matter of fact, an underlying theme in the Protestant reformers who taught that human nature is so corrupt that no good actions a person performs, even by the help of God's grace, can truly be called the work of a human being. Martin Luther taught that we are saved by the grace of God and the working of the Holy Spirit alone, without any human action. This position is rooted in the belief that no good work a human being does can be attributed to that person at all; the goodness of the action is one hundred percent due to God alone. Those who think like this conclude quite naturally that to honor Mary, the saints or any human being for good deeds performed in grace is to rob God of glory by glorifying a creature.

Catholics, on the other hand, insist on the basic goodness of human nature. A modern Protestant theologian, Karl Barth, sees devotion to Mary as the key to this Catholic belief: "The Mother of God of...Catholic dogma is, quite simply, the principle, prototype and summing-up of the human creature cooperating in its own salvation.... Thus, that Church in which there is a cult of Mary must be itself understood as...that Church of man who, by virtue of grace, cooperates with grace.

Catholics would say, "Yes, what is the problem?" This is because Catholics were never taught that human beings are so incapable of anything good that they can't even cooperate with God by freely accepting the gift of grace. Catholics honor Mary for agreeing to be the Mother of God, and honor the saints and all people who accept and use the graces they are given to do the beautiful things they do. We say that the saints are the glory of God because they show the triumph of Christ's death over sin. The proof that Jesus really did win is that we are actually healed and restored, made holy by grace inside and out.

The Immaculate Conception requires us to believe that human beings have a part to play in redeeming the world. God became a man by taking real human flesh from a real human being. That is why Jesus is truly one of us. And that is the mystery of the way God "has mercy" on us: God comes to our aid as one of us. The Lord, the Christ we ask to have mercy, comes to our aid out of a sense of relationship based on our shared humanity.

And this is the reason why Mary, from the first instant of her conception in her mother's womb, had to be preserved from all sin: it was so that the flesh she gave to be the flesh of God, the flesh which would save the world from sin, would never itself have been under the power of sin. Because of the Immaculate Conception, God could take pure flesh from Mary and have mercy on us as one of our own race. Every time we pray "Lord, have mercy," we thank God for the gift of the Immaculate Conception, which is a sign to us of what that mercy is.

Third Sunday of Advent

Seeing What Is There

Isaiah 35:1-6a, 10; James 5:7-10; Matthew 11:2-11

John the Baptist was in Herod's dungeon, expecting the Messiah to deliver him. Since John could not understand why Jesus did not do so, he finally sent a poignant message through his disciples, "Are you the one who is to come, or are we to wait for another?" Jesus tells John not to let his preconceived ideas of what the Messiah should do block John from understanding what Jesus is doing: He is ministering to the poor and afflicted. If it isn't exactly what John expected, he must not let that be an obstacle to accepting Jesus as he is.

Jesus is calling on John—and through him on us all— to believe in Jesus by a free choice. He wants us to believe because we freely choose to recognize him as Savior and as God. Every rational conclusion, as a matter of fact, is a free choice, a judgment for which we take responsibility. Faith is no exception to this. But because faith is an acceptance of the person of Jesus Christ, the choice to believe in him is also an act of love. In the last analysis, to believe in and hope in Christ unconditionally, we need to love him unconditionally. It is a theme of the Gospel According to John that our recognition of truth depends on our love for goodness (see John 8:42-47).

Isaiah invites us to keep our love alive by dreaming of what God's messenger comes to do: The desert shall rejoice and blossom; we will see the glory and majesty of our God; the blind will see, the deaf hear, the speechless will sing, the lame shall leap like deer. Those whom the Lord has ransomed shall return and come to Zion with singing. Sorrow and sighing shall flee. Our God is coming. We need to recall this in order to strengthen weak hands and feeble knees and to reassure ourselves when we are frightened.

James writes similarly in his letter: "Strengthen your hearts, for the coming of the Lord is near." James offers three practical suggestions: (1) Be patient like farmers who wait for the earth to produce its crop. (2) Don't criticize one another. Focusing on faults and failings in the Church often fosters only discouragement. (3) Look to the prophets for encouragement, to those who have borne witness to Christ regardless of the cost to themselves.

In effect, James simply reworks what Jesus said to John: "Persevere in faith and hope out of love. Do not judge God or the Church by what is not happening or get fixated on what you think God should be accomplishing through the Church. Look at what *is* happening. Those blind to faith are beginning to see; those deaf to God's word are beginning to listen; the poor are having the gospel preached to them. Ministry is taking place and God's power is working through all of it. Grace is visible in human beings, in human actions in the Church, right now for those who have eyes to see."

When we see God embodied in the human—as in Jesus, the "shoot from the stump of Jesse"—or when we see in the Church grace made visible in human actions grounded in faith, hope or love, this encourages us. It confirms our faith, strengthens our hope, excites our love. When God's presence and action through grace are made visible in human actions, we find it easier to believe the divine promises, the vision of joy and peace which Isaiah holds out to us.

That is why we need saints and modern-day prophets. Such prophets point out to us how the general, abstract teachings of Jesus apply to the concrete circumstances of our time and place. We are consecrated by Baptism to do this for each other by enfleshing in our lives the attitudes and values of the gospel.

Note: There are special readings for December 17-24. When some of these dates fall in the Third Week of Advent, omit the readings below and use those following the Fourth Sunday of Advent. See the Liturgical Calendar on page x.

Reflecting on This Week's Gospels

Third Week of Advent

Pray daily: Lord, give me the grace never to turn away from you or from your Church because my own expectations are not being met. Teach me to look always at what is most authentic and most inspiring; help me to embrace these for myself. Amen.

Monday: Matthew 21:23-27. Jesus said to them in reply, "I will also ask you one question.... Did the baptism of John come from heaven, or was it of human origin?" Can you say without hesitation that the Church is of divine origin? How does that help?

Tuesday: Matthew 21:28-32. Jesus said to them, "Truly I tell you, the tax collectors and the prostitutes are going into the kingdom of God ahead of you." Do you take the benefits of your religion for granted? Who are some modern-day prophets?

Wednesday: Luke 7:18-23. "John summoned two of his disciples and sent them to the Lord to ask, 'Are you the one who is to come, or are we to wait for another?'" What disappoints you in the Church? Does it come more from human weakness or from malice? Would focusing more on the blessings of God's word, the sacraments, the example of the saints help you deal with this disappointment? Does it require other action?

Thursday: Luke 7:24-30. "What did you go out into the wilderness to look at? A reed shaken by the wind? ...Someone dressed in soft robes?.... A prophet?" What are you really seeking from the Church's ministers? Are you willing to be shaken up? Challenged? How have you responded to modern-day prophets?

Friday: John 5:33-36. "He was a burning and shining lamp, and you were willing to rejoice for a while in his light." Has anyone in the Church inspired you? How? Have you ever changed something in your own life because of someone else's example?

Saturday. *See readings for December 17-24.*

Living This Week's Gospels

As Christian: Make a fully conscious, deliberate, personal, adult act of faith in Jesus as the world's Savior and your Savior.

As Disciple: Read the Sermon on the Mount (Matthew 5—7), looking for what Jesus taught. Has any of this been so watered-down by the actions of Christians that we now take a lower ideal for granted? Which parts?

As Prophet: Choose from Scripture one principle which Jesus taught; you could start with Matthew 5:38-42. Focus on living it out this week. Find a new and creative application of this principle to your own circumstances.

As Priest: Select one thing that bothers you in the Church or in other people. Then follow the advice in James 5:7-10.

As King: Look around you at work, at home, in your social life. Ask what is not yet the way it should be when Christ returns. Make the appropriate changes.

Fourth Sunday of Advent

An Unambiguous Sign

Isaiah 7:10-14; Romans 1:1-7; Matthew 1:18-24

Matthew and Isaiah both speak of the virgin who conceives as a sign of *Emmanuel*: God-with-us. The Incarnation or enfleshment of God took place when God the Son, the Second Person of the Blessed Trinity, was conceived in Mary and of Mary without any act of human intercourse. Jesus, the fruit of her womb, is called Emmanuel because he is truly God and truly man. He is God-with-us as a human being.

God had to take flesh in Mary in order to be truly human. Jesus was not prefabricated in heaven from some divine stuff and then put into Mary's womb. His body was formed from hers.

Mary had to be a virgin so that it would be clear that Jesus was divine. If he had no human father, it would be clear that Jesus was conceived by the power of God. Mary's virginity was an unambiguous sign that Jesus is both divine and human.

Jesus visible as Emmanuel, God-with-us, is an unmistakable sign of God's love for us. Jesus' "being there" cannot be explained except as the sign, the proof, the expression of God's desire to be with us, to reveal God's self to us and to save us. Jesus' every human word and action flowed from this desire, which reached its apex in Jesus' offering himself for us on the cross. In every Mass we celebrate his death and resurrection to new life.

The Church is the continuation of Jesus' visible, human presence and action in the world. In the Church, Christ's Body on earth, the Incarnation is extended in time; Jesus continues to be Emmanuel, God-with-us. The existence, witness and ministry of the Church cannot be explained except as the continuation of Jesus' divine presence and action in us, the human members of his Body on earth.

For years Catholics have described sacraments as visible signs instituted by Jesus Christ to give grace. A sacrament gives grace through some visible, human action. The sacraments do not depend on any human power, even on the holiness of their ministers. Like the virginity of Mary, they are signs of God's action taking place through human beings, but without using any human power to produce their effect. Unless Jesus Christ is speaking and acting through these signs, the water of Baptism does not cleanse, the bread and wine of Eucharist do not nourish, the words of absolution do not pardon, the vows of marriage do not commit irrevocably, the laying on of hands at Confirmation and ordination do not consecrate and empower, and the oils of Anointing do not heal.

When we receive the sacraments, we give unambiguous signs of faith in Jesus-Emmanuel, God still with us in the flesh. The way we express and experience the invisible faith we have in God, in Jesus and in the Church is through visible, human gestures which do not make complete sense unless we have that faith.

Saint Paul's claim to "be an apostle, set apart for the gospel of God," consecrated and empowered for ministry, is based on this same faith. Beginning in a radically new way with Jesus and continuing in the Church, God has chosen to act with divine power through human words and actions. Jesus was born of Mary "according to the flesh and was declared to be Son of God with power"—not with the human power that comes from wealth, education, connections or the authority to command armies, but "according to the spirit of holiness," by abandoning all human power on the cross and by his "resurrection from the dead." The Church's ultimate refusal to rely on human power to spread the Good News is the clearest sign of its reliance on God's power.

Reflecting on This Week's Gospels

December 17-24

Pray daily: God, you chose to redeem the world through human beings acting with divine power, beginning with Jesus, your Son. Teach me to open myself to your power so that you might do through me what you desire. Amen.

December 17: Matthew 1:1-17. Matthew's Gospel begins: "An account of the genealogy of Jesus the Messiah, the son of David, the son of Abraham." If God despised the human race, would God have become in Jesus a member of the human family? Do you recognize Jesus as a fellow member of the human race?

December 18: Matthew 1:18-24. "Now the birth of Jesus the Messiah took place in this way. When his mother Mary had been engaged to Joseph, but before they lived together, she was found to be with child from the Holy Spirit." Was it necessary for Mary to be a virgin? What did it prove? What absence of human resources in your life proves the power of God acting in you?

December 19: Luke 1:5-25. The angel said, "Do not be afraid, Zechariah.... Your wife Elizabeth will bear you a son, and you will name him John." How did John's birth differ from that of Jesus? What does this difference show about them? How were you reborn as a Christian? Was this simply human training or the power of God? How does it make you different?

December 20: Luke 1:26-38. Mary said, "Here am I, the servant of the Lord; let it be with me according to your word." What are you ready to surrender to God, to be done according to God's word?

December 21: Luke 1:39-45. Elizabeth, filled with the Holy Spirit, cried out, "And why has this happened to me, that the mother of my Lord comes to me?" What does it mean to say that Jesus Christ comes to you in Holy Communion? Is your appreciation for that growing?

December 22: Luke 1:46-56. And Mary said: "[T]he Mighty One has done great things for me, and holy is his name." What great things has God done for you? How do you remember and celebrate them?

December 23: Luke 1:57-66. "Now the time came for Elizabeth to give birth, and she bore a son." Was John's birth more important to God than yours? Than anybody else's?

December 24: Luke 1:67-79. "Blessed be the Lord God of Israel, for he has looked favorably upon his people and redeemed them." What signs in the world proclaim this same truth today?

Living This Week's Gospels

As Christian: Put a picture of Mary where you will see it frequently. Imagine her pregnant. Remember that you are also giving flesh to God.

As Disciple: Reread one of the Sunday readings. Then reflect on it, ask questions about it and make a decision in response to it.

As Prophet: Realize that you belong to the Body of Christ. Each day consciously do something that can be explained only by your faith.

As Priest: Through some word or action, minister to someone else, conscious that you are sharing the love of Jesus Christ within you.

As King: Before each thing you do this week, remind yourself that God's power enables you to bear fruit for the Kingdom of God.

CHRISTMAS
SEASON

Christmas Vigil

A Name Among Names

Isaiah 62:1-5; Acts 13:16-17, 22-25; Matthew 1:1-25

In this seldom-used afternoon Christmas Vigil Mass, the Church presents the entire first chapter of Matthew's Gospel, which gives us five key ideas to help us appreciate Jesus as Savior.

Matthew begins with the family tree of Jesus, focusing our attention on two things: First, Jesus is presented as a name among names. Matthew shows us Jesus as God who has come to share in the vast drama of human interaction. He is among us; he is one of us. Therefore, through Jesus it is possible for us to interact humanly with God and to enter into true human friendship with him.

Is Jesus your friend? Do you think of him as a friend, treat him and use him as a friend? Do you interact with other friends in any way that you don't with Jesus? Why? What can you do to make him more of a friend?

The family tree of Jesus also shows us Jesus as "the Messiah, the Son of David," the fulfillment of all God's promises to Israel. Matthew presents Jesus as the goal and fulfillment of Jewish history, of all history. As the focal point of all human achievement, Jesus gives meaning and eternal value to our work, to the time we spend on earth. He saves our lives from meaninglessness.

Is Jesus the goal of everything you do, the fulfillment of all you expect from life?

The angel tells Joseph to name the child Jesus "God saves" because "he will save his people from their sins." Jesus not only takes away the sins we have committed, but he also frees us from the distorted attitudes and values which predispose us to sin. We can interact with Jesus, the Light of the world, and be delivered from the darkness of this world's false hopes and expectations.

How do you see Jesus as your Savior? How can you give him a more active, influential part in everything you do?

"The child conceived in her is from the Holy Spirit": Jesus is the Son of God. He did not come merely to save us from sin but rather to lift us up to a divine level of life and action. He came not simply to help us live good human lives but to give us grace, a sharing in God's life. Jesus is the Savior who came to give us abundant life (see John 10:10) by making us divine.

What behavior of yours is consciously and specifically inspired by goals or ideals that go beyond human goodness? How can Christ's standards permeate more of what you do?

Finally, Jesus is Emmanuel, God-with-us to enable us to interact humanly with God. Because he expressed himself in human words and gestures and because he continues to do this through the sacraments as well as all the graced actions of his Body on earth, Jesus is still Emmanuel for us, still God-with-us until the end of time. He is the Savior who saves, delivers and encounters us through human words and actions.

In how many concrete, physical, human ways do you interact with Jesus every day? In how many simple, humble ways does he communicate with you?

Reflecting on This Week's Gospels

December 26-31

Note: Holy Family Sunday (see page x) will replace one of these days. See below.

Pray daily: Lord, you came to be the light of the world. Your life is the light that enlightens us. Your light is the light that enlivens us. Be my light and my life. Amen.

December 26 (Saint Stephen): Matthew 10:17-22.
"When they hand you over, do not worry about how you are
to speak or what you are to say, for what you are to say will
be given at that time." When you are put on the spot because
of your values, are you conscious that Jesus is your friend?

December 27 (Saint John): John 20:2-8. "Then Peter and
the other disciple set out and went toward the tomb.... [The
other disciple] bent down...and saw the linen wrappings lying
there." What did Jesus accomplish during his time on earth?
What does his life and death help you accomplish now?

December 28 (Holy Innocents): Matthew 2:13-18. "Then
Joseph got up, took the child and his mother by night, and
went to Egypt." Was Jesus equally a savior to Mary and
Joseph when they fled into Egypt as when they were feeling
safe at home? How is he saving you right now? From what?
By what means?

December 29 (Fifth Day in Octave of Christmas):
Luke 2:22-35. "[F]or my eyes have seen your salvation /
...a light for revelation to the Gentiles / and for glory to
your people Israel." How have you experienced salvation?
By what light do you live? What glory have you seen?

December 30 (Sixth Day in Octave of Christmas):
Luke 2:36-40. "[Anna] never left the temple but worshiped
there with fasting and prayer night and day." What visible,
physical reminders can you use to remind you constantly of
God's love and presence?

December 31 (Seventh Day in Octave of Christmas):
John 1:1-18. "And the Word became flesh and lived among
us, and we have seen his glory." How do you experience the
physical, human presence of Jesus in your life? How does he
influence your life today?

Living This Week's Gospels

As Christian: Choose a visible sign to wear or keep close by, something which reminds you that Jesus is your Savior. Use it to keep you interactive with him in everything you do.

As Disciple: Put the Bible on your pillow and make a commitment never to go to sleep at night without reading at least one verse. Ask yourself constantly how you can let the light of Christ enlighten and transform your choices, your life-style.

As Prophet: Set a regular time when you can examine the choices you have made each day, asking whether they bore witness to Christ and if not, how they could have.

As Priest: Form a community of faith with at least one other person with whom you can pray and express your faith, your feelings about God.

As King: Choose one area of your life—a group of people or an environment in which you live, work, study or play—that you think you have a chance of changing. Decide on a first step you can take to make things better.

Sunday After Christmas (Holy Family)

Bride-Love Revisited

Sirach 3:2-7, 12-14; Colossians 3:12-21; Matthew 2:13-15, 19-23

God's treatment of Joseph, Mary and Jesus is shocking. God lets them be driven from their country, their relatives and their family house (see Genesis 12:1) into the poverty and isolation of refugees in a foreign land. God sends an angel only to warn them, not to protect them (see 2 Kings 19:35). This is certainly a strange way to show love!

Compare that treatment to the blessings God promises to those who show love and respect for their parents; we can extend this to good family life in general. God promises riches, gladness, a long life, and answers to their prayers. Sirach says, "[A] father's blessing strengthens the houses of the children" (3:9), but here we see God the Father letting his special family be uprooted from their homeland!

Saint Paul provides the key to God's new way of dealing with us since Jesus came: "[Because you are] God's chosen ones, holy and beloved...." What? Will God bless you or give you long life? No. Paul continues: "...clothe yourselves with compassion, kindness, humility, meekness, and patience. Bear with one another... forgive...." And "Above all, clothe yourselves with love, which binds everything together in perfect harmony."

Paul invites us to think in terms of living and giving in love, not of receiving. He urges us to surrender our hearts to that peace which comes from Christ, to dedicate ourselves to thankfulness. His practical advice is to let God's word dwell in us; that is, to shape all our thoughts, speech and action; to help one another understand Christ's words and live by them ("teach and admonish one another"); to pray and celebrate our faith together ("sing psalms, hymns and spiritual songs to God"). "And whatever you do, in word or deed," he says, "do everything in the name of the Lord Jesus."

This is a change in perspective. Under the terms of the old covenant, people kept God's law for the sake of getting the most out of life. God's laws are instructions for using the human nature the Creator gave us. If we follow them in personal and community life, human society on earth will be what it is supposed to be, and we will all be "healthy, wealthy and wise." When we sin we ruin things for ourselves and others and that is still true. But Jesus has given us a whole new perspective.

We live not simply to enjoy good human lives, but to let Christ live in us and continue his saving work (see Romans 6:4 and Galatians 2:20). We know that people frequently do not follow God's law. Our aim as Christians is not to separate ourselves from others, forming an isolated community to enjoy the fruits of right living while the rest of the world destroys itself. Our goal is to join Jesus in giving ourselves for the life of the world (see John 6:51). This means offering ourselves along with the "Lamb of God," choosing to endure suffering and injustice. In this way we allow our lives to reveal God's love, which calls the world to new life, the life which God alone can give, which was revealed to us in Jesus Christ.

Living by the New Law of Jesus, the law of total abandonment of self in love, is the fruit of the Spirit (see Galatians 5:22 and Colossians 3:12-15). The law of Jesus reflects the wisdom of the cross (see Matthew 11:25 and 1 Corinthians 1:18-25). Now we can identify fulfillment with "emptying" ourselves (see Philippians 2:7) and superiority with being least and last (see Matthew 20:25-28; Mark 9:35; Colossians 3:18-21).

Marriage and family life are a school of love; whatever teaches, enables or calls us to love more selflessly, even heroically, is the blessing God promises. Love is true "riches, gladness," and fullness of life. The power to love is God's answer to our prayers.

January 1 • Solemnity of Mary, Mother of God

To See and Understand

Numbers 6:22-27; Galatians 4:4-7; Luke 2:16-21

W e begin the new year by celebrating Mary as Mother of God. This is an invitation from the Church to think about the mystery of our lives. Who are we? What are we? What have we become through grace?

Who is Jesus? What difference has he made in our lives? What difference did he make in the life of Mary?

Jesus did not change the life of Mary merely by asking her to act differently, to give him birth and raise him. Becoming a mother is not simply starting a job; it is the beginning of a relationship.

What difference has Jesus made in our lives? How do we think of ourselves now that the relationship is established between Jesus and us? How do others think of us? Do they see us as Christians, followers of Jesus? Or as Catholics, members of a particular Church with unique beliefs and practices?

Do we habitually, constantly, from waking to sleeping every day, think of ourselves as the living Body of Christ? Do we see ourselves as the continuation of his living, embodied presence on earth? Is this the way others see us? Is this the way we see other Christians?

We celebrate Mary as Mother of God to remind ourselves of who she is; this reminds us of our own identity. When we celebrate what the grace, the favor of God, made her, we celebrate what grace has made us. When we celebrate what her relationship with Jesus made her, we celebrate what our relationship with Jesus has made us.

In both cases, the essence of the relationship is union: sharing one life. We do not merely imitate Jesus or act differently because of our relationship with him. We live by his life. Because we live by the life of Jesus, we are what he is. Because he is divine, we are divine.

The mystery of becoming a mother is the mystery of one life taking place within another. It is the mystery of a baby living by the life of its mother; the mystery of one human body, one person, living and growing within the body of another and sharing the other's life. Although a baby in the womb is human, it does not have everything it needs to live a human life. It needs to share its mother's life until it is fully formed. Although it has its own distinct life as an individual person, it cannot live except by sharing its mother's life.

This is the mystery of Mary's relationship with Jesus. As God, Jesus had his own divine life. In order to become human, however, he had to share in Mary's life. To become God-made-one-of-us, Jesus had to experience shared life.

This is the mystery of our relationship with Jesus. We have our own distinct human lives. But in order to become divine—to become children of God in fact and not just in a manner of speaking—we need to share in the divine life of Jesus. We need to be united with him in a shared life. We do this by being baptized into membership in his Body. As members of Christ we live by the life of his Body as surely as Jesus in the womb lived by the life of Mary's body. This is the meaning, the mystery of grace.

Reflecting on This Week's Gospels

January 2-7

Note: The reflections for these days are used until the celebration of Epiphany, which falls on the Sunday after January 1.

> *Pray daily: Lord, by taking flesh of Mary you made her the Mother of God. By continuing your life and mission in me you have made me the Body of Christ. Join me to you in mind and heart and desire. Amen.*

January 2: John 1:19-28. The Jews sent priests and Levites from Jerusalem to ask John, "Who are you?" How would you answer that question? Do you identify yourself primarily by your relationship with Christ? What is that relationship?

January 3: John 1:29-34. John the Baptist saw Jesus coming toward him and said, "Here is the Lamb of God who takes away the sin of the world!" Since you are the Body of Christ, you are also the "lamb of God." How do you live it out?

January 4: John 1:35-42. Jesus said to them, "What are you looking for?" How would you answer? What are you looking for in life? How has that changed over the years?

January 5: John 1:43-51. Jesus found Philip and said to him, "Follow me." What did Jesus actually invite Philip to do? Why? How can you "follow" Jesus in your daily choices instead of simply hearing or reading about him occasionally?

January 6: Mark 1:7-11. "I have baptized you with water; but he will baptize you with the Holy Spirit." What does it really mean to be baptized with the Holy Spirit? How does this differ from repenting and believing?

January 7: John 2:1-12. The chief steward called the bridegroom and said to him, "[Y]ou have kept the good wine until now." In what way is the life of grace like good wine?

Living This Week's Gospels

As Christian: Decide how you would define yourself in relation to Jesus. Write that down and put it where you will see it every day.

As Disciple: Each day ask yourself how Jesus used one of his bodily powers—sight, hearing, taste, touch or speech—and compare this with the way you, as a member of his Body, use yours.

As Prophet: Once a day look back over your actions and ask, "Did I do that as the Body of Christ?"

As Priest: Each day offer yourself deliberately as the "lamb of God" through a word or act that is healing for others.

As King: Each time you move from one place to another, remind yourself that you are the Body of Christ, charged to continue his mission on earth. Ask yourself how you can do this at your destination.

What Is the Glory of God?

Isaiah 60:1-6; Ephesians 3:2-3a, 5-6; Matthew 2:1-12

The story of the Magi or wise men was included in Matthew's Gospel to show that from the beginning God intended to call the Gentiles (non-Jews) into unity with the Chosen People. This story was probably an answer to the fundamentalists of the early Church, who opposed Paul's work with the Gentiles on grounds that this was just a "human decision" of the Church; and that "Jesus himself " never preached to non-Jews.

The problem was that the Jews—like everyone else— were tempted to be nationalistic. They could say "Israel first" the way we might say "America first." Isaiah's prophecy, "Arise, shine; for your light has come, / Nations shall come to your light.... [T]he wealth of the nations shall come to you" could mean that Israel would dominate the earth with a universally respected Jewish culture. In reality, this prophecy meant that by the light which came to earth through the Jews, every nation would be enlightened without being absorbed; every human culture would be transformed without losing its identity. All the human "wealth of the nations"—both material and cultural—would be shared among all without being lost to any.

God's plan from all eternity was to "gather up all things in him [Christ], things in heaven and things on earth" (see Ephesians 1:10). Jesus did not come to make one nation or culture dominant over others but instead to glorify the entire human race by bringing everything human, in all its variety and diversity, to its full potential—not only to its natural perfection, but to the glory it can have when transformed by grace.

Jesus came that we might "have life and have it abundantly" through the life of grace (see John 10:10). Saint

Irenaeus says, "As those who see light are in the light sharing its brilliance, so those who see God are in God sharing his glory, and that glory gives them life." He adds that, if we persevere in love, obedience and gratitude to God, "we will receive greater glory from him, a glory which will grow ever brighter until we take on the likeness of the one who died for us." Saint Paul spoke of building up the Body of Christ, "until all of us come to the unity of the faith and of the knowledge of the Son of God...to the measure of the full stature of Christ" (see Ephesians 4:13).

The glory of God and the glory of the human race become one and the same reality in "the full Christ"— head and members—and that glory is "all humanity, fully alive." According to Saint Paul, we are called, consecrated and commissioned to bring about the glory of God, shining through a glorified human race united, with all its individual and cultural diversity, into one Body in Christ.

To celebrate Epiphany is to celebrate not just the light of Christ but the revelation of that light to the whole world. To celebrate this means to rejoice in it, to "single out for grateful remembrance" that people of every race, culture and nation are called to be one Church, one assembly. We are called to be one with each other in faith, in hope and in love, without suppressing diversity or differences. We are called to rejoice in the fact that our Church is *catholic*—that is, a composite of cultures and nations, and does not express itself in the same way all over the world.

Above all, this feast calls us to reach out to others and invite them to celebrate with us the light of Christ. Epiphany reminds us that it is not catholic to want to keep a parish homogeneous—a community of people comfortable with each other because they share the same language, customs, culture or social background. We should not be comfortable until we have invited everyone to join us as believers in Jesus.

Reflecting on This Week's Gospels

Week After Epiphany

> *Pray daily: Lord, you took flesh as a human being so that all might see the glory of God shining through the humanity you created. And you have called every human being to become your Body through Baptism. Pour out your life into every heart, and open our eyes to see your glory shining in every person of every race and nation and temperament. Amen.*

Monday: Matthew 4:12-17, 23-25. "He left Nazareth and made his home in Capernaum...so that what had been spoken through the prophet Isaiah might be fulfilled." Jesus lived in the mixed culture of Galilee to show he came for all people. How much do you reach out to different ethnic groups and races?

Tuesday: Mark 6:34-44. "As he [Jesus] went ashore, he saw a great crowd, and he had compassion for them." Do you feel a kinship with the whole human race that makes you want to help every person you see, regardless of race, nationality or social status?

Wednesday: Mark 6:45-52. "But when they saw him walking on the sea, they thought it was a ghost." Do you look for Jesus to come to you in unexpected persons, thoughts or other ways?

Thursday: Luke 4:14-22. Jesus said to them, "Today this scripture has been fulfilled in your hearing." How have you experienced Jesus as glad tidings to the poor, liberty to captives, sight to the blind and freedom for the oppressed?

Friday: Luke 5:12-16. The man covered with leprosy said, "Lord, if you choose, you can make me clean." Jesus touched him and said, "I do choose. Be made clean." What has Jesus shown that he wants to do for you? What are you asking him to do?

Saturday: John 3:22-30. John answered, "No one can receive anything except what has been given from heaven." Do you realize that God is constantly giving light and inspiring love to all the people with whom you live and work? Do you deal with each person accordingly?

Living This Week's Gospels

As Christian: Write down three things you like most about the customs, ceremonies, and so on, of the Church. How many of these are essential and how many are cultural, changeable, particular ways of expressing Christianity?

As Disciple: Read something (in the *New Catholic Encyclopedia*, for example) about the Eastern rites in the Catholic Church. Do any have parishes where you live?

As Prophet: Identify one way the glory of God hines through your life-style and behavior, a way that is particularly, personally, uniquely your own.

As Priest: Invite someone of a different religion, race or perspective to come to Mass with you one Sunday.

As King: For a day count how many times you or those around you speak negatively about other races, ethnic groups, political parties or people in other departments at work.

ORDINARY TIME

First Sunday of
the Year
Through
Eighth Sunday of
the Year

First Sunday of the Year (Baptism of the Lord)

Jesus' Baptism and Ours

Isaiah 42:1-4, 6-7; Acts 10:34-38; Matthew 3:13-17

J esus' baptism was not for repentance or to wash away sins. It revealed the purpose of our Baptism, which is a new identity. Jesus' baptism symbolized entrance into his mission as Messiah.

Jesus' baptism summed up the three determining moments of his life: his incarnation, crucifixion and resurrection. By asking John for baptism, Jesus accepted his identification with the sinful human race. By going under the water, Jesus accepted his identity as "Lamb of God," who would take into his body on the cross all the sins of the world and annihilate them by carrying them down into the grave. By rising out of the water he prefigured his Resurrection and entrance into glory as *Son of God* (concealed by his Incarnation; see Philippians 2:6-7), *Messiah* (contradicted by his crucifixion; see Matthew 27:42) and as *Lord* (completely revealed at his final coming; see Matthew 26:64).

Our Baptism expresses these same three realities. First, it is an acceptance of identification with God by sharing in Jesus' divine life (see 2 Corinthians 4:10-11; 1 John 5:11-12). We receive this divine life, however, only by dying to our human lives (see Matthew 16:25; Romans 6:3-4 and 12:1-2). We are also baptized into identification with Jesus as "Lamb of God" crucified for the life of the world (see Mark 10:38; Luke 12:50). Finally, our Baptism expresses a rising out of the darkness of death and sin to live as members of Christ, children of God the Father, and temples of the Holy Spirit (see Ephesians 4:1-6; Romans 8:14-27; Galatians 4:6; John 14:15-23). When we rise out of the waters of Baptism, we too hear the Father's voice saying, "This is my beloved, with whom I am well pleased."

God's words to Jesus in baptism recalled Isaiah's prophecy quoted in Matthew 12:18; our baptism makes them applicable to us: "Here is my servant, whom I have chosen, / my beloved, with whom my soul is well pleased. / I will put my Spirit upon him...." Because we are in Christ, his Spirit enables us to carry out his mission: to establish justice on earth, to set free the addicted as well as those enslaved by false promises, to lead blind people out of darkness and bring all things in heaven and on earth into unity and fulfillment as reconstituted in Christ (see Ephesians 1:10).

We are consecrated, anointed, *chrismed* for this vocation as sharers in Christ's anointing as prophet, priest and king. As prophets we continue Christ's Incarnation in a special way, enfleshing his words through action, embodying his truth, his message, in our time and place, allowing our every word, choice and action to bear witness to the attitudes and values he taught. As priests we continue to offer the sacrifice he offered, which reached its climax on the cross. We offer ourselves as his Body on earth: ourselves made one with the "Lamb of God" given and received in Communion, ourselves given to each other through ministry in the faith community, our flesh for the life of the world. As sharers in Christ's kingship we proclaim his resurrection and lordship over all creation by taking responsibility for promoting the Kingdom, the reign of Christ over every area and activity of human life. We devote ourselves to the transformation of society, to the renewal of all things according to his will and desire.

Just as Jesus was "filled with the power of the Spirit" (Luke 4:14) and "went about doing good and healing all who were oppressed by the devil" (Acts 10:38), we are anointed with the same Spirit and the same power—a power which works through gentleness, through patience with the bruised weed and smoldering wick (see Isaiah 42:3), to heal and not to destroy. Through Baptism we die to the way of the world and rise to Christ's way, identifying with sinners and enemies in order to bring all of them lovingly to share his life.

Reflecting on This Week's Gospels

First Week of the Year

Pray daily: Lord, you were baptized into the human race to be one with us. You were not ashamed to be identified with us. You were not afraid to take on our human condition. Lord, let me never be ashamed to be identified with you. Let me never hold back in fear from living your divine life in everything I do. Amen.

Monday: Mark 1:14-20. Jesus said to them, "Follow me, and I will make you fish for people." When you accepted Baptism, what did you or your parents accept as your future direction?

Tuesday: Mark 1:21-28. "They were all amazed, and they kept on asking one another, 'What is this? A new teaching—with authority!'" What have you read in the Gospels that amazes you? What can you do to allow Jesus to become your teacher?

Wednesday: Mark 1:29-39. "That evening, at sundown, they brought to him all who were sick or possessed with demons. And the whole city was gathered around the door." How do people recognize the healing, ministering power of Jesus in you? In what way can you heal those you meet today?

Thursday: Mark 1:40-45. "A leper came to him begging him, and kneeling he said to him, 'If you choose, you can make me clean.'" How have you experienced Jesus curing you, making you clean? Is there any sin or fault from which you think he cannot free you? Do you believe he wants to set you free?

Friday: Mark 2:1-12. Once, when people heard that Jesus was at home at Capernaum, so many came together that there was no longer room for them, not even around the door. Is there room for more worshipers in your parish church at Sunday Mass? At daily Mass?

Saturday: Mark 2:13-17. Jesus said, "Those who are well have no need of a physician, but those who are sick; I have come to call not the righteous but sinners." Is deeper relationship with Jesus, more intimate knowledge of Jesus, an "extra" with you? What can you do without his help?

Living This Week's Gospels

As Christian: Wear on your person or put on your desk at work some visible sign that identifies you with Christ. Notice those times when you would prefer it not be seen.

As Disciple: Choose to make the Scriptures the user's manual, the guidebook for your life. Decide when, where and how long you will read them each day.

As Prophet: Move one way of acting from the human level to the divine level at work, at home or in your social life.

As Priest: Find some practical way to remind yourself when you get up, go to work, come in or go out that you are identified with Jesus and committed by Baptism to share in his ministry of healing and redeeming others.

As King: Have you accepted responsibility for changing things in your life, to remake every area according to God's will? Write down what you are working to change in your family, social circle, workplace, city or neighborhood.

The Scope of Our Baptism

Isaiah 49:3, 5-6; 1 Corinthians 1:1-3; John 1:29-34

Jesus was consecrated "Lamb of God" for the whole human race. Isaiah's prophecy begins, "Listen to me, O coastlands, / ...The LORD called me before I was born, while I was in my mother's womb.... [The LORD] says, 'It is too light a thing that you should be my servant / to raise up the tribes of Jacob / and to restore the survivors of Israel; / I will give you as a light to the nations, / that my salvation may reach to the end of the earth.'"

We too are consecrated in Christ Jesus and called to be a holy people, a people set apart, dedicated to a special mission. By Baptism we were made one with Jesus, the "Lamb of God," and designated to carry out his saving mission to the ends of the earth (see Matthew 28:18-20). We are sent to be a light to everyone around us, to share our faith with all those with whom we live and associate.

What does being identified with Jesus as "Lamb of God" mean? The first and obvious meaning is that we are destined to be sacrificed. Lambs were sacrificial victims. And at our Baptism we are to present our bodies as a living sacrifice (see Romans 12:1-2) so that wherever we are, we sacrifice ourselves in order to carry out the saving mission of Jesus, whose Body we have become. Whether at home, at work or at play, our overriding goal must be to continue and complete the redemptive work of Jesus Christ.

Always to be sacrificed does not mean to be suffering continuously, but we do need always to be selfless. And our goal in everything should be not just our own satisfaction but pleasing Jesus Christ by fulfilling his mission on earth. We must desire his purposes, not our own, in all that we do. Then, even when his desires coincide with our own, we are constantly sacrificed with him, the Lamb of God, for the life of the world. The key to everything is our goal.

If we have deeply embraced the mission of Christ as the goal of our lives, we have made the first step in understanding our Baptism. At Baptism we died to all other reasons for living. Throughout life, any goal we pursue must be sought as part of our primary goal of completing Christ's mission. If that sounds radical, think how radically senseless living for anything else is! To pursue any other goal is to cut ourselves off from the roots of our lives, namely our creation by God and rebirth at Baptism, and to float loosely like a leaf in the wind.

Being a Lamb of God says more than this, however. Jesus was sacrificed precisely for the sins of the world. Thus our attitude toward aggressors must be one of redeeming love.

The stance we take toward the enemies of our country is not to kill them but to come to agreement with them through peaceful means. The stance we take toward criminals is not to punish them but to rehabilitate them. The stance we take toward those who sin in any way—and specifically against us—is not to condemn them but to convert them. Our first concern is not to defend ourselves or seek revenge but to heal and help those who threaten us or do us wrong. Like Jesus we are not on this earth to save our lives but to lose them (see Matthew 10:39; 16:25). Our goal is not to protect ourselves but to offer ourselves in love. What do we gain if we successfully protect everything we own yet in doing so lose our identity with Christ? What will we accept in exchange for being one with the "Lamb of God"? (See Matthew 16:26.)

Reflecting on This Week's Gospels

Second Week of the Year

Pray daily: Lord, at every Eucharist you are presented to us as the Lamb of God who takes away the sins of the world. As I receive you in Communion, transform my heart so that I may endure all things with love to reverse the sin of the world. Amen.

Monday: Mark 2:18-22. "[N]o one puts new wine into old wineskins.... But one puts new wine into fresh wineskins." How do you need to go about changing your heart, your attitudes and values, your reactions and responses in order to live as someone sacrificed with the Lamb of God?

Tuesday: Mark 2:23-28. The Pharisees said to Jesus, "Look, why are they doing what is not lawful on the sabbath?" The law of sabbath rest teaches us that we exist for relationship with God, not just for what we accomplish on earth. Besides refraining from work, how do you observe this law?

Wednesday: Mark 3:1-6. Jesus said to the people in the synagogue, "Is it lawful to do good or to do harm on the sabbath, to save life or to kill?" Is your normal attitude at work, at home, in the city one of "saving life" by affirming, understanding and helping people, or do you manipulate and overpower people to get things done?

Thursday: Mark 3:7-12. "[H]earing all that he was doing, they came to him in great numbers...." Do people seek you out for help, for understanding or sympathy? Do they feel free to? Why or why not?

Friday: Mark 3:13-19. "He went up the mountain and called to him those whom he wanted, and they came to him." Does Jesus want you? For what? Has he summoned you? When? To what is he calling you now?

Saturday: Mark 3:20-21. "Then he went home; and the crowd came together again, so that they could not even eat." What limits do you set on being available to others? To your family? Friends? To people who simply want to talk? What are your limits for sharing yourself? What limits are good?

Living This Week's Gospels

As Christian: When you hear the words "Lamb of God" at Mass, offer yourself to be used by God and by others for the life of the world.

As Disciple: Each time you get angry or impatient, try to think of something Jesus said or did that teaches you how to respond. (You may have to look for this after the fact!)

As Prophet: Think of one concrete thing you could do to show that you want, like the "Lamb of God" to be for others, instead of acting out of power. For example, do your clothes or the arrangement of furniture in your office speak more of friendliness or of power?

As Priest: Make yourself vulnerable; take a risk by being honest with someone about your feelings, your faith or your fears, or really listening to another person's point of view.

As King: Think of something you would like to change at home, at work or in your neighborhood. Ask how you could do it by exerting power; then ask how you could do it by love.

Third Sunday of the Year

Shades of Light and Dark

Isaiah 8:23—9:3; 1 Corinthians 1:10-14, 17; Matthew 4:12-23

Matthew uses Isaiah to present Jesus as a "great light" shining on those who before had "walked in darkness" in a "land of gloom." Jesus is good news because he shows us how to avoid the errors of a culture which diminishes the quality of life for us, makes life destructive. Jesus came that we might "have life, and have it abundantly" (John 10:10). His light, his teachings guide us to it.

If we truly understood and believed everything Jesus taught and lived by it, then we would have the fullest, happiest lives possible on this earth. This does not, however, mean lives without suffering. That is hardly possible in the world we know. For Christians sent to offer themselves as "living sacrifices" for the life of the world, that is not even desirable. A football player can escape pain by sitting on the bench, but then he is not in the game. Jesus says a woman has pain giving birth but forgets it in the joy of giving new life. Saint Paul wrote that the message of the cross which he preached is foolishness to those without faith, but to believers it is the way to the fullness of life, even on this earth (see 1 Corinthians 1:18-24).

Do we really believe and understand what Jesus taught? Christians, even in the same Church, are not always united in what they believe. Saint Paul urged the Corinthians to be in agreement in the name of Jesus and allow no division among them, to be united in one mind and purpose.

Catholics have the advantage of belonging to a Church which can teach with authority as Jesus did (see Matthew 7:29; 2 Corinthians 10:8). But since infallible teaching is rare, on most practical issues Catholics are just as free to disagree with each other as Protestants are—and we do!

Yet insofar as we fail to understand and live by what Jesus teaches, we will walk in darkness and in the gloom of death. So where do we look for light?

First we believe everything in Scripture; most of it is so clear that Church leaders have not needed to interpret it officially. Second we also believe with absolute faith whatever the Church has defined as dogma in Church councils since the earliest days. And third, unless we have very serious reasons to disagree, we believe whatever is officially and commonly taught throughout the whole Church. Finally, when it comes to ordinary letters (encyclicals) and teachings of popes and bishops, we try respectfully to understand and accept what they say whenever possible. But we can disagree on the last two levels without denying our faith. This is always risky, but we need to know it is our right.

Unfortunately, we frequently do not ask about a teaching's level of authority. For example, Andrew Greeley reported in *America* (October 7, 1992) that only seventeen percent of American Catholics think that premarital sex is always wrong, compared to thirty-three percent of other Americans (and compared to seventy-five percent of U.S. Catholics in 1963). Greeley thinks that the birth control issue has made Catholics turn off everything Church authorities say about sex. Yet the law against fornication comes straight from Scripture (see 1 Corinthians 6:9; 7:2); the meaning of the word is disputed, however.

Freedom to disagree does not free a person from the consequences. If we do not walk in the light of Christ, we will walk in darkness. This always puts us in the "gloom of death" by destroying our life to some degree. To live life abundantly, we want and need to know what Christ teaches.

Reflecting on This Week's Gospels

Third Week of the Year

Pray daily: Jesus, you came to be the Word of God made flesh and the law of God made flesh. I believe that in your words and in your example I can find the law of love to live by. Give me fullness of life through the fullness of your light. Amen.

Monday: Mark 3:22-30. "If a kingdom is divided against itself, that kingdom cannot stand." Do you pursue Christ's goals in some areas of your life and then selfish goals in other areas? Do you want your every decision to be guided by Christ's teachings?

Tuesday: Mark 3:31-35. "Whoever does the will of God is my brother and sister and mother." By "will of God," does Jesus mean just keeping the Ten Commandments? What would identify you to others as belonging to Jesus' family?

Wednesday: Mark 4:1-20. "Other seed fell into good soil and brought forth grain, growing up and increasing and yielding thirty and sixty and a hundredfold." How is God's word visibly bearing fruit in your life? Can you identify the ways? What can you do to make yourself "good soil" to receive the words of Jesus?

Thursday: Mark 4:21-25. "For to those who have, more will be given; and from those who have nothing, even what they have will be taken away." We have all been taught the same faith. In what ways do you foster its growth or hinder it?

Friday: Mark 4:26-34. "[The kingdom of God] is like a mustard seed, which...grows up and becomes the greatest of all shrubs, and puts forth large branches...." Must the entire doctrine, behavior and liturgy of Christians be today exactly what it was in the time of the apostles? How have you seen the whole Church grow in understanding and response to the Gospel?

Saturday: Mark 4:35-41. The apostles were filled with great awe and said to one another, "Who then is this, that even the wind and the sea obey him?" Do you try to know and obey all the teachings of Jesus with this kind of awe and wonder?

Living This Week's Gospels

As Christian: For a week, take the Bible and some other book or magazine you read often. Put them side by side on a table and ask yourself daily, "Which of these do I really follow as my 'bible'?"

As Disciple: For a week, in everything you read, underline any value or attitude that seems contrary to the ideals and attitudes taught by Jesus.

As Prophet: At least once this week, at home, at work or in your social life, raise the question with someone else whether some attitude or practice that seems commonly accepted truly reflects Jesus' teaching.

As Priest: Try to bring someone a little more out of "darkness and the gloom of death" through words of encouragement, advice or invitation.

As King: Look at something that is not as it should be, at home, at work or in your social life, and use the light of Christ's teachings to see how you should change it.

Fourth Sunday of the Year

Consider Your Situation

Zephaniah 2:3; 3:12-13; 1 Corinthians 1:26-31;
Matthew 5:1-12a

We expect Jesus, the light of the world, to teach a way of living radically different from our culture. In the Beatitudes he challenges our basic values. He says we are blessed (fortunate) if we are conscious of being inadequate (poor in spirit), experiencing the dark side of life (mourning), powerless or unwilling to resist injustice with force (meek), unsatisfied by anything life offers (hungering and thirsting for righteousness), involved in others' problems (merciful), looking at everything through the eyes of religion (single-hearted), ready to lose face, possessions and freedom for the sake of peace (peacemakers), and suffering insults, lies and persecution for righteousness' sake, that is, for our faith.

The key to such a life is love. God is love, and Jesus' great command is to love one another as he has loved us, even to lay down our lives for others. Humility makes love possible; pride always obstructs it. We have to make ourselves the least of all as Jesus did in order to love as Jesus did. Hate springs from pride, taking our own judgment of others as the criterion of truth and falsity.

According to Saint Ignatius of Loyola, the devil's basic strategy is to tempt us to two things which are not sins— affluence and status—in order to lead us into the deadliest sin of all—pride. Jesus' basic strategy is to encourage us to be voluntarily poor and to welcome the humiliations which come from this so that we might grow in humility. Jesus' approach flatly contradicts our cultural values.

Are not people with money treated with more respect than poor people? If we receive more respect or recognition than others, are we not tempted to consider ourselves better than others? If we only think this way about particular qualities, it is not yet pride—simply vanity or conceit. But if because we are "worth more" than others financially we begin to think we are worth more than others as human beings, very shortly we will begin seeing ourselves as the criterion, the standard of what is right and good. Then we are deeply into pride.

If we are rich and respected, it is very hard not to begin thinking of ourselves as the "right kind" of people, to think that our way of living, of thinking, of evaluating things, is therefore the "right" way for everyone. Such ideas make us the standard and that is pride, making ourselves like God.

It is dangerous to be treated as if we were more important than other people because this makes us begin thinking that we are. This makes us assume, perhaps unconsciously, that satisfying our needs is more important than fulfilling the needs of others, the poor and marginalized, for example. Then we may use our economic and political power to favor the established class. The rich grow richer while the poor suffer exploitation and injustice. But it seems right to us because the "right kind of people" are doing it and what the "right kind of people" think and do must be right.

Riches, prestige and pride contribute to *forced poverty, injustice* and *marginalization*, which Pope John Paul II identifies as the basic causes of war in our day. Echoing Zephaniah ("Seek righteousness, seek humility"), the pope calls Christians to live evangelical poverty, respect human dignity and form community with the poor and disadvantaged (World Day of Peace message, January 1, 1993). And Saint Paul reminds us that to begin the Church God "chose what is low and despised in the world, things that are not, to reduce to nothing things that are." If we want to love as Jesus taught, a three-step program is laid out for us: Refuse affluence, shun the prestige which often goes with it and seek the Lord with the "humble of the land."

Reflecting on This Week's Gospels

Fourth Week of the Year

Pray daily: Lord, I believe that you are the Way, the Truth and the Life. Strengthen me to turn away from the way of life that affluence makes possible, from the distorted perceptions into which prestige can lead me and from the living death of indifference to the poor, which is the fruit of pride. Amen.

Monday: Mark 5:1-20. "He lived among the tombs; and no one could restrain him any more, even with a chain." What unrestrained, destructive conduct do you see coming from those who live "among the tombs" of affluence and prestige?

Tuesday: Mark 5:21-43. "When he had entered, he said to them, 'Why do you make a commotion and weep? The child is not dead but sleeping.' And they laughed at him." Have you ever been ridiculed for expressing the truth you know from faith? Has it made you afraid to express your faith?

Wednesday: Mark 6:1-6. When Jesus began to teach in the synagogue, many who heard him were astounded. They said, "Where did this man get all this?... Is not this the carpenter?" Do you think the work you do makes you more important than others? Can you treat with dignity people who do jobs you consider "less important"?

Thursday: Mark 6:7-13. "He ordered them to take nothing for their journey except a staff; no bread, no bag, no money in their belts." Why did Jesus send his disciples to preach in poverty? What in your life bears witness to the gospel as strongly as this?

Friday: Mark 6:14-29. Herod "was deeply grieved; yet out of regard for... the guests, he did not want to refuse her." Do you ever do wrong from fear of losing prestige or status in others' eyes?

Saturday: Mark 6:30-34. The apostles gathered around Jesus and told him all they had done and taught. He said to them, "Come away to a deserted place all by yourselves and rest a while." When you have a successful day, does it lead you to go aside with Jesus and pray?

Living This Week's Gospels

As Christian: Treat someone with special respect because you recognize him or her as the Body of Christ, and not because of that person's position, status or prestige.

As Disciple: List three things that give people status in this world. Match them with something Jesus said about what gives people value in God's eyes.

As Prophet: Identify something you wear, do or display mostly to impress others. Change it.

As Priest: Notice the ways some people around you are treated with less respect. Show them special respect.

As King: Select some way you can live just a little more simply; use the money you save to benefit the poor.

Fifth Sunday of the Year

Mercy and Light

Isaiah 58:7-10; 1 Corinthians 2:1-5; Matthew 5:13-16

Isaiah tells his listeners to share their bread and shelter the homeless. "Then your light shall break forth like the dawn." And not only light but help will come from God: "[Y]our healing shall spring up quickly.... Then you shall call, and the LORD will answer...."

This light is not only for us but for the whole world. Isaiah goes on to give the promise which the Church quotes on Epiphany: "For darkness shall cover the earth,...but the LORD will arise upon you.... Nations shall come to your light..." (Isaiah 60:3).

Jesus said to us, "You are the light of the world.... Let your light shine before others so that they may see your good works and give glory to your Father in heaven." This command brings us back to the works of mercy. If we share, shelter, clothe and help all those in need, God's light will shine in us and through us—through our actions as well as in our words.

This was the power of Saint Paul's preaching. He did not rely on "plausible words of wisdom" but on the evidence of spiritual power, "so that your faith might rest not on human wisdom but on the power of God." And what was this power? Paul describes it as the power of the cross; he decided to know nothing among them "except Jesus Christ, and him crucified." In other words, it was the power of love revealed, made visible, expressing itself in human flesh for the world's salvation. The power behind Paul's preaching was the mercy of God.

What will bring us, what will bring our faith community, to that level of life we desire and which God desires to give us? What will make the "light rise for us" and "break forth like the dawn" to give light to all around us? Mercy. Works of mercy. Living the light in action. Sharing our bread, sheltering the homeless.

We need to think in terms of the works of mercy. The "corporal" (physical) ones are: feeding the hungry, giving drink to the thirsty, clothing the naked, visiting the sick and those in prison, sheltering the homeless, burying the dead. The "spiritual" works of mercy—though all are spiritual acts!—are: being honest with people about their sins, sharing knowledge with those who are ignorant, working with people in doubt, comforting those who feel emotional distress, loving even when wrong is done to us, forgiving every offense, praying for the living and the dead.

The physical help and spiritual help we give others makes our faith credible. We cannot expect people to "come to our light" unless they see us first living in it.

Each parish is responsible not just for its own members but in a special way for everyone within its boundaries. How many people live within your parish boundaries? How many are lonely? How many are overaged? What is the ethnic mix? What are their special needs and how is your parish addressing them? These especially are the ones we must think of when we read Isaiah's warning "not to turn your back on your kin."

Who will lead us in addressing these needs? The Holy Spirit, if we ask. Through whom? Not just through the pastor! Through anyone in the parish open to the Spirit's voice. We are the Church; we are the parish, all of us. No one of us is more called to the works of mercy than another is. So what do we do?

Reflecting on This Week's Gospels

Fifth Week of the Year

Pray daily: Lord, you came to make us the salt of the earth, the light of the world. And you have sent us to heal the wounds of the world, so that all people may walk in the gladness of your light. Have mercy and make me your mercy to all I meet. Amen.

Monday: Mark 6:53-56. "People rushed about that whole region and began to bring the sick on mats to wherever they heard he was." When there is a talk or reconciliation service in your parish, do you go looking for someone to invite to it?

Tuesday: Mark 7:1-13. Jesus said, "Isaiah prophesied rightly about you hypocrites.... 'This people honors me with their lips, but their hearts are far from me.'" Do you pray at Mass for anything that you are reluctant to act on after Mass?

Wednesday: Mark 7:14-23. "[T]here is nothing outside a person that by going in can defile, but the things that come out are what defile." Can thoughts or feelings that just come to you defile you? Why is it that free choices come only from within a person?

Thursday: Mark 7:24-30. She replied, "Sir, even the dogs under the table eat the children's crumbs." How much of what is offered to you in the Church, in your parish, do you leave untouched?

Friday: Mark 7:31-37. Jesus "said to him, '*Ephphatha*,' that is, 'Be opened.' And immediately his ears were opened, his tongue was released, and he spoke plainly." The word *Ephphatha* was probably spoken over you at Baptism. Do you know what prayer was said for you then?

Saturday: Mark 8:1-10. When a great crowd of people had nothing to eat, Jesus called the disciples and said, "I have compassion for the crowd...." When you think of people without Eucharist, do you think of Jesus saying this?

Living This Week's Gospels

As Christian: Light a candle where you pray or put a container of salt where you work to remind you that Jesus calls you to be the light and salt of the earth.

As Disciple: Every day for a week write down one way in which you are closed to the teaching of Jesus. Make appropriate changes.

As Prophet: Look at one detail of your life-style and ask, "Is this how the salt of the earth acts? How does this give light to the world?"

As Priest: Identify one person who may be tempted not to believe in God because of some personal or family difficulty. Try to minister respectfully to that person.

As King: Each time you make a decision, ask yourself, "What value or attitude is guiding this decision?" Then look at the decision in the light of Christ's teaching and change it if necessary.

Sixth Sunday of the Year

Choices Beyond Choice

Sirach 15:15-20; 1 Corinthians 2:6-10; Matthew 5:17-37

The most wonderful and yet the scariest thing about being human is our freedom of choice. Because we are free we can love or hate, do good or evil, choose happiness or misery forever. Sirach says God has set before us "fire and water...life and death." What we choose will be given us.

Sirach says something else very significant: "If you choose, you can keep the commandments." God does not force anyone to sin. We can never say that we are so weak or wounded that we cannot love, that we cannot refuse to do evil.

But, as a truck going seventy miles an hour downhill cannot be stopped immediately, habit or passion may make us, for all practical purposes, unable at a particular moment to avoid something we have set ourselves up to do. We can even be programmed because of abuses we have suffered to react to certain situations without thinking, without free choice. Fear can make us react automatically. This is not choosing evil and sin but rather suffering the effects of evil and sin.

What we can do, however, and must do to accept our humanity, is work toward freeing ourselves from the habits, conditioning and knee-jerk reactions which cause us to act in evil, self-destructive ways. There are, for example, Twelve-Step Programs for addiction to alcohol, drugs and sex—and for woundedness caused by someone else's abuse of these. We must take care not to let our feelings of fear or anger become so strong that they overwhelm us. We are responsible for doing everything we can to become free, to avoid letting ourselves get to the point where we lose control.

Jesus, however, calls us to act in ways that are beyond human freedom, ways made possible for us only by God's grace. In the Sermon on the Mount he changes the commandments from laws of good human behavior into laws for acting on God's level. It is no longer enough not to kill; we must love one another as God loves us. It is no longer enough to avoid adultery; we must see each other as God sees us: as the Body of Christ and temples of the Holy Spirit. It is no longer enough not to lie; we must be as honest with each other as God is with us, realizing that our words, like God's words, are sacred because we are sacred.

Just as human choices depend on human understanding, divine choices depend on divine understanding. We humans choose freely only when we choose on the basis of what we understand—normally, on the basis of reason. But when we have become divine by grace, by sharing in the life of God, we understand not by human reason alone but by the light of faith. A fully alive faith shares in God's own act of knowing; we can have such knowledge only by sharing in God's own life by grace. The same gift of grace which enables us to see by the power of God's light allows us to choose through the power of God's love. In this way the gift of grace, sharing in the divine life of God, empowers us to live on the level of God. Acting on God's level is the morality taught by Jesus, beginning with the Sermon on the Mount.

Saint Paul presumes all this when he speaks of the "wisdom" he expects to find only in the spiritually mature. The ideals, the values, the attitudes which Paul preaches as the teaching of Jesus are simply beyond the range of natural understanding. The "wisdom of this world" regards them as plain foolishness, absurd. And that gives us a new choice: to follow the wisdom of the world or the wisdom of the cross, darkness or light, death or life. What we choose will be given us.

Reflecting on This Week's Gospels

Sixth Week of the Year

Pray daily: Lord, you came to give us life, life to the full. Inspire and strengthen us to take responsibility for the choices that give shape to our souls. And direct us by your love in all that we choose to be and to do. Amen.

Monday: Mark 8:11-13. Jesus sighed from the depth of his spirit and said, "Why does this generation ask for a sign? Truly I tell you, no sign will be given to this generation." What greater sign can there be of God's grace to you than your choices?

Tuesday: Mark 8:14-21. Jesus said, "Watch out—beware of the yeast of the Pharisees...." Pharisaism, or legalism, is a way of escaping the responsibility of choices by blindly obeying the letter of the law. Do you do this at times?

Wednesday: Mark 8:22-26. Jesus laid his hands on the blind man and asked, "Can you see anything?" The man replied, "I can see people, but they look like trees, walking." When Jesus laid hands on the man's eyes again, the man saw clearly. What kind of encounter with Christ will help you see clearly when you make choices? How do you seek this encounter?

Thursday: Mark 8:27-33. Jesus asked his disciples, "Who do people say that I am?" After they offered various answers, he asked them, "But who do you say that I am?" How have you personally chosen to interact with Jesus? Who, what is he for you?

Friday: Mark 8:34—9:1. Jesus called the crowd and his disciples and said to them, "If any want to become my followers, let them deny themselves and take up their cross and follow me." The key question is, do you really want to follow Jesus? How closely? How much is it worth to you?

Saturday: Mark 9:2-13. Peter said to Jesus, "Rabbi, it is good for us to be here." Have you ever explicitly said to yourself, "It is good that I am in the Church!"? Can you say it now?

Living This Week's Gospels

As Christian: Describe in one sentence why you choose to follow Jesus.

As Disciple: Write down what helps people recognize that you are not a believer in name only but rather are a disciple, a student, of the teachings of Jesus Christ.

As Prophet: Each day this week make one choice which is based not just on the Ten Commandments, on what is right or wrong, but on some more generous and demanding ideal taught by Jesus.

As Priest: Perform some daily act of kindness for someone else, a conscious act of expressing the healing, helping love of Jesus who is within you, acting through you.

As King: Reconsider some rule or policy you obey but do not feel comfortable about. Accept responsibility for deciding whether this rule or policy reflects the highest ideals of Jesus. Discuss the situation with someone you consider wise.

Seventh Sunday of the Year

Be Holy as I Am Holy

Leviticus 19:1-2, 17-18; 1 Corinthians 3:16-23; Matthew 5:34-48

As Christians we are not called to be good; we are called to be godlike. That is why Paul keeps saying Christian values are absurdity to people whose thinking is dictated by their culture and, in the same way, the "wisdom of this world is foolishness with God."

If our starting point, our goal, is life in this world and all it has to offer, then what we spontaneously do in our society makes sense. We acquire property, pass laws which make orderly living in society possible; we equip a police force and an army with sufficient force to defend our property and our way of life against internal or foreign aggressors. If we are focused on "life, liberty and the pursuit of happiness" in this world, this is the only course which makes sense. If we want a decent life in this world, we have to be willing to defend our way of life against anyone who would threaten it.

This is so obvious that it has been followed by every nation and human society since the beginning of time. It is so natural, so reasonable, that no one would call it into question—no one except Jesus Christ.

Jesus' starting point is not that we are called to the "pursuit of happiness" in this world, but that instead we are called to "be perfect" as our "heavenly Father is perfect." Then Jesus spells out very concretely what this means: offer no resistance to injury; do not fight back to defend your dignity (even if slapped in the face), your property (even if someone wants to take your coat) or your freedom (be willing to go the extra mile for someone). We are to love our enemies, to pray for those who mistreat and oppress us. Our focus is on living like God, now and forever.

To make it even plainer, Jesus later boiled everything down to one commandment: "Just as I have loved you, you also should love one another" (John 13:34). Jesus left us the image of himself on the cross to show us what such love means. The only grace-filled, Christian response to insult, injustice or injury is to look at Jesus on the cross and ask, "How can I love like that?"

In fact, God prepared us for this teaching by giving the law of the sabbath rest. By commanding us to stop one day a week and do no work that could seem to justify our existence, God taught us that human beings are different from everything else in the universe. Everything else exists only for what it can contribute to life on this planet. Humans, however, exist immediately for God. Therefore no government has a right of "eminent domain" over any human life. We cannot take a human life for the good of society because humans exist for something greater. Like God, we have a *raison d'etre*, a reason for living, that is independent of what we do in this world. The sabbath was God's way of saying, "You shall be holy, for I the LORD your God am holy." Like God, humans are holy—that is, separated or set apart—not simply a part of the created world. The sabbath observance is a sign of this (see Exodus 31:13).

Saint Paul applies this teaching specifically to the human body. "Do you not know that you are God's temple and that God's Spirit dwells in you? If anyone destroys God's temple, God will destroy that person. For God's temple is holy, and you are that temple." Anyone who takes a human life—for any reason whatsoever—is presuming to destroy God's temple, something that does not belong to life just in this world. We are not justified in doing that to preserve any value which simply contributes to "life, liberty and the pursuit of happiness." Anyone who presumes to destroy human life will answer to God.

Reflecting on This Week's Gospels

Seventh Week of the Year

Pray daily: Lord, you call us to be perfect as God alone is perfect. You have shared with us your Spirit and your divine life so that we might live on the level of God. Give us faith to believe, hope to trust, and love to do all that you empower us to do. Amen.

Monday: Mark 9:14-29. Jesus said to him, "If you are able!—All things can be done for the one who believes." Has the world, have Christians, ever taken seriously Jesus' teaching about love of enemies? If we did, could Christians contribute to this world's violence?

Tuesday: Mark 9:30-37. Jesus told his disciples: "'The Son of Man is to be betrayed into human hands, and they will kill him, and three days after being killed, he will rise again.' But they did not understand what he was saying and were afraid to ask him." Do you understand why Jesus chose to save the world through love instead of through power? What keeps you from following this example?

Wednesday: Mark 9:38-40. "Whoever is not against us is for us." How often, when people offend you, are they really against you? How often are they just hurting or insecure?

Thursday: Mark 9:41-50. "And if your eye causes you to stumble, tear it out...better for you to enter the kingdom of God with one eye than to have two eyes and to be thrown into hell." Is saving one's life, body or property the highest value? What would you kill for? What would Jesus kill for?

Friday: Mark 10:1-12. Jesus told them, "Because of your hardness of heart [Moses] wrote this commandment for you." On what points has Christian morality become clearer, more loving and more demanding in the last thousand years?

Saturday: Mark 10:13-16. "Truly I tell you, whoever does not receive the kingdom of God as a little child will never enter it." Are you willing to be taught by Jesus and his Spirit a whole new outlook on life? To make the necessary changes in your values and priorities?

Living This Week's Gospels

As Christian: Place a small crucifix on top of whatever book or tool you use most often, to remind you what you really trust for what you want in life.

As Disciple: Divide a page into two columns. At the top of the left one write, "Love your neighbor." Over the right column write, "As yourself." On the left side list three people who aggravate you. In the right column write what you would want others to do for you if you were that person.

As Prophet: Change one action of your day from good to Godlike.

As Priest: Identify three things you do that you do not think a member of God's priestly people should do. After each one write, "The temple of God is holy and I am that temple."

As King: Ask yourself what is sacred about your work. (For Christians, "work" includes retirement and sickness.) Does this change your understanding of the way you should do your job or live your life?

Eighth Sunday of the Year

A New Freedom From Fear

Isaiah 49:14-15; 1 Corinthians 4:1-5; Matthew 6:24-34

Before Christmas one year our parish received a letter from a fund-raising company. The letter began, "As we prepare for one of the most holy and happiest holidays, many pastors are looking forward with great anticipation to...." The birth of the Savior? Celebrating Midnight Mass? No. The letter continued: "the largest offertory collection of the year"! The company went on to explain, "Finances will remain as a pastor's number one challenge [for the next ten years]."

This company was totally out of touch with the way most pastors think. If any parish's financial situation becomes so critical that its pastor thinks first and foremost of the need to raise money, sees this as his "number one challenge," and sees great liturgical feasts like Christmas as settings for enhancing the offertory collection, then for the sake of his own survival as a Christian, that pastor needs to leave parochial ministry and go into some other kind of priestly work. The priesthood should draw priests deeper into the spiritual life, not focus their hearts on finances. The same holds true for every other Christian way of life.

Pastors are supposed to be "examples to the flock" (1 Peter 5:3). And so, when Jesus says, "Strive first for the kingdom of God and his righteousness," he means that pastors should model this attitude. But that would not be possible—it would not be real—if pastors had no financial worries. If pastors had no anxiety about paying bills, they could not be an example to those who do. It is easy not to "worry about your life, what you will eat or what you will drink" when the bank account is fat! Thus it is precisely when the parish is short on funds and the needs are great that the pastor is forbidden to worry! If he cannot do this, he should work seriously at converting his own heart since the temptations of the job are so great for him that he can no longer be an "example to the flock" who have financial worries also.

Today's Gospel is our Lord's teaching about idolatry, which is essentially dividedness of heart. Idolaters are people who overemphasize human values—who worship technology (the god Vulcan), bravery (Mars), sexual love (Venus), prosperity (Pluto), relaxation (Bacchus) or speed of communication (Mercury)—and organize their lives around these values. This organizing can occur through a religious cult, as it does in societies that frankly turn these values into "gods," or it can occur by giving visible priority to one of these values in a person's life or in a nation's public policies. In a parish, for example, if the offertory collection becomes the high point and central focus of the liturgy, the Mass becomes a worship of Pluto, not of Jesus and his Father.

This Gospel invites us all to examine our priorities. How many of our decisions are determined by fear? Fear pushes into a priority position something to which we ordinarily would not assign such value. Fear of another country drives us into giving first priority in the national budget to weapons for killing foreigners rather than to programs for housing, educating, healing and rehabilitating our own citizens. Fear of losing our desired standard of living can drive us into giving priority to work over family, to productivity over preserving people, to hardheartedness over concern for human needs. Fear of unemployment may drive a city or state into accommodating industries which pollute the environment. We can all expand this list and tailor it to fit our own experience. It is worth taking time to do so.

Jesus' teaching is that the focus of our hearts should be one thing and one thing alone: "striving first" to surrender to God's kingship over us, to pursue and follow "his righteousness." The focus of our hearts should be on giving priority to God, giving priority to whatever will help us know, love and follow God more intensely. If we do this, God promises, everything else we need "will be given" as well. If we take this promise seriously, what priorities might we need to reexamine in our lives?

Reflecting on This Week's Gospels

Eighth Week of the Year

Pray daily: Lord, you overcame sin and death that we might be free. You have told us not to worry about anything on earth because our Father in heaven knows what we need. Teach us to trust in the Father and be free. Amen.

Monday: Mark 10:17-27. "Jesus, looking at him, loved him and said, 'You lack one thing; go, sell what you own, and give the money to the poor, and you will have treasure in heaven; then come, follow me.'" What do you fear most about poverty? What did Jesus say about this fear?

Tuesday: Mark 10:28-31. "Truly I tell you, there is no one who has left house...or children or fields, for my sake...who will not receive a hundredfold now in this age...and in the age to come eternal life." Do you believe this? How do you show it?

Wednesday: Mark 10:32-45. "...whoever wishes to be first among you must be slave of all. For the Son of Man came not to be served but to serve, and to give his life a ransom for many." How important is recognition or status for you? What in your life shows Jesus' attitude toward these?

Thursday: Mark 10:46-52. "Jesus said..., 'What do you want me to do for you?' The blind man said to him, 'My teacher, let me see again.'" Would this be your answer? In what ways are you blind?

Friday: Mark 11:11-26. "My house shall be called a house of prayer.... But you have made it a den of robbers." What in your life keeps you from praying? What takes up your time? What can you do about it?

Saturday: Mark 11:27-33. Jesus said to them, "I will ask you one question; answer me, and I will tell you by what authority I do these things." If you really ask, "Who is Jesus Christ for me?" how might the answer change your priorities?

Living This Week's Gospels

As Christian: List in descending order how much money you spend on shelter, insurance, education, the offertory collection at Mass, charity to others, food, drink, clothes, entertainment and other expenses.

As Disciple: Divide the expenses above into categories such as: "necessary or unavoidable," "bears witness to proper care for myself," "shows love for others," "irrelevant to the Kingdom of God."

As Prophet: Ask which expenses show explicit faith or hope in God. Which are explicit expressions of your love for God? (The emphasis here is on "explicit." All expenses should be this implicitly, at least.)

As Priest: Decide how much you can spend specifically on helping the poor or ministering to others in need.

As King: Explicitly, formally, prayerfully give all your possessions to God. Write out a deed! Then accept responsibility for managing them according to God's desires.

LENT

Ash Wednesday and Weekdays After Ash Wednesday

Reflecting on This Week's Gospels

Pray daily: Lord, you call me out into the desert with yourself. You want to speak to my heart. Give me the motivation to break with the distractions in my life and focus my attention on your words. Amen.

Ash Wednesday: Matthew 6:1-6, 16-18. Jesus said, "Beware of practicing your piety before others in order to be seen by them; for then you have no reward from your Father in heaven." What personal, private acts of devotion tell you that religion is very personal to you and not just something you were "brought up in"?

Thursday after Ash Wednesday: Luke 9:22-25. "If any want to become my followers, let them deny themselves and take up their cross daily and follow me." How much of a cross is it to make time for daily Mass or prayer? How might this save you from greater crosses?

Friday after Ash Wednesday: Matthew 9:14-15. Jesus said, "The wedding guests cannot mourn as long as the bridegroom is with them, can they? The days will come when the bridegroom is taken away from them, and then they will fast." What does fasting express for you? What does it make you aware of?

Saturday after Ash Wednesday: Luke 5:27-32. Jesus said, "Those who are well have no need of a physician, but those who are sick; I have come to call not the righteous but sinners to repentance." What is healthy in your spiritual life? Where is growth needed? Have you experienced Jesus inviting you to more?

Several Suggestions for Lent

Prayer: Do something different. Add or change something in the way of you pray.

Fasting: Change something in your life-style: Make it simpler.

Almsgiving: Find a new way to give love, help or more acceptance to someone in your life.

First Sunday of Lent

Life on What Terms?

Genesis 2:7-9; 3:1-7; Romans 5:12-19; Matthew 4:1-11

All three temptations in the desert are attempts to turn Jesus' Kingdom into another worldly kingdom: a kingdom of prosperity, power and productivity; a kingdom focused on satisfaction, security and success. These temptations invite us to ask what we are looking for in life and what we are asking from the Church.

Prosperity includes more than what money can buy. It can be any self-satisfaction that comes from feeling we "have it made" in terms of health, education, career, human relationships, self-development, even moral behavior. Churches fall into this temptation when they center on people's need to feel blameless through law-observance (legalism), on their need for healing (as opposed to knowing God) or on their need for "community" (meaning supportive human relationships). All of these concerns are good, provided they do not become the main focus of our religion.

Power does not simply mean dominating others. It also presents itself as security or invulnerability: the power to survive, to maintain one's position, to defend oneself and one's family, friends and possessions against any threat. This temptation makes us want the Church to be for us the reassuring image of a well-ordered, unchanging world where God keeps everything under control through an established authority system: a Church of legalism, clericalism and triumphalism—in short, a no-risk religion.

Productivity is good if we are working out of the servant stance of responsible stewardship under God. But when we want success for its own sake—for what it says to us about ourselves, for the self-esteem that achievement offers—then we are tempted to make the accomplishment of our will and purposes the supreme law of life. This is idolatry and pride.

When we find ourselves tempted to compromise our obedience to God by accepting forbidden means to a desirable end, it is a sign that our religion is turning into idolatry. This has led Christian Churches into burning heretics and persecuting other religions; it was the spirit behind the Inquisition and the Crusades. And it is the spirit behind any current religious movement or crusade which sacrifices love and respect for opponents to the achievement of a seemingly desirable goal. Such conduct rejects Jesus, "the Lamb of God" and Isaiah's Suffering Servant (see Isaiah 42—53); it denies everything Jesus taught through the cross.

Adam and Eve disobeyed God for the sake of a human value which they thought would enhance their lives by making them Godlike. The pride of their disobedience to God brought destruction on the human race. Jesus, on the other hand, "though he was in the form of God, / did not regard equality with God / as something to be exploited, / but emptied himself, / taking the form of a slave.... [H]e humbled himself and became obedient to the point of death—even death on a cross" (Philippians 2:6-8). As a result, Saint Paul says, "[J]ust as by one man's disobedience the many were made sinners, so by the one man's obedience the many will be made righteous."

Lent is a time of choice. The desert is a place of choice. To observe Lent, to "go out into the desert," is to confront the choices we have made, the choices we are making, consciously or not, and the choices we have yet to make. It is to ask what we are actually looking for now—from life, from our religion. Are we living for satisfaction, security, success? Are we basing our hopes on prosperity? On power? On productivity? Are we hiding behind "fig leaves" of illusions because we are afraid to stand naked in truth before God?

Lent invites us to turn away from every desire, defense or idol which prevents us from focusing on Jesus as Savior and basing our lives on him as the Way, the Truth and the Life.

Reflecting on This Week's Gospels

First Week of Lent

Pray daily: Father, through our observance of Lent, help us to understand the meaning of your Son's death and resurrection, and teach us to reflect it in our lives. Grant us this through Christ, our Lord.

Monday: Matthew 25:31-46. And the king will "say to those at his left hand, 'You that are accursed, depart from me' for I was hungry and you gave me no food, I was thirsty...a stranger...naked...sick and in prison, and you did not visit me." Whom does society reward or write off in this world? The achievers or the humble? Those with power or those with no way to defend themselves? The rich or the poor? How does God judge people?

Tuesday: Matthew 6:7-15. "When you are praying, do not heap up empty phrases as the Gentiles do; for they think that they will be heard because of their many words. Do not be like them, for your Father knows what you need before you ask him." When you want something from God, do you look for novenas and devotions which promise surefire results, or do you just pray trustingly to God who loves you?

Wednesday: Luke 11:29-32. "This generation is an evil generation; it asks for a sign, but no sign will be given to it except the sign of Jonah." How much do you think about the sign of Jesus' Resurrection after three days in the grave? What does it mean to you? What do you do about it?

Thursday: Matthew 7:7-12. "If you then, who are evil, know how to give good gifts to your children, how much more will your Father in heaven give good things to those who ask him!" What do you want, or what would you want most for your children? Is this what you ask God to give you?

Friday: Matthew 5:20-26. "So when you are offering your gift at the altar, if you remember that your brother or sister has something against you, leave your gift there before the altar and go; first be reconciled to your brother or sister, and then come and offer your gift." Is "winning your case" in a way that satisfies you a way to be reconciled with another? What is the best way to resolve conflicts?

Saturday: Matthew 5:43-48. "You have heard that it was said, 'You shall love your neighbor and hate your enemy.' But I say to you, Love your enemies and pray for those who persecute you." How does this teaching match the slogans and attitudes of our society?

Several Suggestions for Lent

Prayer: This week do something which indicates you believe that you live not by bread alone but by the word of God revealed to us in the Bible. Read each day's gospel passage.

Fasting: Sacrifice ten minutes of time you spend on something else and then use it to pray.

Almsgiving: Go to Mass one day this week to pray for someone who does not have or does not appreciate the riches of the Eucharist.

Second Sunday of Lent

Man of the Promise

Genesis 12:1-4a; 2 Timothy 1:8b-10; Matthew 17:1-9

Abraham was chosen by God to be the father of the Jewish race. To be born a Jew meant to be born a descendant of Abraham. It was only through their relationship with Abraham that the Chosen People shared in God's first covenant and promises. God told Abraham, "This is my covenant, which you shall keep, between me and you and your offspring after you...." (see Genesis 17:1-23).

Saint Paul begins his second letter to Timothy by recalling God's promise to give life to the whole human race through Jesus, according to the plan God made "before the ages began" (see 2 Timothy 1:1, 9). The grace, the favor of God is held out to us "in Christ Jesus." It is through our relationship with him that we share in God's New Covenant and its promises.

Jesus, however, did not have an impressive presence on earth while walking the roads of Galilee. He was an ordinary man, dressed in ordinary clothes, who traveled on foot and generally attracted the poor and uneducated as followers. The large crowds that followed Jesus were usually small by our standards: small enough for Jesus to teach them while sitting down, without a microphone. Important people, like the Sanhedrin leader Nicodemus, were afraid to be seen with him. When a low-ranking Roman officer asked for a cure, Jesus was amazed. Mostly, he was a small-time preacher on a small-town circuit.

Today Jesus is still not that prominent. He does not have high visibility in most countries' national life. And when he does, in the person of the pope or Church dignitaries, it may be because they are using the same status symbols (private jets, motorcades, clothing, protocol) that other political figures use. But in most of Jesus' ministry today—his quiet

influence on family and social life, business and politics;
the daily initiatives and decisions of all the members of
his Body; his daily presence through everyone engaged in
teaching, preaching and healing ministries—Jesus keeps a
very low profile, so low that many people hardly notice
his presence.

That is why God gave us the Transfiguration and why
we celebrate this liturgy. Here, as on the mountain of the
Transfiguration, God invites us to look at Jesus in his glory:
to see his face shining like the sun, to hear the Father saying
to us, "This is my Son, the Beloved;...listen to Him!" In the
liturgy Jesus is recognized for what he truly is: the Good
News, the Light of the world, the Lamb of God who takes
away the sins of the world, the Bread of Life. In the liturgy
bread and wine, ordinary things, symbols of ourselves and
of our ordinary lives, are given back to us transfigured,
transformed into Eucharist, into the Bread of Life and our
spiritual drink. The host and the chalice are held up to us,
lifted up as Jesus was on the cross, and a voice proclaims,
"This is my body. This is the cup of my blood. Take this,
all of you. Eat. Drink." And we adore.

After the Transfiguration, Jesus said to his disciples,
"Tell no one about the vision until after the Son of Man has
been raised from the dead." Now Jesus is risen. Now is the
time to proclaim him to the world as what he is: the Savior,
the Lord, the fulfillment of all God's promises, Abraham's
descendant in whom "all the families of the earth shall
be blessed."

It is time for us to focus our own hearts on the grace
given to us in Christ Jesus, "who abolished death and
brought life and immortality to light through the gospel."
It is time to look, to see and to believe.

Reflecting on This Week's Gospels

Second Week of Lent

> **Pray daily**: *God our Father, help us to hear your Son. Enlighten us with your word, that we may find the way to your glory. Grant us this through Christ, our Lord. Amen.*

Monday: Luke 6:36-38. "Be merciful, just as your Father is merciful." The expression "be merciful" means to come to the aid of another out of a sense of relationship. On the basis of Jesus' teaching, can you see every person as God the Father does and treat every person as a brother or sister? How will doing this change your life?

Tuesday: Matthew 23:1-12. "The greatest among you will be your servant." Can you serve everyone, wherever you are, whatever you are doing? What are you seeking in your work, social and family life, civic involvement or participation in your parish? Is it service?

Wednesday: Matthew 20:17-28. "...[T]he Son of Man came not to be served but to serve, and to give his life a ransom for many." How is Jesus serving you now? In what ways are others sacrificing themselves for you? How are you responding?

Thursday: Luke 16:19-31. "And at his gate lay a poor man named Lazarus, covered with sores, who longed to satisfy his hunger with what fell from the rich man's table." Who would gladly receive from you a "scrap" of notice or attention, a smile, a thoughtful act or some help you can give? Whom do you know who is "covered with sores"— wounded by life experiences? How can you help?

Friday: Matthew 21:33-43, 45-46. "Have you never read in the scriptures: 'The stone that the builders rejected / has become the cornerstone; / this was the Lord's doing, / and it is amazing in our eyes'?" Is Jesus the cornerstone of your life, the key to everything you think, say and do? Have you rejected him in favor of building your life around something else, some other goal, value, program or attitude? If you stopped believing in Jesus tomorrow, what concrete things would you change in your life-style?

Saturday: Luke 15:1-3, 11-32. "But we had to celebrate and rejoice, because this brother of yours was dead and has come to life; he was lost and has been found." When people sin against you, insulting or treating you unjustly, is your first reaction to defend yourself? To get even? Or do you pray that they will be converted and "come to life"?

Several Suggestions for Lent

Prayer: Put the Bible on your pillow. Read one line before going to sleep each night and again on waking up.

Fasting: Pick one activity of your day that you enjoy. Decide not to satisfy yourself by doing that until you have done something kind for someone else.

Almsgiving: Each time someone (including God!) is nice to you or does you a favor, do something right away for someone else.

Third Sunday of Lent

Striking the Rock

Exodus 17:3-7; Romans 5:1-2, 5-8; John 4:5-42

After Jesus spoke to the Samaritan villagers, they said to the woman who had told them about him, "It is no longer because of what you said that we believe, for we have heard for ourselves, and we know that this is truly the Savior of the world."

We need to be able to say this to the Church, the "woman" we met at the well of Baptism. Our faith in Jesus must be the result of personal encounter with him. We cannot truly know him through others' experience of him, through what we have been told by our parents, friends and community. The witnesses to Christ invite us to come and see; it is only when we have "heard for ourselves," when we have "seen with our eyes" and "touched with our hands" that we can say we truly know Jesus as the Word of life (see John 1:39, 46; 1 John 1:1).

This requires discipleship: reading and reflecting on Scripture, thinking about Jesus, talking to him, interacting with him in all the ways we interact with friends and teachers and those whom we love, encountering him in the sacraments of Reconciliation and Eucharist, celebrating in liturgy his life and recognizing the continuing impact of his self-offering for the world's salvation.

Faith is the foundation of discipleship; discipleship turns faith into experience. Do we recognize God's gift? Do we believe that Jesus is the Messiah, the Anointed One who will tell us everything? Do we believe that Jesus will give us living water that will become in us a "spring, gushing up to eternal life"? If we believe, why do we not come and drink? Why do we fail to keep coming to see for ourselves?

Hope is what keeps discipleship going. We must not doubt as Moses did when he struck the rock in Horeb.

Because he feared that God would not keep the promise, Moses asked the community, "Listen, you rebels, shall we bring water for you out of this rock?" (Numbers 20:10). And then Moses struck the rock a second time, just to be safe.

We have to pray, to read and reflect on Scripture, not as an experiment to see if it will work, but realizing that it will work if we persevere. Jesus is the rock; he has promised us "living water." Unlike Moses, we have been told to strike the rock calmly and consistently, not expecting instant results but trusting absolutely that if we ask we will receive, if we seek we will find and, if we keep knocking, the heart of Christ will open to us.

Christ's love is the reason for our hope. We dare not expect to find living water in the word of God because we are good at praying or because we are especially virtuous or have a special gift for understanding Scripture. It is because Christ loves us. He wants to share his heart with us, to teach us the truth which sets us free, to lead us into deeper love, joy and peace—into the fullness of life. This is why he came. Saint Paul says, "Hope does not disappoint us, because God's love has been poured into our hearts through the Holy Spirit that has been given to us." (See John 8:32; 10:10; 14:12-27; Romans 5:5.)

It is true that the more we love God, the more clearly we will be able to understand his word. "Blessed are the pure in heart, for they will see God" (Matthew 5:8). But the real source of our hope is that God "proves his love for us in that while we were still sinners Christ died for us." It is God's love, demonstrated through Jesus' death on the cross, which gives us confidence, hope and strength to persevere. God's love for us sweetens even what is bitter in the waters of life (see Exodus 15: 22-25).

Reflecting on This Week's Gospels

Third Week of Lent

Pray daily: Father, you have taught us to overcome sin by prayer, fasting and works of mercy. When we are discouraged by our weakness, give us confidence in your love.

Monday: Luke 4:24-30. Jesus said, "Truly I tell you, no prophet is accepted in the prophet's hometown." Are you so used to having the word of God that you fail to read it? So used to having Jesus as Teacher that you do not consult him?

Tuesday: Matthew 18:21-35. Jesus said that Peter must forgive "Not seven times, but, I tell you, seventy-seven times." Do you believe that the right, the best response to hurt and injustice is forgiving as God forgives us? Are you waiting to forgive someone? Who has hurt you "just one time too many"?

Wednesday: Matthew 5:17-19. "Do not think that I have come to abolish the law or the prophets; I have come not to abolish but to fulfill." Have you seen how each of the Ten Commandments has been transformed and perfected by the teaching of Jesus? What concrete choices in your life show that you aim at more than just avoiding sin?

Thursday: Luke 11:14-23. "Every kingdom divided against itself becomes a desert.... Whoever is not with me is against me, and whoever does not gather with me scatters." Do you try to be "with" Jesus in your daily actions or do you seek simply not to go against him? How can you seek nothing except "the Kingdom of God and his righteousness" in your work, social life, family life?

Friday: Mark 12:28-34. One of the scribes asked Jesus, "Which commandment is the first of all?" Which commandment is first for you? First in your consciousness? How do you show that?

Saturday: Luke 18:9-14. "[F]or all who exalt themselves will be humbled, but all who humble themselves will be exalted." According to Jesus, in what does your true value consist? Do you need to win the approval of others to believe you are good and lovable? Do you feel a need to explain away your faults? Do you act as though you must "win" God's love or do you accept it as a totally free gift?

Several Suggestions for Lent

Prayer: Read the Gospel for each day this week. Ask yourself what point in it you would preach on if you were giving the homily at Mass. Then practice what you would preach.

Fasting: Ask if there is any sacrifice you could make which would let God work through you better at home, at work, in your social life.

Almsgiving: Each day share with another person the living water you receive from Jesus Christ.

Fourth Sunday of Lent

Anointing for Sight

1 Samuel 16:1b, 6-7, 10-13a; Ephesians 5:8-14; John 9:1-41

When John says Jesus spread mud on the eyes of the man born blind, the word John uses (*epechrisen*) actually means "anointed." Anointing has been part of the baptismal rite from the earliest days of the Church. At Baptism we who were "born blind," culturally conditioned by the darkness of this world's attitudes and values, were anointed to see. Like David, whom Samuel anointed to be king, we were chosen by God and anointed, and "the spirit of the LORD came mightily" upon us.

We were anointed to be prophets, people who see how the general teaching of Jesus applies to our world. We become prophets not when we learn the teachings of Jesus but when we see how they call us to change the way we do things in family and social life, business and politics. The blind man in the story became a prophet when he was anointed with mud, earth mixed with Jesus' saliva, and then was "washed" (baptized) in the pool whose name (Siloam) means "sent." When we confront the reality of this world with the truth that comes from Jesus' mouth, then we accept our baptismal mission and thereby become prophetic.

Pope John XXIII convened Vatican Council II with a call to bring the contemporary world into contact with the life-giving energies of the gospel. The Church's mission is to bridge the gap between this world and God, between the darkness of the culture and the light of Christ. We do this by being earth ourselves. Our physical bodies are made into "mud"—something moist and pliable, a matrix of life like the primordial ooze from which life emerged on earth—by being blended with the truth coming from the mouth of Jesus. When our own transformed and prophetic life-styles— our "baptized" words, choices, policies, behavior—are applied to the eyes of the culture, the world can see again. By living in this world and yet apart from it, we become for others what Baptism anoints us to be. As Christians we are not simply involved in family, school, social life, business and politics; we are "applied to" all these areas of life like an ointment. We do not merely exist in the world; we are sent in, sent to model a different outlook.

For this we must come of age. The parents of the man born blind would not answer for him; they said, "He is of age; ask him." And the man spoke fearlessly. To be prophets we cannot hide behind the skirts of the Church's teaching. We cannot defend our attitudes, our values, our choices by saying, "The Church teaches..." or even "The Bible says...". We have to think about what God teaches through the Church or the Bible until we are transformed and can say for ourselves, "I see it." We are not mere channels to pass on the living water of Christ's teaching; we are "mud paste," people impregnated with his truth, warm bodies transformed by his words, people in daily, physical contact with this world to heal it. We are ointment, not pipelines. We heal by what we are, not just by what we "pass on."

Our impact on the world is not automatic. We too were "born blind," and we acquire clear vision only gradually. Saint Paul reminds us, "For once you were darkness, but now in the Lord you are light. Live as children of light." God's light is within us, but if we are to produce every kind of goodness, justice and truth, that light must permeate our family and social life, school life, work and politics. This means we need to read and reflect on Christ's teachings and on his example. We need to see our lives under his light. Then the values which are now overshadowed by our culture's preoccupations become clearly visible; then all the dark corners that no one ever talks about will be bathed in light.

Reflecting on This Week's Gospels

Fourth Week of Lent

> *Pray daily: God our Father, your Word, Jesus Christ, spoke peace to a sinful world. Teach us, the people who bear his name, to follow the example he gave us. May our faith, hope and love turn hatred to love, conflict to peace, death to eternal life. Amen.*

Monday: John 4:43-54. Jesus said to the royal official, "Unless you see signs and wonders you will not believe." The official replied, "Sir, come down before my little boy dies." Can you pray with absolute trust that, regardless of what you see, God loves you enough to provide everything you need?

Tuesday: John 5:1-16. Jesus asked the paralyzed man, "Do you want to be made well?...Stand up, take your mat and walk." Do you believe that Jesus is offering what you need to live the life of grace more fully? Do you want it?

Wednesday: John 5:17-30. Jesus said, "I can do nothing on my own. As I hear, I judge; and my judgment is just, because I seek to do not my own will but the will of him who sent me." Do you consciously base every judgment and decision on what you hear Jesus saying in the Gospels?

Thursday: John 5:31-47. "But I have a testimony greater than John's. The works that the Father has given me to complete, the very works that I am doing, testify on my behalf that the Father has sent me." What visible behavior of yours shows that you are conscious of being sent by Jesus to establish the Kingdom of God?

Friday: John 7:1-2, 10, 25-30. Jesus said, "I have not come on my own.... I know him [the Father], because I am from him, and he sent me." How would your life change if you remembered that you do not go to work or to social events on your own but rather are sent by God? Do all your actions at home, at school, work and recreation show that you know Jesus?

Saturday: John 7:40-53. The guards sent to arrest Jesus said, "Never has anyone spoken like this!" Would the people you deal with say that you speak and act in a way that is different from others? Do they ever say, "No one does that!" or "Nobody thinks like that!"? Is that because you are thinking and speaking the truth as Jesus teaches it?

Several Suggestions for Lent

Prayer: At the end of each day, ask what you have done that day which was different because it was consciously based on something Jesus said or did.

Fasting: Change something in your life-style. Ask "How does this bear witness to the values of Jesus?" until you find something you have, do or say that could become more radically Christian.

Almsgiving: Choose to improve something in your work or school environment, or in your family or social life, simply by changing your behavior in some specific way. Be "salt of the earth" by adding taste from the gospel to something you do.

Fifth Sunday of Lent

"Lord, If You Had Been Here..."

Ezekiel 37:12-14; Romans 8:8-11; John 11:1-45

Where Jesus is, there life is; where he is not, sin has power to wound and to kill. Martha said to Jesus, "Lord, if you had been here, my brother would not have died." How many people can say today: "Lord, if you had been here, the war that killed my brother would never have happened; the driver who killed my sister would not have been drinking; the hunger and disease that kill children every day would not have been ignored"? How many deaths are due to human cruelty? When we exclude God from our world, from our thoughts and our decision-making processes, we invite selfishness, cruel indifference, destructive greed and violence.

It is not just physical death we are talking about. How many times can we say, "Lord, if you had been here, if you had been speaking through these people, acting in this community, our brothers and our sisters would not have turned away from love or given up hope. They would not have lost faith in themselves, in other people, in the Church, in God. Something in them would not have died."

Jesus is "the resurrection and the life." But he is this not only in himself but also in his Body on earth. He acts through us. The woundedness we see around us need not "lead to death." We can respond to sin and to sickness of heart in such a way that "the Son of God may be glorified." Jesus' risen presence in the world can be revealed and his power made manifest through the life-giving, healing love we show to all in need—to victims and violators alike.

When Jesus said, "Let us go to Lazarus," the apostle Thomas said, "Let us also go, that we may die with him." Thomas spoke as a prophet; Jesus indeed gave life to the world by dying. And we can give life only if we die with him in order that others may live. The dying we must accept is giving our flesh for the life of the world as Jesus did. And this means to give expression in the flesh to truth, to hope, to love.

Jesus came as the Word made flesh. He was the truth of God expressed visibly on earth. In his teaching God's words were "made flesh" in the physical sounds of his voice. In his life-style the values of God were literally embodied. He was killed for bearing witness to the truth. And on the cross, more important than the pain he suffered was the love he expressed through it.

To express ourselves is to be vulnerable. We are afraid to drop all the masks we hide behind, to be ourselves, to reveal ourselves, to express ourselves. Just as we use clothes to hide our bodies, we often use our bodies to hide our emotions and thoughts. We don't want the "word" of our souls to be "made flesh" in nakedness, even to give life to those around us.

This is what our baptismal priesthood is all about: We were anointed at Baptism to share in the priesthood of Jesus. But a priest has no function except as a minister within a community. To accept our baptismal consecration as priests is to accept our role of *active ministry in the community of the Church*. And this means *giving expression* to the truth and love within us by grace. Saint Paul writes, "You are in the Spirit, since the Spirit of God dwells in you." God is revealed through our words and actions so that no one will ever have to say, "Lord, if you had been here...." Every member of Christ has "the manifestation of the Spirit for the common good" (see 1 Corinthians 12:7). This is the fulfillment of God's promise made to Ezekiel, "I am going to open your graves, and bring you up from your graves.... I will put my spirit in you, and you shall live." When we surrender ourselves to let God express his truth, his love through us, Jesus can empower us as a community of priests to "roll away the stone" that keeps others in their tombs, and can say to us, "Unbind them and let them go free."

Reflecting on This Week's Gospels

Fifth Week of Lent

Pray daily: Father, help us to be like Christ your Son, who loved the world and died for our salvation. Inspire us by his love and guide us by his example. Amen.

Monday: John 8:1-11. "The scribes and the Pharisees brought a woman who had been caught in adultery...making her stand before all of them." People are frequently exposed in their sinfulness. Are you ready to "stand before" your friends expressing your faith? Do you respond and sing at liturgy? Do you express your faith at work, home and in your social life?

Tuesday: John 8:21-30. Jesus said, "[T]he one who sent me is true, and I declare to the world what I have heard from him." Are you willing to tell the world that what you have learned from Jesus in the Church is true? How do you feel when unpopular truths are criticized? To whom are you sent to speak about Jesus?

Wednesday: John 8:31-42. Jesus said, "If you continue in my word, you are truly my disciples; and you will know the truth, and the truth will make you free." Are you confident that you can make people free by sharing with them Jesus' teaching? Do you do it?

Thursday: John 8:51-59. Jesus said, "I know [the Father], and if I would say that I do not know him, I would be a liar like you. But I do know him and I keep his word." How do you show publicly your love for the Father, for Jesus, for Mary? Are you willing to share your experiences of God? With whom?

Friday: John 10:31-42. Many came to Jesus and said, "John performed no sign, but everything that John said about this man was true." Do you realize and accept the power you have to bring others to Jesus through the witness of your own faith and life-style? What do people see in your life that indicates that you take Jesus and your faith seriously?

Saturday: John 11:45-57. Caiaphas, the high priest, said, "[I]t is better...to have one man die for the people than to have the whole nation destroyed." Is it better that you should suffer for speaking the truth, or that little by little, through everyone's silence, whole nation or culture should accept many falsehoods, prejudices and wrong values?

Several Suggestions for Lent

Prayer: Try praying with someone this week—at home, at work, on a date—anything from just saying the Our Father together or talking over a Scripture passage.

Fasting: Is there anything in your life you could stop doing (or stop not doing!) just because it doesn't express your real values and beliefs?

Almsgiving: How could you give someone a gift out of the riches of your faith and religion? What do you have as a Catholic that others may not have but might like to know about? How can you make a gift to others by expressing your devotion in liturgy?

Passion (Palm) Sunday

An Unassuming Triumph

Gospel Before the Procession: Matthew 21:1-11;
Isaiah 50:4-7; Philippians 2:6-11; Matthew 26:14—27:66

The key word in Matthew's report of Jesus' triumphal entry into Jerusalem is *praus*, which is translated as "meek," "humble" or "without display." Jesus' entry is seen as the fulfillment of Zecharaiah's prophecy: "Lo, your king comes to you; / ...humble [*praus*], and riding on a donkey, on a colt, the foal of a donkey." This text includes the king among the "lowly," the poor in spirit "whose poverty did not allow them the arrogance and assertiveness of the wealthy but imposed habitual and servile deference." The way Jesus chose to enter Jerusalem proclaimed him as one of these; "This was the only type of Messianic claim Jesus would publicly profess—the claim to be the Messiah who was one of the lowly" (*Jerome Biblical Commentary*, Prentice-Hall, 1968, 30:43, 142).

The description of Jesus as humble or lowly is very important because this entry into Jerusalem was the only triumphal entry that Jesus, the Son of David, would ever make into David's city. Perhaps Jesus' disciples saw this entry as a preview of the triumphal procession they would have once he defeated all his enemies and took over the government as king. But this was all there would ever be. Jesus would never reign on earth as the Messiah-king they expected. And that is the whole point: He was born poor and lowly, would die poor and lowly and never intended to become anything else. His Kingdom would be a reign established by no other power than the power of truth and love.

Jesus' entry into Jerusalem was in fact a victory parade. He entered as king to establish his reign. But he would triumph by being defeated; he would establish his reign by dying; the only throne he would ever have on this earth was the cross. If we are going to join the crowd in shouting "Hosanna"—as we do at the *Sanctus* (Holy, Holy, Holy) of every Mass—we ought to know what kind of Messiah we are accepting. The only Messiah who comes "in the name of the Lord" intends to win by losing, to give life by dying, to conquer by loving and to reign by identifying himself with the poor and powerless.

This is not ancient history; this is now. Jesus still refuses to save the world with what we recognize as power. He still does not use divine force to wipe out disease, crime, poverty, oppression or error. He still tries to convert rather than to control. He still chooses to love instead of trying to look good. As a result, his Church and his followers on earth make him look like a loser. Jesus still identifies himself not only with the powerless but also with sinners. He works through sinful people: popes, bishops, clergy and laity. He uses a Church which is still trying to understand the gospel after two thousand years of learning by trial and error. Jesus works through human intelligence, teaching truth at a human pace to those who seek rather than impose truth on everyone with a blast of divine enlightenment. He works through human freedom, allowing evil to have its way until evildoers freely turn away from sin. Jesus respects human nature so much that the only way he will establish his reign on earth is through human beings freely cooperating with him, freely uniting themselves to him in mind, will and action.

At Baptism we were anointed as "kings" or sharers in the kingship of Christ through stewardship. We were consecrated to work with him to establish his life-giving reign over every area and activity of human life. But since Jesus chose to respect freedom rather than use force, to convert rather than control, the condition for working with him is a commitment to unconditional perseverance. We must keep trying to transform society, to renew human life on earth through love and powerlessness—regardless of visible results—while, as we say at Mass, "we wait in joyful hope for the coming of our Savior, Jesus Christ."

Reflecting on This Week's Gospels

Holy Week

*Pray daily: Almighty Father of our Lord Jesus
Christ, you sent your Son to be born of a woman
and to die on a cross, so that through the obedience
of one man estrangement might be dissolved for all.
Guide our minds by his truth and strengthen our
lives by the example of his death, that we may live
in union with you in the kingdom of your promise.
Amen.*

Monday: John 12:1-11. Jesus said, "You always have the
poor with you, but you do not always have me." How do you
find Jesus in prayer? In the poor?

Tuesday: John 13:21-33, 36-38. Jesus asked Peter, "Will
you lay down your life for me? Very truly, I tell you, before
the cock crows, you will have denied me three times." When
do you take risks because of faith and love for Christ?

Wednesday: Matthew 26:14-25. Jesus said, "The one who
has dipped his hand into the bowl with me will betray me."
In what ways do you express one thing in liturgy and
something quite different at work or in your social life?

Holy Thursday: John 13:1-15. "And during supper Jesus,
knowing that the Father had given all things into his hands,
and that he had come from God and was going to
God...poured water into a basin and began to wash the
disciples' feet and to wipe them with the towel." Then Jesus
said to the apostles, "If I, your Lord and Teacher, have
washed your feet, you also ought to wash one another's feet.
For I have set you an example...." Do you live your life in
service to others—at home, at work, in social and civic life?
Is your attitude always one of humble service, not wanting to
be first, not asking to be served? Do you recognize and
reverence Christ in other people as you do in the Eucharist?

Good Friday: John: 18:1—19:42. Jesus answered Pilate: "You say that I am a king. For this I was born, and for this I came into the world, to testify to the truth." How do you testify to the truth through your words and actions at home, at work, in your social and civic life? Is your witness changing things? Is it causing hostility?

Several Suggestions for Lent

Prayer: Try to spend Holy Week in greater reflection and quiet. Participate in the Easter Triduum services: Holy Thursday, Good Friday and the Easter Vigil.

Fasting: Think about Jesus' Passion, seeing his love expressed. Ask yourself, "What have I done for Christ? What am I doing for Christ? What will I do for Christ?"

Almsgiving: Ask what contribution you can make to improve conditions at home, at work, in your social life, in your city or country. How can you help bring people together into unity and peace according to Christ's desire? (See Ephesians 1:9-10.)

EASTER
TRIDUUM
and
EASTER

Easter Triduum
   (Holy Thursday, Good Friday, Easter Vigil)

A Three-Day Sunday

Mass of the Lord's Supper (Holy Thursday)
Exodus 12:1-8, 11-14; 1 Corinthians 11:23-26;
John 13:1-15

Good Friday
Isaiah 52:13—53:12; Hebrews 4:14-16, 5:7-9;
John 18:1—19:42

Easter Vigil
*At least three of seven Old Testament readings with
Psalm responses, always including the Exodus account:*

Genesis 1:1—2:2; Genesis 22:1-18; Exodus 14:15—15:1;
Isaiah 54:5-14; Isaiah 55:1-11; Baruch 3:9-15,32—4:4;
Ezekiel 36:16-17a,18-28; Romans 6:3-11; Matthew 28:1-10

Many people think that we celebrate the Resurrection on Easter Sunday. To them, Good Friday is a tough day for remembering the crucifixion and Holy Thursday a sort of nice day when we think about the Eucharist and visit church. But Easter is Sunday.

At some point they may have been told that Easter is the greatest feast of the year, greater than Christmas. But that doesn't seem true: Nobody gets into Easter as much as into Christmas. And besides, at Christmas school is out for a week or more; Easter doesn't rate that.

Easter is really a three-day Sunday: a celebration of the resurrection that lasts from Holy Thursday evening to Easter Sunday evening.

Good Friday is all about resurrection, not crucifixion! Holy Thursday is a celebration of resurrection, too. The three last days of Holy Week are one long celebration of the Resurrection—and of Baptism.

The Easter liturgy (all three days) developed as the one great celebration of the year. It was the time when new Christians were baptized—and their Baptism was an initiation into the mystery of our redemption; that is, of our rebirth as children of God. The mystery is that we are saved and reborn only by dying and rising, by being baptized into the death and resurrection of Jesus. And this mystery is so central to our whole understanding of the Good News of Jesus that the Church spends three days every year celebrating it; presenting it to our senses; reading the Scripture texts that explain it; walking us through it; helping us feel it, appreciate it, experience it.

These three days bring home to us the meaning behind the words that invite us to celebrate on Sunday: "May the grace of our Lord Jesus Christ, and the love of God, and the fellowship of the Holy Spirit be with you all." They are the most important days of the year.

If Holy Thursday, Good Friday and Holy Saturday are part of the Easter Sunday celebration, why aren't we obliged to attend services those days? The answer is that ours is a religion of meaning, not of laws. Rules are necessary, of course, in any human community. But the early Christians would no more have thought of making a rule about attending Mass than they would have thought about making it a rule that parents should attend the weddings of their children! Some things are just obvious. The three days of Easter are the most important celebration of the liturgical year.

If we really understand Baptism, and what it means for us to be the Church, what it is to be the living Body of Christ on earth, we understand that the "liturgical year" is just everybody's year, everybody's life—with its meaning made explicit. We don't have any "real" life or "ordinary" life apart from our life as Church, our life as the Body of Christ. We have died, and our lives are hidden now in Christ. We live now, not just human lives, but Christ is living in us (see Colossians 3:3). To celebrate Easter, then, is to celebrate the meaning of life itself, of our lives. Given the relationship we have with Jesus Christ, it would make more sense for us to stay home from a daughter's wedding than from the Easter liturgy. If we felt our graced bond with Christ our Head as strongly as we feel the natural bonds of kinship, this would be obvious to us.

A meaningless life is hardly worth living. And meaning unrecognized cannot give direction to our love. During the Easter liturgy we celebrate the meaning and direction of life itself. That is why we give it three days.

Easter Sunday

"He Saw and Believed"

Acts 10:34a, 37-43; Colossians 3:1-4; John 20:1-9

When John entered the empty tomb, he "saw and believed." The body of Jesus was not in the tomb. His body was risen. The Incarnate God, the Word-made-flesh is still alive and with us. This is our basic faith.

When Peter explained Christianity to the Romans at Cornelius's house, he called for faith in four basic truths: (1) Jesus is the Christ, the one anointed by God with the Holy Spirit and power; (2) he was sent to deliver us from the devil's oppression and reconcile us to God; (3) God raised Jesus from the dead and made him judge of "the living and the dead"; (4) the Church is commissioned to preach and bear witness to Jesus. All four of these truths are implicit in the Resurrection. John read them all in the "wrappings on the ground" of the empty tomb, which no longer held Jesus' body.

What the Resurrection says to us is that God has affirmed Jesus and all he taught; that he has accepted his death on the cross to "take away the sins of the world"; that he has glorified Jesus; that Jesus is "seated at the right hand of the Father" as Lord and King, with power to judge every human person and to share his glory with all who believe in him. To believe in the Resurrection is to know Jesus as the savior who has power over sin and death, can reconcile us to God, raise us from the dead, and give us the fullness of life and joy both in this life and forever. That is why Jesus' Resurrection is the source of the *hope* we have in our own resurrection and glorification.

When Jesus rose he rose *multiplied*, like the grain of wheat that falls into the ground and dies. The Resurrection is the reality of the Church. Paul says we "died with Christ"

and "were raised in Christ" because at Baptism we became
the Body of Jesus offered and resurrected. We "offered our
bodies" to him that he might live in us and continue his
human, embodied presence on earth. Because Jesus is risen
he lives now in us, his Church. And in us he continues his
"ministry of reconciliation."

Every letter attributed to Saint Paul has the words *grace*
and *peace* in the greeting. *Peace* is the word Jesus used to
greet the disciples after his Resurrection. Jesus is the source
of our peace because it is through him and in him that we
have been reconciled to God—not only in forgiveness, not
only in love, but in that union of one shared life which we
call grace—the favor of sharing in God's life. God's love
totally purifies us, embraces us and unites us to the Trinity
in an unreserved sharing of mind, will and heart.

"All this," Saint Paul tells the Corinthians, "is from God,
who reconciled us to himself through Christ, and has given
us the ministry of reconciliation" (2 Corinthians 5:18). "All
this" is implicitly expressed and contained in his Resurrection.
"All this" is the reason why we should believe in God's love
for us and love him back with confidence, in unreserved
surrender and abandonment of all we have and are to him.
And "all this" comes to us through Jesus Christ, who
loved us and gave himself up for us. "All this" invites us
to surrender our lives to Christ and to live in a loving
relationship with him in everything we do.

Saint Paul told the Colossians: "If then you were raised
with Christ, seek the things that are above, where Christ is
seated at the right hand of God. Set your minds on things
that are above, not on things that are on earth, for you have
died, and your life is hidden with Christ in God. When Christ
your life is revealed, then you also will be revealed with him
in glory."

Reflecting on This Week's Gospels

Easter Week

Pray daily: May the risen Lord breathe on our minds and open our eyes that we may know him in the breaking of the bread and follow him in his risen life. Amen.

Monday: Matthew 28:8-15. Jesus said, "Go and tell my brothers to go to Galilee; there they will see me." Jesus told those who saw him after the Resurrection to tell others about him. Whom have you invited to come and see Jesus present and acting in his Church?

Tuesday: John 20:11-18. Jesus said, "Go to my brothers and say to them, 'I am ascending to my Father and your Father, to my God and your God.'" Do you treat everyone in a way that reflects your belief in the Father of Jesus—your belief that we are brothers and sisters to each other?

Wednesday: Luke 24:13-35. They said to each other, "Were not our hearts burning within us while he was talking to us on the road, while he was opening the scriptures to us?" These two disciples immediately set out and told the apostles how Jesus was revealed to them in the breaking of the bread, the Eucharist. Have you ever felt your heart "burning" inside you at Mass? In prayer? Have you shared this experience with others?

Thursday: Luke 24:35-48. Jesus told the apostles that it was written that "the Messiah is to suffer and to rise from the dead on the third day, and that repentance and forgiveness of sins is to be proclaimed...to all nations.... You are witnesses of these things." How do you share what you know about forgiveness of sins? Whom do you know who needs to hear it?

Friday: John 21:1-14. Jesus said, "Cast the net to the right side of the boat...." After they cast the net, they were unable to pull it in because of the number of fish. How are you trying to bring people into the boat that is the Church?

Saturday: Mark 16:9-15. Jesus told the disciples, "Go into all the world and proclaim the good news." How do you share in that evangelizing ministry?

Living This Week's Gospels

As Christian: In one or two lines write down what you have "seen and believed" of Jesus Christ.

As Disciple: Read a Gospel passage used this week and imagine how Jesus would explain it to you. See if your heart is "burning within you."

As Prophet: Change something in your life-style to make it express better the truth that you are the risen Body of Jesus.

As Priest: Ask one or two Christians what makes Jesus real to them. Be ready to say what makes him real to you, if asked.

As King: Show your faith in the power of the risen Lord by trying to change some situation you are involved in— at home, at work, in your social life, in civic life.

Second Sunday of Easter

Keeping Life Alive

Acts 2:42-47; 1 Peter 1:3-9; John 20:19-31

Believing in the Resurrection gives a person cause for rejoicing. Since Jesus came out of the tomb with new life, all tombs have become wombs for those who enter them as Jesus did. We who were baptized into Christ's death have entered into the tomb to be reborn into his life. Baptism is the tomb-womb of our birth to hope, to an imperishable inheritance and to a salvation which will be revealed in all its inexpressible joy only at the end of time.

What sustains our hope in the promise of our Baptism? What helps us believe in the reality of Jesus' Resurrection and of our own? What keeps alive the love we have for him whom we have never seen?

The answer is multiple: the gift and power of grace, prayer, expressing our faith, choosing hope and love. But what sustains us in our daily activities? What keeps us faithful in fulfilling our duties? The oldest answer for Christians is community: the expression of faith in discipleship, liturgy and sacraments and in a life-style flowing from these. The earliest Christians "devoted themselves to the apostles' teaching and fellowship, to the breaking of bread and the prayers.... [They] had all things in common...."

A believing Church is a Church eager to learn. A parish that studies the teachings of Jesus grows in faith. All those who use the continuing education programs offered in parishes sustain not only their own faith but also the faith of all the others who attend. Although we certainly have to spend time alone with Jesus to let his message penetrate our hearts, we listen to him first in community. Jesus sent his disciples out not one by one but two by two.

Only witnesses are credible—and teachers to the extent

they are witnesses. Discipleship only flourishes in a Church that lives out what it learns. A Church that bears witness in action is a Church that experiences the reality of the risen life. To bear witness to the Resurrection we must live the risen life, "be intent on things above, not on things of earth" (Colossians 3:2) and show it in our life-style. We were baptized not only to know the truth but to make the truth credible to others by professing our faith in visible acts of prophetic witness.

A celebrating Church is a Church that experiences the joy of the risen life. Liturgical prayer, prayer offered together, the public expression of faith and commitment—this is one way to "have all things in common." We don't hoard the riches of our faith to ourselves, to gloat over them in private; we make a party out of the gifts God has given us. The truth of the eucharistic banquet is not manifest unless it is a potluck supper. The Mass is not said by a priest for a congregation; the Mass is celebrated by a community of priests, with one who is ordained to preside. When we give ourselves "to the breaking of the bread and the prayers," we give life to one another. But we have to "devote" ourselves, not just be passively present. We are a community of priests, not of onlookers.

Finally, like Thomas, we need to sustain our faith by human contact with the living Jesus: to see him, hear his words and feel his touch. We do this especially through the sacraments, special ways in which Jesus still ministers to us in human words and gestures. When we sin, for example, we do not silently ask forgiveness in our hearts from an invisible God and then trust that it is granted—any more than we do that with each other. A line in an old movie claimed that love means you never have to say you're sorry, but no one who loves could stand not to say it. So when we sin we say it in human words to Jesus present in a human priest; we hear human words of forgiveness spoken in response. All the sacraments are human encounters with the risen Jesus. When we act as sacraments, visible signs of faith, hope and love, to one another, we sustain Jesus' life in the world and give his peace.

Reflecting on This Week's Gospels

Second Week of Easter

Pray daily: Heavenly Father and God of mercy, increase in our minds and hearts the risen life we share with Christ and help us to grow as your people toward the fullness of eternal life with you. Amen.

Monday: John 3:1-8. Nicodemus said, "Rabbi, we know that you are a teacher who has come from God; for no one can do these signs...apart from the presence of God." What in your life shows others that God is with you? What shows your belief that God is with the Church?

Tuesday: John 3:7-15. Jesus said, "And just as Moses lifted up the serpent in the wilderness, so must the Son of Man be lifted up, that whoever believes in him may have eternal life." Nothing bears greater witness to the truth of Jesus Christ than responding to evil with love. When and how can you do this?

Wednesday: John 3:16-21. "For God so loved the world that he gave his only Son, so that everyone who believes in him may not perish but may have eternal life." Spend some time absorbing the fact that Jesus loves you this much.

Thursday: John 3:31-36. "He whom God has sent speaks the words of God, for he gives the Spirit without measure." Do you believe Jesus shares his Spirit with you abundantly? How can you open yourself to receive more light and love from the Spirit?

Friday: John 6:1-15. "There is a boy here who has five barley loaves and two fish. But what are they among so many people?" Do you believe you have something to offer the community, some contribution which will nourish others' faith? How do you try to share your gifts with others?

Saturday: John 6:16-21. Jesus said to them, "It is I; do not be afraid." What are your greatest fears? Your daily ones? How can you turn them over to Jesus in trust?

Living This Week's Gospels

As Christian: Put some visible symbol in your home or worksite as a reminder that you are living the risen, divine life of Christ; for example, holy water, a beeping watch, a white cloth.

As Disciple: Ask yourself if there is some parish Scripture study or faith-sharing group in which you could participate.

As Prophet: Change one thing in your life or life-style precisely as a way of sharing your faith through witness, that is, through some way of acting which makes no sense apart from your faith in Jesus Christ.

As Priest: Reexamine how you participate in the liturgy. Do you consciously take an active part as a priest? Does your body-language, posture, words and actions help others experience joy in these celebrations?

As King: Try to be a sacrament of hope to others through your words and actions. Refuse to look glum. Speak of what gives hope, not of what is depressing. Try to promote peace around you.

Third Sunday of Easter

Risen—"So What?"

Acts 2:14, 22-33; 1 Peter 1:17-21; Luke 24:13-35

The most reverent response we can make to the good news of Jesus' Resurrection is "So what?" Asking this question sincerely shows we are taking the Good News seriously, considering how we should respond to it in action through choices which restructure our lives.

Some scholars think that 1 Peter 1:3—2:10 quotes an earlier baptismal ritual. In fact, it describes clearly and powerfully how a life based on Baptism should be restructured. Through Christ we believe in a God who raised Jesus from the dead, will raise us from the dead and has already shared with us the divine life. Because of this faith all our attitudes and values rest on a new foundation. Our whole perception of this world is different: We see everything in the light of the new meaning that Christ's Resurrection has given to our lives. All our desires have a new focus. As Peter puts it, we have been delivered from the "futile ways" our culture hands down to us. Now all that we believe in and value, all our faith and all our hope for fulfillment, are "set on God." The life we live begins and ends in God.

Peter first explains the faith to nonbelievers by proclaiming Resurrection and new life through the gift of the Holy Spirit. Because of this we can sing with the psalmist, "[B]ecause [the Lord] is at my right hand, I shall not be moved /...my body also rests secure. / For you do not give me up to Sheol, / ...You show me the path of life" (Psalm 16:10). The path we follow is not the way of life our culture invites us to live; that life looks no further than the grave. Think about it. In our society everything—education, business, politics, social life—is organized around a single goal: finding fulfillment in a life that stops cold at death. Neither God nor grace is in the picture.

A new hope, based on faith in Resurrection, characterizes and shapes an authentically Christian life here on earth. Hope involves two things: hope for and hope in. We hope for those things we desire. We hope in whatever or whomever we trust to make them achievable.

Hope is a free choice. We hope for those things we choose to desire. We might feel desire for all sorts of things, but we only hope for those things on which we freely focus our desire. Although we might wish to lose weight, this becomes a hope only when we adopt it as a goal. In the same way, although we might want to be happy forever with God after death, this only becomes a hope when we organize our lives around it. The virtue of hope which we received at Baptism (along with faith and love) is the gift of being able not just to believe in, but also to accept personally the fulfillment which Jesus holds out as the practical, guiding goal of our lives.

We can set our hopes only on what we believe is achievable. That is why hope also means trust. And trust is also a free choice. Even when something seems clearly possible, we must choose to trust the evidence before we can try to achieve the goal. When something seems obviously impossible—such as life after death—we cannot hope for it or choose it as a goal unless we trust that something will make it possible. Our hope for life with God after death is based on our trust in the death and resurrection of Jesus Christ.

That is why we need liturgy, specifically the Eucharistic celebration. The disciples on the road to Emmaus who had hoped in Jesus but were hoping no longer, who doubted the reports that Jesus had risen from the dead, only came to know him "in the breaking of the bread." In every Mass we celebrate and proclaim through word and sacrament the reality of Christ's death and Resurrection. By expressing our hope together, we grow in it together. In liturgy we give life and receive it.

Reflecting on This Week's Gospels

Third Week of Easter

Pray daily: God our Father, may we look forward with hope to our resurrection, for you have made us your sons and daughters and restored the joy of our youth. Amen.

Monday: John 6:22-29. "Do not work for the food that perishes, but for the food that endures for eternal life, which the Son of Man will give you." What motivates you to get up in the morning? What motivated Jesus? What motivated the apostles after the Resurrection?

Tuesday: John 6:30-35. Jesus said, "I am the bread of life. Whoever comes to me will never be hungry." What hunger of yours has Jesus satisfied? What else could he satisfy? How?

Wednesday: John 6:35-40. "And this is the will of my Father, that all who see the Son and believe in him may have eternal life." What does this tell me about God as Creator? As Father? As One I can trust? As One who loves me?

Thursday: John 6:44-51. "It is written in the prophets: 'And they shall all be taught by God.' Everyone who has heard and learned from the Father comes to me." How does God teach you? How can you "hear the Father"? What draws you to Jesus?

Friday: John 6:52-59. "Just as the living Father sent me, and I live because of the Father, so whoever eats me will live because of me." How did the Father's life appear in Jesus? What did it empower him to do? How does Jesus' life reveal itself in your words and actions?

Saturday: John 6:60-69. "Lord, to whom can we go? You have the words of eternal life." To whom do you turn for help, guidance, comfort in life? Can you find these in the words of Jesus?

Living This Week's Gospels

As Christian: Ask in detail how in everything you do each day you can be part of God's work. Plan how to use reminders throughout the day. For example, symbols, watch beeps, association with other actions, like opening a door or starting your car.

As Disciple: Read a passage of Scripture every day, looking to see how these words are "words of eternal life."

As Prophet: Decide on some specific action or choice which will show (to those who have eyes to see) that in each area of your life (work, recreation and so on) you are looking for more than this life can give.

As Priest: Ask who in particular can have life because of you. Decide what you can do to share your faith, hope, love with that person in a life-giving way.

As King: Start pinpointing the goals held up to you by others at work, in your social life, when you watch TV, by those who sell you things. How can you help everything you are involved in more toward the goal of establishing Christ's reign on earth?

Fourth Sunday of Easter

Know "With Certainty"

Acts 2:14a, 36-41; 1 Peter 2:20b-25; John 10:1-10

The response Peter sought when he preached the Good News was "know with certainty" that the crucified and risen Jesus is Messiah and Lord, the "shephered and guardian of your souls" (1 Peter 2:25).

Jesus called himself the gate: "Whoever enters by me will be saved." Jesus is the Good Shepherd who calls his own by name, leading them to pasture. He described in one line what he will do for all who believe in him: "I came that they may have life, and have it abundantly." This is what we are called to believe with certainty.

Easter is the season of light, of power, of new life, of victory, of the outpouring of the Spirit. Here we take to heart the Good News that the apostles preached in their Pentecost enthusiasm. Easter invites us to be caught up and carried along in the faith-hope-love tidal wave which swept across the world after Jesus burst out of the tomb. Easter helps us to surrender ourselves to Jesus and celebrate our risen life in every action, every word, every thought on each extraordinary/ ordinary day. The key to our Easter life is this: "Know with certainty" that God has made both Lord and Messiah the Jesus who was crucified.

In the power of this belief we make the double response which flows from believing with certainty that Jesus is Lord: "Repent and be baptized." Because we experience in our hearts the power of the risen Jesus, we confidently rebuild and restructure our lives from the ground up. We live now as his Body, offering our own bodies as living sacrifices, pledging that wherever we are, whatever we are doing, we are ready to do Jesus' will, enabling him to live and act in us, carrying out the work of his Kingdom. Our repentance is not just a turning away from what is bad, not even a simple dedication to doing good works. It is a total surrender of our lives, our being, our every choice and action to the risen One now living within us, making our flesh his own. Our repentance is a consecration, a commitment to living and acting on God's level because we have been baptized into sharing divine life in Jesus Christ.

Because we are now one with Jesus, the Christ, the anointed Lamb of God, we know with certainty that we have been anointed as he was. With Jesus we are anointed as sacrificial victims, bearing witness in love to the truth of God's love for the world and for each person in it. Jesus showed that love by putting the salvation of every single person ahead of his own interests in this world. "When he was abused, he did not return abuse; when he suffered, he did not threaten" (1 Peter 2:23). Jesus did not protect himself by retaliating. "But he entrusted himself to the one who judges justly." He allowed sinners to overcome him; he loved them back. By enduring evil with love he loved evil out of existence. Jesus sends us to do the same. By our wounds, accepted in love, our world will be healed.

Do we know, are we willing to affirm "with certainty" that this Jesus who was crucified has been raised up as Messiah and Lord? Do we know and are we willing to affirm beyond any doubt, that when we are crucified by injustice, hostility, betrayal, physical and emotional abuse or bodily injury and death and yet we respond with love as he did, that we are allowing Jesus to triumph in us? Do we believe that by speaking the truth courageously in love, without defenses or threats, by challenging evil with no weapons except truth and love, we are letting him reign in us as Messiah and Lord? Do we believe that in union with him we will "have life and have it abundantly"?

Reflecting on This Week's Gospels

Fourth Week of Easter

> *Pray daily:* God and Father of our Lord Jesus
> Christ, though your people walk in the valley of
> darkness, no evil should they fear; for they follow in
> faith the call of the Shepherd you have sent for their
> hope and strength. Attune our minds to the sound of
> his voice and lead our steps in the path he has
> shown that we may know his strength and enjoy the
> light of your presence forever. Amen.

Monday: John 10:1-10. Jesus says that sheep recognize
their shepherd's voice and will follow it. How is Jesus
speaking to you today? Through whom? What obstacles
do you encounter in trying to follow that voice?

Tuesday: John 10:22-30. Jesus said, "My sheep hear my
voice. I know them, and they follow me." Do you recognize
Jesus' voice as the voice of your Shepherd, always leading
you to safety and greater life? How do you listen for
his voice?

Wednesday: John 12:44-50. "I have come as light into
the world, so that everyone who believes in me should not
remain in the darkness." How can you shed more of Christ's
light on the realities of your daily life at work, at home and
when you recreate?

Thursday: John 13:16-20. "I tell you this now, before
it occurs, so that when it does occur, you may believe
that I am he." What does it mean to you that the words
of Scripture are the words of God? That the example of
Jesus is the way God chose to live as a human being?

Friday: John 14:1-6. "Do not let your hearts be troubled.
Believe in God, believe also in me." How does the event of
the Resurrection give you comfort when you are afraid? Do
you think about the power shown in Jesus' Resurrection
when you are anxious?

Saturday: John 14:7-14. "Very truly, I tell you, the one who believes in me will also do the works that I do and, in fact, will do greater works than these, because I am going to the Father." What is Jesus doing in you, through your situation and gifts, that he could not have done in his own circumstances or in the body he received from his mother?

Living This Week's Gospels

As Christian: If you believe "with certainty" that Jesus is the Way, put some visible reminder of this every place where you make choices: in your home, car, workplace, TV room or where you socialize.

As Disciple: If you believe "with certainty" that Jesus is the Truth, put the Bible on your nightstand and tell God you will never go to sleep without reading at least one line.

As Prophet: If you believe "with certainty" that Jesus is the Way, decide each morning before you set about your day's business what actions that day will bear witness to his values.

As Priest: If you believe "with certainty" that Jesus is the Life, share his life with someone else by a word or act of love.

As King: If you believe "with certainty" that Jesus is the Lord, try to improve something, however small, in your environment this week.

"Come to the Lord!"

Acts 6:1-7; 1 Peter 2:4-9; John 14:1-12

Jesus says, "Do not let your hearts be troubled! Come to me! I am *the way, the truth, the life.* I have prepared a place for you, that you might be with me forever. Come to me! Come to me believing I am alive."

We know "with certainty" that Jesus is the *Way* that leads to the fullness of life, both now and forever. He is the *Truth.* What he tells us is true. He has seen the Father. In knowing him, we know the Father, we know God. Jesus teaches the truth that makes us free from the fears that paralyze us, the allurements of a culture which leads us into dead-end streets empty of life, the pressures which drive us to work without let-up, without conviction or joy, for the "bread that does not satisfy." We know "with certainty" that Jesus is the *Life.* He came that we might "have life, and have it to the full." He will give us what he promises—if we "come to the Lord" believing that he is alive.

Jesus is the "living stone," rejected by the world but approved and precious in God's eyes. He is—he must be for us—the cornerstone, the way we structure our lives. We need to make his words, example and mission the foundation of all our decisions, all the directions we take in life. He is the keystone of the arch, the cornerstone of our lives, the living stone present to us every moment of the day, penetrating our minds with truth, filling our hearts with love, giving strength and life and joy to everything we do.

We, too, are living stones. We are not dead, inert building blocks to be hauled around by God and set in place in the Church to just "be there" until Jesus comes again. God has made us coworkers with Christ, prophets "full of the Holy Spirit and of wisdom" in order to share Jesus' truth with others, show others his way and be a community of love and truth. We do so by celebrating his Resurrection, living his risen life, bearing witness to his presence in the world, living his teachings joyfully, proclaiming in word and action the glorious works of God, who calls the world from darkness into his marvelous light.

We are "a chosen race." God has selected us, chosen us, gifted us with Baptism to live as the Body of Christ on earth, to continue his mission. We are "a royal priesthood." We are ordained and consecrated by God, each one of us, to offer together until the end of time the Holy Sacrifice which redeems the world. In every Mass, we join with Jesus in lifting up to the Father the sins of the world. We offer ourselves with Jesus as priests in the Priest, victims in the Victim, our flesh with his, given for the life of the world—given to others, offered in love, sacrificed passionately in our every word and action so that others may have life.

We are "a royal priesthood." We are stewards of the kingship of Jesus the Lord, who came to establish his loving reign over every area and activity of human life. We are sent to transform, to consecrate every human undertaking on earth. We are priests who lift up the bread of human labor, love and dreams so that every human activity may be transformed by grace into life-giving bread for the world: life without end, life to the full. When we consecrate bread at Eucharist to be the Body of Christ, we also consecrate ourselves as the Body of Christ, bread for the world. We sacrifice ourselves to the work of transforming society until Christ is all in all.

Why should our hearts be troubled? Jesus has promised to keep doing in us and through us the works he did. And we will do "greater works than these" if we come to the Lord believing he is alive in us and we are alive in him.

Reflecting on This Week's Gospels

Fifth Week of Easter

> ***Pray daily****: Father of our Lord Jesus Christ, you have revealed to the nations your saving power and filled all ages with the words of a new song. Give us voice to sing your praise throughout this season of joy. We ask this through Christ our Lord. Amen.*

Monday: John 14:21-26. Jesus said, "[T]hose who love me will be loved by my Father, and I will love them and reveal myself to them." Do you believe that Jesus will draw you into intimacy with himself in knowledge and love if you invite him? Have you invited him?

Tuesday: John 14:27-31. Jesus said, "Peace I leave with you; my peace I give to you. I do not give to you as the world gives. Do not let your hearts be troubled, and do not let them be afraid." Do you experience his peace? Do you believe in his words? Do you read them?

Wednesday: John 15:1-8. "I am the vine, you are the branches. Those who abide in me and I in them bear much fruit...." How do you "abide in Christ"? How would you affect others if you were always consciously aware of Christ's presence in you?

Thursday: John 15:9-11. "As the Father has loved me, so I have loved you; abide in my love." How often do you deliberately recall and believe in God's love for you?

Friday: John 15:12-17. "I have called you friends, because I have made known to you everything that I have heard from my Father." Do you believe Jesus delights in sharing his heart—his thoughts, feelings, desires and dreams—with you? Do you want to share yourself with those you love? Does Jesus feel the same way?

Saturday: John 15:18-21. "If you belonged to the world, the world would love you as its own. Because you do not belong to the world, but I have chosen you out of the world—therefore the world hates you." Jesus is the stone rejected by the world's builders but approved by God. Do you tend to forget about him because our culture ignores him? When you base your choices on him, do you experience intimacy with God?

Living This Week's Gospels

As Christian: Plan how you can make Jesus the cornerstone of your life. What are your key goals or motives at work? At home? In your social life? How can Jesus transform them?

As Disciple: Ask what you can do to become "full of the Spirit and wisdom." What books could help you in this? Are there Scripture study groups you could join? Adult religious education talks you could attend?

As Prophet: Each morning choose one particular area of your life—home, work, recreation, civic life—where you can proclaim the glorious works of Christ. Choose an action which will speak without need of words.

As Priest: Consciously offer yourself with the bread and wine at the Offertory of the Mass, and again with Christ when his Body and Blood are lifted up at the Consecration. Be given, offered and lovingly sacrificed for the good of others at home, at work, at play.

As King: Ask how Jesus can work through your special gifts and situation to extend his reign in the world. Try to improve something in your environment.

Sixth Sunday of Easter

"To Be With You Always"

Acts 8:5-8, 14-17; 1 Peter 3:15-18; John 14:15-21

The Father has given us a Paraclete, a Comforter, an Advocate, the guiding Spirit of truth and love to be with us forever: to dwell with us, remain with us, abide in our hearts and be with us always!

Those Philip baptized in Samaria did not experience the coming of the Spirit until Peter and John came and imposed hands on them, praying that they might receive the Holy Spirit. And yet the Spirit had already been given to them, as to everyone, at Baptism, and was in fact already dwelling in their hearts.

Baptism gives us divine life: a share in the infinite, eternal life of God. Just as we must grow and develop as persons in order to experience being fully alive as human beings, so we have to grow in the life of grace in order to experience the Holy Spirit within us. As we grow in grace, we reflect more deeply as disciples on the words of Jesus. As we embody them more creatively in our lives, we bear witness to Gospel values as prophets. As we accept our baptismal priesthood and offer ourselves with Christ in the Eucharist and ourselves with him for the life of the world, we learn to let go of our inhibitions and live out our faith and love in life-giving ways. As we show our concern for the world and take responsibility for renewing society as stewards of the kingship of Christ, we act as a "royal priesthood." As we enter more and more fully into the commitment and consecration of our Baptism, we experience more and more the gift of the Holy Spirit abiding with us: Guiding us, strengthening and comforting us, speaking through us, acting with us, dwelling within us, given to us to be with us always!

The Spirit is not someone we experience or relate

to as "out there"—not even in the way we can relate to the Father and to Jesus as "out there." Even though Father, Son and Spirit dwell in our hearts, in the most intimate depths of our being, still it is possible for us to think of the Father "in heaven" as being "on high," to pray to the Creator "up there." It is possible to relate to Jesus "out there"—to imagine him walking the roads of Galilee or standing in front of us, speaking to us, touching, teaching or healing us. Since we can see him offering himself on the cross, we can offer ourselves with him. We can receive him from the outside in the gift of Holy Communion.

But we experience the Spirit not as Someone "out there," but as the abiding Presence within us through whom we relate to the Father as Father and to the Son as Son. Through the gift of the Spirit we know God as only the Son can know the Father. We call the Father *Abba* (the Hebrew equivalent of "Daddy") with the intimacy of sons and daughters in Christ. Only through the gift of the Spirit abiding within us can we call Jesus "Lord" and know him in truth as he really is: Savior, Teacher and Leader, Head of the Body, Bridegroom, Lover, Redeemer and Lord. Knowing the Father as Father and the Son as Son, we know the Spirit as Spirit: Indwelling Gift as abiding within us, acting within us, remaining within us *to be with us always*!

Like all God's gifts, the Spirit is a gift to be used for others. Through the Spirit we can give others "an accounting for the hope" in us; we can keep our consciences clear, always answering "with gentleness and reverence." Through the Spirit we can appear to the world as people who live by God's life, bearing witness to the risen Christ, who lives and shares his life with us.

Reflecting on This Week's Gospels

Sixth Week of Easter

Pray daily: Ever-living God, help us to celebrate our joy in the Resurrection of the Lord and to express in our lives the love we celebrate. Grant this through our Lord Jesus Christ, your Son, who lives and reigns with you and the Holy Spirit, one God for ever and ever. Amen.

Monday: John 15:26—16:4. Jesus said, "When the Advocate comes...the Spirit of truth..., he will testify on my behalf." How has the Spirit shown you that God is truly your Father? That Jesus is your Savior? That God loves you?

Tuesday: John 16:5-11. Jesus said, "[I]t is to your advantage that I go away, for if I do not go away, the Advocate will not come to you." If Jesus had stayed with the apostles, how much responsibility would they have taken for the Church? How do you exercise your responsibility for it?

Wednesday: John 16:12-15. "I still have many things to say to you, but you cannot bear them now. When the Spirit of truth comes, he will guide you into all the truth." How has your understanding of God changed as you have grown? How is it changing now?

Ascension Thursday: Matthew 28:16-20. Jesus said, "Go therefore and make disciples of all nations." How do your dealings with others reflect this command?

Friday: John 16:20-23. Jesus said, "[Y]our hearts will rejoice, and no one will take your joy from you." Do you experience a deep-down joy that nothing can take away? After Communion, close your eyes and ask yourself this prayerfully.

Saturday: John 16:23-28. "Very truly, I tell you, if you ask anything of the Father in my name, he will give it to you." We ask "in Jesus' name" when we ask as members of his Body, sharing in his mission. When do you pray like this?

Living This Week's Gospels

As Christian: Find a way to keep yourself aware of the new life you received at Baptism and of the gift of the Holy Spirit present within you. For example, put a holy water font in your home by the doorway you use most; bless yourself each time you pass by it.

As Disciple: Prayerfully ask the Holy Spirit, the Spirit of truth, to guide you to all truth as you read the Scriptures each day.

As Prophet: Ask the Holy Spirit to show you which actions or choices in your life can bear witness to the divine life in you. Look for concrete ways your life can testify to Christ's victory over sin, death, selfishness and fear. What shows your focus on eternal values?

As Priest: Be deliberately conscious at liturgy that you are praying in Christ's name, with his Spirit, as a member of his Body. Lift up the world—with its sin and its needs, its beauty and its promise—to the Father when Christ is "lifted up" during the Mass.

As King: Ask how you can persuade those you live, work or play with to "carry out all that Jesus has commanded" because it would be better for everyone. (Don't mention religion unless it is appropriate!) What does your group do that falls short of the abundant life Jesus promises? Ask the Holy Spirit's help.

Ascension of the Lord

"The Lord Be With You"

Acts 1:1-11; Ephesians 1:17-23; Matthew 28:16-20

Before Jesus ascended into heaven he did two things: He sent his disciples to carry out his mission in the world: "Go...and make disciples of all nations..." (see Matthew 28:19) and he promised to be with them and to work with them forever: "...I am with you always, to the end of the age" (see Matthew 28:20).

What does Jesus mean when he says "I am with you"? An echo of this is one of the most frequent expressions in the Mass: "The Lord be with you!" It is the same expression as our English departure-prayer, good-bye, which is an abridgment of "God be with you." This wish became such a standard Christian expression that we have stopped paying attention to what it means. Even when we do think what we are saying, we may not be conscious of the depth and mystery we as Church express when we use those words.

"The Lord be with you" is both a prayer and a reminder. It reminds us that by grace the Lord is with us. But he doesn't just watch over us and hover above us to be our guide and help. The Lord is not with us just as a companion, the way human beings often are with each other. The Lord is with us within us! He is with us as only he can be: sharing his life with us, sharing our actions with us, speaking and smiling and touching and working through us, with us and in us.

The most solemn and significant response we make during the whole Mass is the Great Amen that concludes the Eucharistic Prayer. In this Amen we own—express union of heart with—everything the ordained priest has said during the Eucharistic Prayer. And the words which invite this Amen are always the same: "Through him, with him, in him, in the unity of the Holy Spirit, all glory and honor is yours, almighty Father, forever and ever."

This is what "The Lord be with you!" means. It is the recall of what each one of us as a Christian has recognized and celebrated during the Mass: that in everything we do we are acting "through him, with him, and in him" because we are one with him and he is acting through us, with us and in us at every moment of our lives. "The Lord be with you!" sums up the Mass. To say it to each other is to say in one phrase everything we say to God and to one another in the Mass, because being with Christ as his Body on earth is the fruit of his passion and the commitment we make in response to it. This is the Christian life.

To be with him is to be dedicated to Christ's mission. It is to accept Jesus' words to the Father—"As you have sent me into the world, so I have sent them into the world" (John 17:18). And it is to accept this mission knowing that the world as Saint John uses the word is an environment alien to the gospel, even closed and at times hostile to it. To go into the world is to go as the Lamb of God, expecting the sacrifice. It is to offer one's body as the bread is offered at Mass, to become the bread of life for others: blessed and broken and given for the life of the world.

We do this by offering the truth of Christ embodied in our lives. We offer proof of the Good News by maintaining the purity of our ideals within a culture where deadly poison and the demonic assail us daily (see Mark 16:17-18). Our resistance is the sign of Christ's presence.

This is scary. The prospect of his passion made Jesus sweat blood beforehand. He even asked the Father to take this mission away from him. If we don't feel eager to confront the world of business and politics or even of family and social life with the differentness of lives lived in radical witness to the gospel, that does not mean we love less, any more than Jesus' feelings diminished his love. Love consists in choices, not feelings. And our strength comes from trust in our union with Christ, not from any confidence we feel in ourselves. That is why Jesus told his disciples not to begin their mission until they were "clothed with power from on high" by the outpouring of the Holy Spirit (Luke 24:49).

And it is why we keep saying to each other, "The Lord be with you!" It reminds us that the Lord is with us and within us to be our strength.

Seventh Sunday of Easter

"Give Glory to Your Son"

Acts 1:12-14; 1 Peter 4:13-16; John 17:1-11a

"Father, the hour has come; glorify your Son...." This is the prayer of the Easter season, indeed the prayer of all seasons. It is the prayer of the Church living the risen life; it is our prayer today and every day because it is in us that Christ is glorified. We are his "hour." Through us he lives that hour, his death, resurrection and life-giving presence to the world. The hour has come—our hour—the hour to live out fully the life entrusted to us, the hour to give glory to the Son.

"Father,...glorify your Son so that the Son may glorify you, since you have given him authority over all people, to give eternal life to all whom you have given him." We glorify Jesus Christ by receiving eternal life from him, by holding fast to it, by surrendering ourselves to the Spirit, our constant guide. We glorify Christ by valuing the gift of eternal life higher than this world's empty promises of fulfillment apart from him, by refusing to be separated from him or from the life-giving Body of his Church for anything this world offers. We glorify Jesus by living what he died for.

"And this is eternal life, that they may know you, the only true God and Jesus Christ whom you have sent." We glorify Jesus by becoming his disciples, by allowing his words to soak in, by nurturing his teachings in our hearts, by keeping his example before our eyes—day by day, hour by hour. We glorify Jesus by knowing his Father as our Father, as only the Son can know the Father. We can only know the Father through the Spirit who has been given to be with us always, the Spirit dwells in our hearts crying, "Abba! Father!" (Galatians 4:6).

We glorify Jesus by accomplishing his work as prophets called out of darkness into his wonderful light, a holy priesthood offering spiritual sacrifices acceptable to God, a royal priesthood transforming the world as stewards of Christ's kingship.

We glorify the Son whenever we let his saving message take flesh in our lives, embodying in our life-style what he took flesh to embody. When we bear prophetic witness by keeping his word and living out his truth, we show that we belong to him, that we are given to him, that he is alive and living in us.

We glorify Jesus as sharers in his priesthood when our lives give striking evidence that we have not only accepted and believed him but have also understood and known that Jesus comes from the Father and that we are truly from Jesus, one with him, united with him in offering ourselves as co-victims with him on the cross. We glorify Christ when we give witness that everything we possess is from him and that we are one with him, offering our flesh—his flesh—for the life of the world.

When the world hates us because we do not belong to it any more than Jesus did, then we know that we, too, have been consecrated in truth and sent into the world to transform and redeem it, to bring all things in heaven and on earth together under Christ's headship. When we take responsibility for establishing his reign over every area of human life on earth, we glorify the Son by accomplishing the work he gave us to do.

"Father, the hour has come; glorify your Son so that the Son may glorify you."

Reflecting on This Week's Gospels

Seventh Week of Easter

> *Pray daily: Father, help us keep in mind that Christ our Savior lives with you in glory and has promised to remain with us until the end of time. We ask this through our Lord Jesus Christ, your Son, who lives*

and reigns with you and the Holy Spirit, one God for ever and ever. Amen.

Monday: John 16:29-33. "I have said this to you, so that in me you may have peace. In the world you face persecution. But take courage; I have conquered the world!" In what ways do you know peace consciously from the fact that Jesus has conquered the world?

Tuesday: John 17:1-11. Jesus prayed about his disciples: "[T]hey have believed that you sent me...and I have been glorified in them." How does your faith glorify Jesus, make his victory visible?

Wednesday: John 17:11-19. "Sanctify them in the truth; your word is truth. As you have sent me into the world, so I have sent them into the world." How can you stay conscious that you have been consecrated to carry Jesus' word, his truth, into your world of work, family and social life?

Thursday: John 17:20-26. "The glory that you have given me I have given them, so that they may be one, as we are one, I in them and you in me, that they may become completely one." How do your intimacy with Christ and your union with others reveal in you the glory that was in Jesus?

Friday: John 21:15-19. Jesus said, "Simon son of John, do you love me more than these?... Tend my sheep." Which of Jesus' sheep are you tending? When and how? Are you aware that Jesus values your love for him?

Saturday: John 21:20-25. "But there are also many other things that Jesus did; if every one of them were written down, I suppose that the world itself could not contain the books that would be written." Do you believe God has more to teach you beyond what you already know? Do you want to learn more?

Living This Week's Gospels

As Christian: Glorify Jesus by selecting something specific to help you stay in touch with "eternal life": regular Reconciliation, a weekday Mass, a break with some sin.

As Disciple: Glorify Jesus by opening yourself in some way to knowing God more deeply; for example, make a retreat, read a spiritual book, meditate through the rosary.

As Prophet: Glorify Jesus by incorporating into your lifestyle something to show that you do not "belong to this world." Identify and challenge racist or sexist language; defend someone who is criticized unfairly.

As Priest: Glorify Jesus by consciously uniting yourself to Jesus on the cross. Believe that by enduring "in him" some suffering that you cannot escape you are contributing to the redemption of the world.

As King: Glorify Jesus by trying to change something in your environment that does not reflect the ideals of Christ. When you wake up each morning, make the sign of the cross on your lips as a reminder that you are "consecrated in truth" to have a life-giving influence on everyone around you. Try respectfully and peacefully to improve something that needs improving; do not yield to fear that the "world will hate you" because of it.

Pentecost

The Promise of Peace

Acts 2:1-11; 1 Corinthians 12:3b-7, 12-13; John 20:19-23

Peace be with you! Peace is the fruit of Christ's Resurrection. "Peace" is his Easter greeting to the disciples. Peace is Paul's greeting in every letter. Peace is the message we announce to the world. And peace is the promise that Pentecost proclaims.

Peace is not simply the absence of conflict. There is not true peace in the home just because spouses are not actually fighting. There is not true peace in the city just because no riots have broken out. True peace between nations means more than not going to war. There is not true peace in schools or worksites just because no one is actively undermining someone else. Peace is unity of mind, heart and will. True peace is what Jesus came to establish on earth.

Christ's peace is a peace that nothing in this world can give. It is the fruit of the Holy Spirit's uniting all peoples of the world in truth and in love, in mutual understanding and acceptance, in a common commitment to the good of all without exception, just as God is committed to the good of all. The peace of Christ is the peace we strive to establish in family and social life, in business and politics, between ourselves and others. It can only be established as Christ established it: through our dying and rising again.

Promoting peace means dying to all that divides us from one another; answering selfishness with self-sacrificing love; acknowledging and moving beyond past hurts through forgiveness; overcoming prejudice with openness; reconsidering our personal opinions through humility; facing our preferences and familiar customs with a willingness to change; breaking out of any ethnic exclusivity through a new vision of the human race. Following Jesus along the way of peace means that we must be willing to "turn our back on father and mother," renouncing any loyalty which obstructs our loyalty to God and to the whole human family. We are one people now—not "one nation under God" but one people, one family under a God who embraces all nations, all peoples, all cultures. We can accept no dividing lines; we have died to everything that divides us.

This peace is not just a gift; it is a process, something to work at, a goal to which we dedicate ourselves. To establish this peace we have all been given the gift of ministry through the Holy Spirit poured out in our hearts. When Jesus says, "Peace be with you," that peace is the presence of the Spirit within us. The Spirit of Jesus is an active Spirit, an empowering, impelling Spirit who overflows with gifts of ministry to make us not merely the beneficiaries of peace but its bearers to the world. We do not simply receive peace as a gift; we accept it as a mission.

There are different gifts but the same Spirit; different ministries that serve the same Lord, working to establish his Kingdom. There are different achievements, but they come from the same God working through us. Even in the diversity of our gifts and ministries, we are united through the one purpose, the one power, the one presence in us all.

The miracle of tongues at Pentecost reversed the Tower of Babel, where pride caused such conflicts that the false peace of separation became the only means of survival. Separation breeds mistrust; it distorts communication and destroys peace. Surrender to the Spirit restores communication by making us sharers in a common history "in Christ" and providing us with a common vision, purpose and language. It empowers us to unite the world in love, to proclaim peace with tongues of fire.

Reflecting on This Week's Gospels

Note: You will need to check the Liturgical Calendar on page x to find out what week of the year follows Pentecost

Sunday this year. Once you know which week it is, you can find the weekday Gospel reflections after that week's Sunday Gospel reflection. For example, if the week following Pentecost Sunday is the Ninth Week of the Year, then locate the Ninth Sunday of the Year and the weekday reflections for the Ninth Week will follow.

ORDINARY TIME

Ninth Sunday of the Year Through Thirty-Fourth Sunday of the Year

Ninth Sunday of the Year

Faith Made Flesh

Deuteronomy 11:18, 26-28, 32; Romans 3:21-25, 28;
Matthew 7:21-27

What is it that saves us, faith or good works? And what does it mean to be saved? Is it just getting to heaven, or does our response to Jesus Christ make our lives on this earth different? Is the goal of religion just to keep out of sin or does interaction with Jesus Christ make our lives count for more?

Saint Paul tells us in his Letter to the Romans that doing the "works prescribed by the law" is not enough to make us Christian. On the other hand, Saint Matthew tells us in his Gospel that just acknowledging Jesus as Lord will not get us into the kingdom of heaven. It is not enough to hear God's words and say we believe them—or even think we believe them. Jesus only recognizes as his own the one who "hears these words of mine and acts on them."

What Paul is attacking is something very common in our day and found in people of every religion: the attitude that religion is a matter of doing the right thing—as defined by either the culture or an individual. Whether we follow the laws of some group or think out everything for ourselves, if we see religion (or "upright behavior") as a matter of doing what is right and just, we reduce religion to observance of law. This was the religion of the Pharisees.

When we say "the culture" or "our society," we include the Church insofar as the Church is an organized society with laws and practices. A "cultural Catholic" is someone who does what is expected of Catholics. And if we break with "organized religion" in order to be free and independent thinkers living by our personal lights and conscience, all we do is fall into another subculture. The behavior of independent thinkers is usually predictable because nobody is in fact independent of society's influence. Most of what we call "thinking for ourselves" is just picking and choosing between various cultural trends after trying to analyze where they come from and where they lead. As the Teacher says in the Book of Ecclesiastes, "What has been is what will be; and what has been done is what will be done; there is nothing new under the sun. Is there a thing of which it is said, 'See, this is new'? It has already been, in the ages before us" (Ecclesiastes 1:9-10).

Christians are those who believe that there is something new under the sun, but that it came from outside the cosmos:

In the beginning was the Word, and the Word was with God, and the Word was God.... What has come into being in him was life, and the life was the light of all people.... The true light, which enlightens everyone, was coming into the world.... And the Word became flesh and lived among us, and we have seen his glory, the glory as of a father's only son, full of grace and truth (John 1:1,3-4,9,14).

To be authentically Christian means to believe in the words of Jesus and to live by them. This is not a religion of laws, because Jesus didn't make laws. Instead, he taught new attitudes and values—God's own. And he gave us the gift of divine life so that we could understand and accept what only God understands, and do what only God can do. What we call grace is a sharing in the life of God that enables us to live on the level of God. "From his fullness we have all received, grace upon grace. The law indeed was given through Moses; grace and truth came through Jesus Christ" (John 1:16).

To be a Christian means to give flesh to faith in action; to live by the voice of the Spirit, which we hear in the laws and teachings of the Church, in God's words spoken in Scripture and in the depths of our own hearts. To be Christian is to bear prophetic witness by faith lived out in action.

Reflecting on This Week's Gospels

Ninth Week of the Year

> *Pray daily: Lord Jesus Christ, you said to your apostles, "Peace I leave to you, my peace I give to you." Look not on our sins, but on the faith of your Church, and grant us the peace and unity of your kingdom, where you live for ever and ever. Amen.*

Monday: Mark 12:1-12. "Have you not read this scripture: 'The stone that the builders rejected / has become the cornerstone...'?" Have you rejected Jesus as a teacher of peace? With whom are you willing to fight? Over what? Did Jesus teach this?

Tuesday: Mark 12:13-17. Jesus said, "Give to the emperor the things that are the emperor's, and to God the things that are God's." Which of your other loyalties may cause conflict with your loyalty to God? Do you ever hurt some people out of loyalty to others?

Wednesday: Mark 12:18-27. Jesus said to the Sadducees, "Is not this the reason you are wrong, that you know neither the scriptures nor the power of God?" Can you think of any mistakes you made in the past because you did not keep God's power in mind? Because you failed to think about what is in Scripture? Could anything in your attitudes or decisions today be distorted for the same reason?

Thursday: Mark 12:28-34. When asked what is the first commandment, Jesus replied: "The first is, 'Hear, O Israel: the Lord our God...is one; you shall love the Lord your God with all your heart,...soul,...mind, and...strength.' The second is this, 'You shall love your neighbor as yourself.'" How can you build peace in yourself and among those around you by keeping these commandments?

Friday: Mark 12:35-37. Jesus said, "David himself calls [the Messiah] Lord; so how can he be [David's] son?" How do you think of Jesus? What is he for you?

Saturday: Mark 12:38-44. "Truly I tell you, this poor widow has put in more than all those who are contributing to the treasury. For all of them have contributed out of their abundance; but she out of her poverty has put in everything she had, all she had." Do you ever hold back from offering your service or help because what you have to offer seems insignificant?

Living This Week's Gospels

As Christian: Whenever anything disturbs your peace, stop for a moment and remember that Jesus dwells in your heart as helper, guide and friend. Fear is the enemy of peace. Trusting in God is the foundation of peace.

As Disciple: Read Scripture every day this week, asking specifically how Jesus' teaching can establish peace and unity in your home, at work, in your city and in the world.

As Prophet: Reconsider whether anything you do or your group does expresses an attitude of division from other people. Decide what you can do to express unity.

As Priest: Identify five people who are hurting in some way. Do one thing this week just to show love to each of them.

As King: Divide a piece of paper into two columns. Write "Us" at the top of one column and "Them" at the top of the other. List the people or groups you think of as "us" and "them." Think of one thing you can do to help yourself and those you think of as "us" to begin to think of "them" as "us," too.

Tenth Sunday of the Year

Priests in the Priest

Hosea 6:3-6; Romans 4:18-25; Matthew 9:9-13

To live by the inspiration of the Holy Spirit is to fulfill our baptismal consecration as prophets. The authentic prophet is precisely one in whom the words of God are made flesh in action. And Jesus puts special emphasis on our mission to live out specifically what he taught in word and example about God's compassionate, redeeming love. To do this is to fulfill our baptismal consecration as priests.

To "follow Jesus," as Jesus invited Matthew to do when he sought him out in his tax-collector's booth, means actively to show mercy to others. To those who measured religion by law observance, Jesus said, "Go and learn what this means, 'I desire mercy, not sacrifice.'"

Priests offer sacrifice. But the sacrifice Christians offer is the sacrifice which Jesus offered once and for all on Calvary. Jesus is the one and only Priest, and all who are baptized into him are priests by sharing in his priesthood. To be a Christian is to be a "priest in the Priest." This means that we offer the one and only sacrifice which redeemed the world: the sacrifice of Jesus, who became the compassionate, redeeming love of God embodied on the cross.

Our participation at Mass is not just a "being there" while prayers are said and readings are read. We come to Mass to hear the word of God call us to be like Jesus, to be Christ, and to respond to that word by offering Jesus to the Father—and ourselves with him—for the life of the world. What God's word calls us to be is Christ's Body on earth, priests in the Priest, victims in the Victim, offered in love at every moment of our day as Jesus was offered in love on the cross to bring life and truth to the world. Christianity is by nature a religion of mercy, not laws. If we do everything right, everything we are supposed to do, but do not live out God's redeeming mercy toward others, we are nothing.

To have mercy means to come to the aid of another out of a sense of relationship. To be a "priest in the Priest," then, we have to accept our relationship with others as profoundly as Jesus accepted relationship with the human race. Jesus,

> ...though he was in the form of God,
> > did not regard equality with God
> > as something to be exploited,
> but emptied himself,
> > taking the form of a slave,
> > being born in human likeness.
> And being found in human form,
> > he humbled himself,
> > and became obedient to the point of death—
> > even death on a cross (Philippians 2:6-8).

To be Christian—specifically, to share in the priesthood of Christ as Christians—we have to accept the communal dimension of our lives. We have to see ourselves as sent to those who are "harassed and helpless, like sheep without a shepherd." We have to accept "the work of ministry, for building up the body of Christ, until all of us come to the unity of the faith and of the knowledge of the Son of God, to maturity, to the measure of the full stature of Christ." To be a priest is to be consecrated to the service of others, and all of us are consecrated to this priesthood by Baptism. We cannot be baptized into Christ, as members of his Body, without being baptized into his priesthood.

There is no purely private religion for Christians. If we live only to "save our souls," we will lose them. Jesus didn't come to save his soul, but to save ours. To live as Jesus means that we dedicate ourselves, as he did, to the salvation of others. This salvation Jesus came to give is more than getting to heaven. He said, "I came that they may have life and have it abundantly" (John 10:10). To live as priests, then, means to dedicate ourselves to helping everyone live life to the full.

Reflecting on This Week's Readings

Tenth Week of the Year

Pray daily: Father, you sent your Word to bring us truth and your Spirit to make us holy. Through them may we come to know the mystery of your life. Help us to worship you, one God in three Persons, by proclaiming and living our faith in you. Amen.

Monday: Matthew 5:1-12. "Blessed are the poor in spirit, for theirs is the kingdom of heaven." How does the recognition of our inadequacy help us to grow in faith? In hope? In love?

Tuesday: Matthew 5:13-16. "You are the salt of the earth; but if salt has lost its taste, how can its saltiness be restored?... You are the light of the world.... [L]et your light shine before others, so that they may see your good works and give glory to your Father in heaven." When, where, how is your faith reflected in your actions? Do you experience this as life?

Wednesday: Matthew 5:17-19. "[W]hoever breaks one of the least of these commandments, and teaches others to do the same will be called least in the kingdom of heaven; but whoever does them and teaches them will be called great in the kingdom of heaven." Which commandments is Jesus talking about here? Why does it take far more faith to believe in Jesus' commandments than in the Ten Commandments God gave through Moses?

Thursday: Matthew 5:20-26. "...if you remember that your brother or sister has something against you, leave your gift [before the altar] and go; first be reconciled with your brother or sister, and then come and offer your gift." When you seek reconciliation with someone, how is this an act of emptying yourself as Jesus did in his Incarnation?

Friday: Matthew 5:27-32. "If your right eye causes you to sin, tear it out and throw it away...." How does your faith make your priorities different from those of the society in which you live?

Saturday: Matthew 5:33-37. "Again, you have heard that it was said to those of ancient times.... But I say to you...." How would you describe the difference between the Sinai Covenant (Ten Commandments) and the New Law of Jesus?

Living This Week's Gospels

As Christian: Let Christ save you from some fault by raising you to a divine level. For example, avoid unkind words by dedicating your speech to God each morning, dedicating yourself to give life by expressing to others Jesus' love.

As Disciple: Search the Sermon on the Mount (Matthew 5—7) for three examples of the way Jesus calls us to act, not just as good human beings, but on the level of God.

As Prophet: Do one specific thing—at home, at work, in your social life—which will reveal the grace "of our Lord Jesus Christ" in you.

As Priest: Consciously show the love of God to one person each day at work and at home. If you live alone, show it to yourself!

As King: Make a list of the people you deal with regularly. Note the ones with whom you experience the "fellowship (communion) of the Holy Spirit." Ask what you can do to increase your union of mind, heart and will with the others.

Eleventh Sunday of the Year

Stewards of His Kingship

Exodus 19:2-6a; Romans 5:6-11; Matthew 9:36—10:8

Immediately after telling his disciples to ask God to send out laborers into his harvest, Jesus chose twelve to send out with the authority or power to proclaim the good news, to cure, to raise the dead, cleanse lepers and cast out demons.

The mission of the Church and of every member in the Church who was baptized into identity with Jesus Prophet, Priest and King, is to go out into the whole world, not just geographically, but into every area and activity of human life. We are "sent out" to be the active, transforming presence of Jesus in family and social life, business and politics. This is the particular mission of the laity.

The laity are defined by Vatican Council II, not just negatively as all those who are not either priests or members of a religious order, but intentionally, as those who "by their very vocation seek the kingdom of God by engaging in temporal affairs and by ordering them according to the plan of God. They live in the world; that is, in each and in all of the secular professions and occupations... in the ordinary circumstances of family and social life, from which the very web of their existence is woven."

To be a layperson in the Church is a vocation. Just as people are called into the priesthood or into a religious order, the laity are in their state of life because "they are called there by God." And the reason they are called to be laity is "so that by exercising their proper function and being led by the spirit of the gospel, they can work for the sanctification of the world from within, in the manner of leaven. In this way they can make Christ known to others, especially by the testimony of a life resplendent in faith, hope and charity." (See Vatican II, "The Church," Chapter Four.)

Because the laity are "closely involved in temporal affairs of every sort," that is, in occupations which of themselves belong to the sphere of time, not eternity, it is the laity's "special task to illumine and organize these affairs in such a way that they may always start out, develop and persist according to Christ's mind, to the praise of the Creator and Redeemer." This is to promote the Kingdom, the reign of God, over family and social life, business and politics.

Authority and power are given to the laity to do this. They do not act publicly and officially in the name of the Church (which is why the Church teaches that the mission of the laity to transform the world does not come under the authority of the hierarchy), and they do not have any authority from God to govern others. But they do have a divine mandate, authority directly from God, to engage in the work of transforming society and its institutions. If anyone were to ask a lay Christian, as the Jewish priests and elders once asked Jesus, "By what authority are you doing these things? And who gave you this authority?" the correct answer would be, "God himself. I was baptized into the kingship of Christ to take responsibility for establishing his reign in every area and activity of human life in which I am involved."

There are demons in our society: in church work and politics, in family life and religious orders, in social circles and in the educational milieu. But all who are sent out by Christ have power to cast them out—not dramatically, through ritual exorcisms, but by the power of gospel truth and love lived out courageously. Christians overcome the power of evil by the witness of their life-style, by their evident love, joy, peace, patient endurance, kindness, fidelity, generosity, gentleness and self-control which Saint Paul calls the "fruit of the Spirit," and by the decisions they make, the priorities they establish, the attitudes and values they express in their own fields of activity. God has called us to be a "priestly kingdom and a holy nation."

Reflecting on This Week's Gospels

Eleventh Week of the Year

> *Pray daily:* Lord Jesus Christ, I worship you living within me in the sacrament of your Body and Blood. I surrender to you my undivided love. I invite you to reign in my heart. May my life be poured out in loving service of you and of your Kingdom. I ask this of you, Jesus the Lord. Amen.

Monday: Matthew 5:38-42. "...But I say to you, Do not resist an evildoer. But if anyone strikes you on the right cheek, turn the other also." How does the presentation of Jesus as "Lamb of God" in the Mass invite us to live this teaching?

Tuesday: Matthew 5:43-48. "Be perfect, therefore, as your heavenly Father is perfect." In what sense is this possible? How does Jesus help?

Wednesday: Matthew 6:1-6, 16-18. "But whenever you pray, go into your room and shut the door and pray to your Father...in secret." What kind of sharing requires such privacy? To what level of intimacy with God is Jesus inviting us here?

Thursday: Matthew 6:7-15. "Pray then in this way: Our Father in heaven, / hallowed be your name. / Your kingdom come. / Your will be done, / on earth as it is in heaven." What degree of identification with God in mind, heart and will does this prayer express? What kind of love?

Friday: Matthew 6:19-23. "For where your treasure is, there your heart will be also." What visible actions or evidence say where your heart is, what you seek most on earth?

Saturday: Matthew 6:24-34. "No one can serve two masters; for a slave will either hate the one and love the other, or be devoted to the one and despise the other." What kind of love insists on total, undivided gift and surrender?

How does the Eucharist express this kind of love on
God's part?

Living This Week's Gospels

As Christian: Express (and experience) your belief that
Eucharist gives life by asking again whether daily Mass
might be possible for you.

As Disciple: Take seriously the intimacy with Jesus that the
Eucharist expresses. Ask him to reveal his heart to you through
the Scriptures. Listen for the feelings behind the words.

As Prophet: Give your flesh for the life of the world by
embodying in physical action your acceptance of some
teaching of Jesus.

As Priest: Consciously "be Eucharist" for at least one
person each day by some deliberate act of sharing yourself
with that person.

As King: Ask how in your own circle and environment
people may use or exploit others' flesh (their bodies, their
physical labor) for their own satisfaction. Ask what you can
do to change these attitudes by "offering your flesh" to
enhance the lives of others. What can you do that would
change the tone where you live, work, play?

Twelfth Sunday of the Year

Light in Darkness

Jeremiah 20:10-13; Romans 5:12-15; Matthew 10:26-33

Jesus called us the light of the world. On the day of our Baptism a candle, lit from the paschal candle, which symbolizes Christ, was given to us or to our godparents. We were instructed to keep the light of faith brightly burning until the day of Christ's return.

On that day the light of Christ was enkindled in our hearts; we became bearers of his light to the world. We were sent to let his light shine in us like a lamp set on a lampstand or a city built on a hill; to proclaim from the housetops what is whispered in our hearts; to speak in the light of day what we hear in the quiet darkness of our hours of prayer.

The light in us is a light shining in the darkness. We are sent into a world which loves the darkness of its own distorted light; a world of false values and distorted priorities; a world where people have "loved darkness rather than light because their deeds were evil" (John 3:19); a world which rejected Jesus, the Light of the world, and prefers to live in darkness and the gloom of death. This world will reject us as soon as we let the light within us illumine the darkness of its ways.

All around us, like Jeremiah, we will hear "many whispering." Our situation may not be as terrifying as what Jeremiah faced: "Terror is all around! / Denounce him! Let us denounce him! / ... Perhaps he can be enticed, / and we can prevail against him, / and take our revenge on him." But we will be able to respond with Jeremiah, "The word of the LORD has become for me / a reproach and derision all day long.... All my close friends are watching for me to stumble" (20:8, 10). The light that shines in the darkness is not welcome in a world that prefers darkness to light. It is only the pure of heart who will see God.

But Jesus tells us, "[H]ave no fear.... Do not fear those who kill the body but cannot kill the soul.... Are not two sparrows sold for a penny? Yet not one of them will fall to the ground apart from your Father. And even the hairs of your head are all counted. So do not be afraid; you are of more value than many sparrows." If we acknowledge Jesus before others, he will acknowledge us before his heavenly Father.

We live in an age of cover-ups. Evil is done in high places; laws are broken by those sworn to uphold them. Truth is suppressed while half-truths are fashioned into lies; news stories are slanted. Reputations are dragged through the mud and "dirty tricks" seem to be a part of every political campaign. Often, the higher one rises in business or politics, the lower one's credibility falls. We are accustomed to the "administrative lie." We easily disregard "official versions." We know that news reports and commercials are financed by the same people and that money speaks louder than truth. But Jesus tells us, "nothing is covered up that will not be uncovered...nothing secret that will not become known." John's Gospel tells us, "The light shines in the darkness, and the darkness did not overcome it" (1:5).

Saint Paul reminds us: "[S]in came into the world through one man, and death came through sin, and so death spread to all because all have sinned." In the same way, through one person, Jesus Christ, life came into the world, and his life is the light of the human race, the true light, which enlightens everyone. The life Jesus gives is spreading to all because his light is shining in all who believe. "The light shines in the darkness, and the darkness did not overcome it."

The world was not created in darkness. The darkness of any society is created by innumerable individual acts of sin: of deception, distortion and deliberate entry into darkness which become a way of life. In the same way, society can be brought into light and life by innumerable individual acts of witness. As the words of Jesus are made flesh in us we become the light and renewal of the world.

Reflecting on This Week's Readings

Twelfth Week of the Year

> *Pray daily*: Lord, you are the light of the world, and you send us to be the light of the world. Let me love your light. Call me out of darkness into discipleship. Invite me to learn your heart. Amen.

Monday: Matthew 7:1-5. "Do not judge, so that you may not be judged. For with the judgment you make you will be judged." Do you judge the policies, customs and behavior of your society by the light of Christ's teachings or by what is accepted practice?

Tuesday: Matthew 7:6, 12-14. "In everything do to others as you would have them do to you; for this is the law and the prophets." Is this the standard you use in dealing with others at home? At work? In your social life? In the city?

Wednesday: Matthew 7:15-20. "You will know them by their fruits. Are grapes gathered from thorns, or figs from thistles?" How do you pick your models? By their achievement of success in this world? By their popularity? Their social prestige? What does Jesus mean by "their fruits"?

Thursday: Matthew 7:21-29. "Everyone then who hears these words of mine and acts on them will be like a wise man who built his house on rock." If you build your life on what others do, what they think or expect of you, what are you building on? How long can it last?

Friday: Matthew 8:1-4. A man suffering from leprosy approached, knelt before Jesus, and said, "Lord, if you choose, you can make me clean." Do you want this for yourself? Do you believe Jesus can do it? That he wants to? Have you asked him to do it? When?

Saturday: Matthew 8:5-17. Jesus said to the centurion, "Go; let it be done for you according to your faith." Would you be willing to accept this deal? To what extent do you believe in and base your life on Jesus' promises?

Living This Week's Gospels

As Christian: Each day do one thing consciously and deliberately according to Christ's ideals that is a "break" with what is taken for granted in our society or in your own milieu.

As Disciple: Each morning read a few verses from the Sermon on the Mount (Matthew 5—7) and try to live them out that day.

As Prophet: Each day this week try to give those around you a "clue" that you are a Christian, without saying it in words.

As Priest: Look into your heart; see what gifts you have for helping people and then consciously use one gift each day to minister to someone.

As King: For one day, notice who the people are who influence your decisions and behavior. Count how many times it is Jesus.

Thirteenth Sunday of the Year

Seeing and Saying Truth

2 Kings 4:8-11, 14-16a; Romans 6:3-4, 8-11; Matthew 10:37-42

Jesus tells us that recognition is the key to reward: recognition of prophets and disciples, recognition of his own presence in others, recognition of ourselves as his Body on earth, dedicated to living his divine life in our human flesh and fulfilling his divine mission in our human circumstances.

Saint Paul tells us that we were all baptized into Christ Jesus: baptized into his death, buried with him and raised up with him to live a new life as the members of his risen Body on earth. We are not just human; we are divine. We are expected to live our human lives on this earth on a Godlike level. Our ground-level activity should be a manifestation of the presence of God in us—as that of Jesus was.

The more we realize this, the more likely we are to live it. The more aware we are of the mystery of Christ's presence in us, the more likely we are to let that presence reveal itself in our words and actions. The more radically we believe that we are the Body of Christ, the more we will act like the Body of Christ. Awareness prepares us to act.

This is why we use titles and show special signs of respect for others: It is to remind us of a reality that we might overlook. We use titles such as *Mr.* and *Mrs.*, *Dad* and *Mom*, *Darling* and *Dear*, or even *Ole Buddy*. They are all to remind us of what another person is and means to us.

We need to recognize that some titles can be used just for the sake of prestige, even to imply that some people are superior to others. These titles do not express a Christian attitude. Jesus said, "[W]hoever wishes to be first...must be slave of all" (Mark 10:44). A good rule of thumb for Church titles is to accept and use those which express relationship while rejecting those which simply bestow prestige. For

Christians, true human superiority does not come from position or rank, or even from talents or accomplishments. There is only one way to become authentically a better human being, and that is to become more like Jesus Christ, who "came not to be served but to serve, and to give his life a ransom for many" (Matthew 20:28). Those ready to "lose their lives"—or the self-image based on prestige or success—in response to Jesus' teaching and example will "find their lives" and discover their true value and identity as children of God.

When Jesus said, "[C]all no one your father on earth, for you have one Father—the one in heaven" (Matthew 23:9), and gave the same teaching about rabbi and instructor, titles were not the focus of his concern. We still call our fathers "Father" and our teachers "Professor" or "Doctor." What Jesus meant was that we should not see any earthly relationship as ultimate, as if we owed so much respect to our fathers and mothers that we should please them rather than God. He said, "Whoever loves father or mother more than me is not worthy of me; and whoever loves son or daughter more than me is not worthy of me." We should be on guard against being so impressed by the brilliance of human teachers that we put more faith in their opinions than in the teaching of God. (See Matthew 20:25-28; 23:6-12; Mark 9:35.)

Yet we constantly accept the attitudes and values of our culture, especially those approved by the people we respect, even when these attitudes and values contradict the gospel. There are Christians who would not call a priest "Father" for anything on earth, but they are so subservient to cultural prejudices that they do not accept people of other races or ethnic origins as brothers and sisters in God's family. Christians readily take a military oath to kill others on command, putting blind trust in an officer's judgment about the morality of a particular mission or a president's judgment about the morality of going to war. People who think Jesus is just talking about titles here are focusing on the gnat and missing the camel (see Matthew 23:24)!

Reflecting on This Week's Readings

Thirteenth Week of the Year

Pray daily: Lord, you call us to life in its fullness. You invite us to live in constant awareness of your love for us and your presence within us. You call us to find our value in being your body on earth, your coworkers. Don't let me be distracted by anything less than this. Amen.

Monday: Matthew 8:18-22. Jesus answered a would-be disciple, "Follow me, and let the dead bury their own dead." When it comes to following Jesus, how much concern do you have about the opinions of other people?

Tuesday: Matthew 8:23-27. Jesus said to his disciples, "Why are you afraid, you of little faith?" What, whom do you worry about? What does this say about your beliefs?

Wednesday: Matthew 8:28-34. "Then the whole town came out to meet Jesus; and when they saw him, they begged him to leave their neighborhood." When would you prefer not to have Jesus around? Not to think about him?

Thursday: Matthew 9:1-8. "For which is easier, to say, 'Your sins are forgiven,' or to say, 'Stand up and walk'?" Do you believe more in the power of medicines to heal your body than in the power of the Sacrament of Reconciliation to heal your soul? Which do you use more?

Friday: Matthew 9:9-13. The Pharisees saw this and said to his disciples, "Why does your teacher eat with tax collectors and sinners?" When you are with friends who are not especially religious, are you ashamed to have Jesus around? How can you make him noticeably present?

Saturday: Matthew 9:14-17. Jesus answered them, "The wedding guests cannot mourn as long as the bridegroom is with them, can they?" When you submit to sadness, worry, discouragement, in what sense is Jesus not with you? How can you let him be with you?

Living This Week's Gospels

As Christian: Wear or put where you work some visible symbol that says who Jesus Christ is to you.

As Disciple: Set aside definite times each day, each year (for example, time for a retreat) to read, hear and reflect on the teaching of Jesus.

As Prophet: Ask yourself whose opinion blocks you most from living the gospel as you desire. Talk to that person frankly about your religious beliefs.

As Priest: Each day choose one person to minister to. It does not have to be obvious.

As King: Pretend you are a supervisor for the Kingdom of God. (You are!) Make a report to the Lord on what needs to be changed around you and how you will try to do it.

Fourteenth Sunday of the Year

"Come to Me..."

Zechariah 9:9-10; Romans 8:9, 11-13; Matthew 11:25-30

What, in a sentence, is the mission of the Church, of the parish? What did Jesus come to do?

Saint Paul says God's plan is "to gather up all things in [Christ], things in heaven and things on earth" (Ephesians 1:10). Yes, Jesus came to establish peace between us and God, peace among individuals, races and nations. But the source and support of this peace is one thing alone: *knowing God*, being united in mind, heart and will with God. Jesus came to reveal his own heart to us so that we might know God and, by knowing him, love God and one another as Jesus does. "[L]earn from me; for I am gentle and humble in heart, and you will find rest for your souls."

The problem is, no one can know the heart of Jesus except God. "No one knows who the Son is except the Father..." or "who the Father is except the Son..." (Luke 10:22). Only God can know God completely, totally. The mystery of the Christian religion, and all of its power, rests in this one fact: that through the gift of grace God has made us all *filii in Filio*, "sons in the Son, "sharers in the divine life of Jesus Christ, participants in his own divine act of knowing and loving God and therefore able to be one in mind, will and heart with him. The mission of Jesus and the Church is to bring every mind, heart and will in heaven and on earth together into unity through union with the mind and heart of Christ. This is peace: "[L]earn from me; for I am gentle and humble in heart, and you will find rest for your souls."

Ironically, we look to governments and armies to maintain peace by making war. But God taught us to look to a king, a true savior, who comes "triumphant and victorious" by coming to us "humble and riding on a donkey." He will banish the war chariot and the war horse; the battle bow will be cut off. "[A]nd he shall command peace to the nations; his dominion shall be from sea to sea...to the ends of the earth." If we learn from Jesus, who is gentle and humble in heart, we will find rest for our souls. We will find peace.

If we live "according to the flesh," Saint Paul says—that is, according to the spirit of this world, the prejudices of our upbringing, the natural tendency which is in us all to fight fire with fire, to take an eye for an eye and a tooth for a tooth, to defend ourselves by retaliation and threat of even more violent retaliation—then quite simply, "we will die." The way of the world is death. The way of violence is death. The way of dependence on arms is death. The way of defending our lives by dealing death to others is already death to our souls. "For those who want to save their life will lose it, and those who lose their life for my sake will find it" (Matthew 16:25). Take it or leave it: spirit or flesh, the way of life or the way of death. We can follow the darkness of this world into violence and death or we can learn from Jesus who is "gentle and humble in heart" and we find rest for our souls.

Are we fulfilling our mission as Church when we encourage children to play "killer" with toy guns, to play "war" with toy soldiers, tanks and planes? When we let our hearts approve the violence of the "good guy" who kills the "bad guy" on TV? When we applaud troops who commit themselves to kill on command anyone an officer or a president points to as a "bad guy" who threatens our country?

The mission of the Church is to unite every heart on earth with the heart of Christ. But we are the Church. Every Christian family is the Church assembled on the level of the home. Every group of Christian friends is the Church assembled for recreation or celebration. Every business or office where there are Christians is the Church assembled for service to the world. In every place and situation, at home and in the city, at work and at play, our mission is to help each other recognize Jesus, who is "gentle and humble in heart," so that we may all find rest for our souls.

Reflecting on This Week's Gospels

Fourteenth Week of the Year

> *Pray daily*: *Father, the sufferings your Son endured restored hope to a fallen world. Let the illusion of power never ensnare us with empty promises of passing peace. Make us one with you in gentleness and humility of heart so that our security may come from you and our love may give life, not destroy it. We ask this through Christ our Lord. Amen.*

Monday: Matthew 9:18-26. The woman said to herself, "If I only touch his cloak, I will be made well." If just touching Jesus can heal, what power comes from being united with him in mind and heart?

Tuesday: Matthew 9:32-38. Jesus said, "The harvest is plentiful, but the laborers are few; therefore ask the Lord of the harvest to send out laborers into his harvest." Are you willing to work for peace? What step can you take today?

Wednesday: Matthew 10:1-7. Jesus gave his disciples authority to cast out unclean spirits and to heal every disease and every infirmity. What power do we as Church have today to cast evil out of the world and heal suffering? How can you share in this work?

Thursday: Matthew 10:7-15. "Take no gold, or silver, or copper in your belts." Do you really need money, power, earthly resources in order to live a Christian life?

Friday: Matthew 10:16-23. "See, I am sending you out like sheep into the midst of wolves; so be wise as serpents and innocent as doves." Do you rely on intimidation and force to defend yourself? Or do you use your mind to discover peaceful means to reconciliation through reflection and prayer?

Saturday: Matthew 10:24-33. "A disciple is not above the teacher, nor a slave above the master." If Jesus did not use force or violence, should you?

Living This Week's Gospels

As Christian: Ask what in your life does or could show that you rely on Jesus as the only true Savior of human life on earth.

As Disciple: Check your gut reactions to war news and to the "good guys'" violence on TV. Compare this with specific words of Jesus that seem to address the issue.

As Prophet: Check to see how many things in your home explicitly or implicitly glorify or condone violence. Begin making everything in your life bear witness to Jesus, man of peace.

As **Priest**: Try to "turn the other cheek" consciously once a day, not just in passive endurance but as a positive expression of redeeming love.

As King: Think of some gentle, peaceful step you could take to start changing something in your environment that is not in accord with the mind and heart of Christ.

Omnipotence Plus One

Isaiah 55:10-11; Romans 8:18-23; Matthew 13:1-23

Scripture scholars speculate that Jesus may have told the parable of the sower in answer to the objection, "If you are really sent from God, why are so few people listening to you?"

The answer is a shocking one. It seems to contradict God's words in Isaiah: "For as the rain and the snow come down from heaven, / and do not return there until they have watered the earth, / making it bring forth and sprout, / ...so shall my word be that goes out from my mouth; / it shall not return to me empty, / but it shall accomplish that which I purpose, / and succeed in the thing for which I sent it." Jesus compares his words to seeds. Since their fruitfulness depends in part on the kind of ground which receives them, they do not always accomplish their purpose. Their power is limited by people's willingness to respond.

The key to Christianity is in the phrase, "fully divine and fully human." Jesus was fully God and fully human: eternal yet born in history; omnipresent yet restricted to being in one place at a time; all-knowing yet knowing only what he learned through his human powers; omnipotent yet reduced to human weakness; the God of majesty and glory yet "despised and rejected by others; / a man of suffering and acquainted with infirmity" (Isaiah 53:3). In Jesus omnipotence and powerlessness meet. In him we see the mystery not only of God made human but of God's powerlessness in relationship to human beings created in God's image.

In a sense it is true that "Omnipotence plus one equals powerlessness." Once God created one being in the divine image, one person able, like God is able, to know, love and choose freely, then God was no longer "all powerful."

By choosing to create even one free person, God limited the divine freedom to control everything in the world. "Omnipotence plus one" means that now no one is all powerful—not as long as God allows human beings to be free.

This is why there is pain and suffering. God leaves people free to sin, to act against the divine will, thus hurting other people and themselves. For this reason God cannot possess us entirely, cannot penetrate to the deepest core of our being and be united with us there unless we open our hearts to God in free surrender, inviting God into our life.

That is why "the whole creation has been groaning in labor pains until now." The image of God in us needs to be brought to perfection through perfect likeness to Jesus, the perfect "image of the invisible God, the firstborn of all creation." This is the destiny for which we were created. "For those whom he foreknew he also predestined to be conformed to the image of his Son." Freedom is such an awesome responsibility that anyone who exists in the image of God, by endowment with free will, has a need to share in God's life by grace in order not to abuse it. Being created in the image of God, we need to be recreated in the likeness of the Word made flesh, in whom that image was brought to perfection in word, action and life. This takes time. It takes repeated opening of our minds in discipleship, repeated surrenders of our wills in love. It takes seduction; God must win us.

And so we who "have the first fruits of the Spirit, groan inwardly while we wait" for our bodies, our minds and our hearts to be perfectly conformed to Jesus in total surrender and love. We have "stripped off the old self with its practices" that we might be naked and open to the seduction of the Bridegroom, and have "clothed [our]selves with the new self, which is being renewed in knowledge...." (Colossians 3:10). God's word has the power to win us. If we open ourselves to God's words as the earth opens itself to the seed, if we receive God's word again and again into our hearts, we will gradually be brought to perfect surrender and filled with the life of God. Then God's word will not return void but will achieve the end for which he sent it.

Reflecting on This Week's Gospels

Fifteenth Week of the Year

> *Pray daily*: Father, let the light of your truth guide us to your kingdom through a world filled with lights contrary to your own. May your love make us what you have called us to be. We ask this through Christ our Lord. Amen.

Monday: Matthew 10:34—11:1. Jesus says, "Those who find their life will lose it, and those who lose their life for my sake will find it." What are you afraid of losing if you "lose yourself" in total surrender to everything Jesus desires?

Tuesday: Matthew 11:20-24. "Then he began to reproach the cities in which most of his deeds of power had been done, because they did not repent." In what "deeds of power" has God shown love for you? How have you responded in word and action?

Wednesday: Matthew 11:25-27. Jesus said, "I thank you, Father, Lord of heaven and earth, because you have hidden these things from the wise and the intelligent and have revealed them to infants." Do you believe you can come to know Jesus intimately if you read Scripture? Do you use the excuse that you "haven't studied" Scripture?

Thursday: Matthew 11:28-30. "Come to me, all you that are weary and are carrying heavy burdens, and I will give you rest." How do you "come to" Jesus? How often? With what hopes and desires?

Friday: Matthew 12:1-8. "But if you had known what this means, 'I desire mercy and not sacrifice,' you would not have condemned the guiltless." What difference is there between trying to understand God's words and trying to understand the mind and heart behind those words? Which do you do?

Saturday: Matthew 12:14-21. "Here is my servant, whom I have chosen, / my beloved, with whom my soul is well pleased." Have you chosen to let Jesus serve you? How? Can you say he is your "beloved" with whom your soul is "well pleased"?

Living This Week's Gospels

As Christian: Ask what in your life is hardened against Christ's words because you follow the culture's "beaten path." What teachings of Jesus seem unrealistic to you?

As Disciple: Take one saying of Jesus and reflect on it until it "takes root" in your life, until it gets down to the level of some concrete choice.

As Prophet: Clarify your vision by weeding (purifying) your heart. Give up for one week something that you think you are strong enough to give up, but have not proved it to yourself.

As Priest: Offer yourself consciously with the bread and wine each time you are at Mass, asking Jesus to penetrate your heart with his words, transform you into his likeness, and unite you to himself without restrictions or reserves.

As King: Take one concrete step to make your home, social circle or parish better ground to receive and nurture into fruitfulness the seed of Christ's word.

Sixteenth Sunday of the Year

Time in God's View

Wisdom 12:13, 16-19; Romans 8:26-27; Matthew 13:24-43

Smallness limits everything: vision, perspective, generosity, even our ability to forgive. We see the small picture and panic; God sees the whole picture and waits. We condemn and hurt each other because we are weak and scared; God is lenient and merciful because God is all-powerful. "...[A]nd with great forbearance you govern us; / for you have power to act whenever you choose."

God's actions give us insight into the divine heart, and the Scripture interprets those actions for us. God's example teaches us that "the upright must be kind." God fills us with hope, because he gives time for repentance, conversion and growth. When we are inclined to judge others, therefore, we should "meditate on his goodness"; when we feel guilty, we should "count on his mercy."

Jesus put this teaching into parables that teach us to include the dimension of *time* whenever we make judgments about people whether as individuals or as Church. Time is for growth. Only over a period of time can we see whether growth is taking place. Only after people have had time to grow and change can we make a final judgment about them. And only God knows when anyone's time is enough, which is one reason why only God can judge.

To teach us not to write off the power of God's grace working in the Church, or in groups or individuals within it (ourselves, the priests, the hierarchy), Jesus compares the Kingdom of God on earth to a field in which a farmer sowed good seed. But an enemy came and sowed weeds—literally "darnel," a plant that looks like wheat. When the farmer's overzealous servants heard of this, they wanted to go and root up the weeds, but the farmer told them there was no way to know whether a plant was weed or wheat until it matured. "Let both of them grow together until the harvest," he said. Only then could they tell which each one was.

We sometimes want to clean out all the "bad guys" in the Church—all except ourselves, of course. We may write off the older members because they are fixed in their ways and the young because they are not fixed in ours! We write ourselves off because we do not see within us any power to change that gives us hope. We write off the Church because we do not see anything happening to change things that need to be changed.

But we are small. We have very limited perception of both space and time. One thing we care about passionately can fill our whole screen. If we focus intensely on one problem, everything else goes out of focus. All time and space get reduced to the here and now. If it is not happening now, and especially if it won't happen in our lifetime, it might as well not happen—as if history were not important once it ceases to affect our lives.

Jesus urges us to "look at the big picture, to get a wide-angle lens. The Church existed before you were born and will continue to exist after you are in heaven. God has more time than you do; the game is not over for the Church when the clock stops for you. Do what you can while you are in the game, contribute all the points you can, but keep the big picture in mind. Do not reduce the universe to what you can see or all history to what takes place in your short span of time."

When we write anyone off, we are just experiencing how small we are. We reduce a whole person to one fault; a whole life to one mistake, a whole group of people to one false value they accept. But God, who "searches the heart," sees the Holy Spirit at work deep within each of us, helping us "in our weakness," praying "with sighs too deep for words" for what we do not even know we desire. God sees the Church as a seed growing, leaven working, a woman in labor; God waits for "the whole Christ" to be born.

Reflecting on This Week's Gospels

Sixteenth Week of the Year

Pray daily: Father, let the gift of your life continue to grow in us, drawing us from death to faith, hope and love. Keep us alive in Christ Jesus, watchful in prayer and true to his teaching until your glory is revealed in us. We ask this through Christ our Lord. Amen.

Monday: Matthew 12:38-42. "The people of Nineveh will rise up at the judgment with this generation and condemn it, because they repented at the proclamation of Jonah, and see, something greater than Jonah is here!" Are you constantly reconsidering your values and behavior as you grow in understanding of Jesus?

Tuesday: Matthew 12:46-50. "For whoever does the will of my Father in heaven is my brother and sister and mother." How do you treat Jesus as a brother? How could you?

Wednesday: Matthew 13:1-9. "Other seeds fell on good soil and brought forth grain, some a hundredfold, some sixty, some thirty." What makes a person "good soil" for the word of God? Are you? What fruit shows in your life?

Thursday: Matthew 13:10-17. "Truly I tell you, many prophets and righteous people longed to see what you see, but did not see it, and to hear what you hear, but did not hear it." In what ways are you using the Scriptures in order to understand Jesus better?

Friday: Matthew 13:18-23. "But as for what was sown on good soil, this is the one who hears the word and understands it, who indeed bears fruit and yields, in one case a hundredfold, in another sixty, and in another thirty." What does it take to understand Christ's words? Which do you understand best? Least?

Saturday: Matthew 13:24-30. Jesus said, "No; for in gathering the weeds you would uproot the wheat along with them." How often have you rejected someone instead of waiting for the person to change?

Living This Week's Gospels

As Christian: Identify three influences from your environment that have led you into destructive behavior. Then find something in the example or teaching of Jesus that would counteract these influences.

As Disciple: Set aside a ten-minute period each day to let Christ sow the seed of his words in your mind.

As Prophet: Decide on one thing, large or small, in your life-style that you can change into something that bears positive witness to the values Jesus taught.

As Priest: Take one step this week to make your friends, family members or fellow parishioners into "good soil" for Jesus' ideas to grow. For example, suggest a prayer before some common activity or start a discussion on some issue that involves attitudes and values.

As King: For one day, be alert to all the seeds sown in your mind from various sources, especially advertisements. Decide which seeds are good for your spiritual health and which are not. Take one step to clean up the environment, filtering out all harmful input to the senses.

Seventeenth Sunday of the Year

The Greatest Treasure

1 Kings 3:5, 7-12; Romans 8:28-30; Matthew 13:44-52

If you had one wish, what would you wish for? The choice you make will reveal your own heart and determine who you are.

What Jesus taught is that each of us has only one wish and if we try to make more than one, we lose the whole deal. If we have enough understanding to realize that there is only one choice to make—God—then everything else we need for happiness will be given to us as well. If we fail to make relationship with God our one wish in life, then nothing else we wish for can give us what we desire (see Matthew 6:33).

God taught this in three different ways. To begin with, God gave us the First Commandment: "I am the LORD your God...you shall have no other gods before me" (Exodus 20:2-3). This commandment made it an offense to have a divided heart; God alone must be the focus of all our desires, our hopes, our choices. To seek any other good, any other fulfillment besides God, is idolatry.

God said the same thing in giving the Hebrew people words to live by, which Jesus later called the "first and greatest commandment": "Hear, O Israel: The LORD is our God, the LORD alone. You shall love the LORD your God with all your heart, and with all your soul, and with all your might" (Deuteronomy 6:4-5). This commandment explicitly turns law into love.

Jesus taught this from a different angle when he told the parables of the hidden treasure and the pearl of great price. Here he presents the command to love God unreservedly as a means to life and fulfillment, to coming into possession of all that is best and most beautiful. Jesus appears here as the Master of the Way, the Teacher of Life, the one who instructs us in the art of living and by example shows us what life is all about. He is the Good Shepherd who guides us to the high places where we can experience life most deeply and enjoy it most purely. He is Wisdom incarnate.

"Wisdom" in the Scriptures means the gift of knowing how to live, how to distinguish right from wrong, true from false, helpful from destructive, authentic from fake. It was the gift Solomon chose when he asked for an "understanding heart." Saint Thomas Aquinas gives the key to wisdom when he describes it as the habit of seeing everything in the light of our last end, our ultimate goal: God. In practical terms, what makes us wise is appreciation of God and spiritual things. When we appreciate the true value of the "treasure hidden in the field," we will sell everything we have to possess it. This is what Scripture calls "wisdom" and our culture calls just "being smart."

Those who are wise take the long view. They avoid judging either people or things by what they appear to be here and now. Wise people know that the true value of everything and of everyone is measured by what this person—or this experience, even this joy or suffering— will mean to us at the end of the world. The world we see is like the surface of a lake: what is underneath is what really counts. On the surface, a lake may appear clean, yet the bottom could be full of trash; or it can look scummy on top and yet be clear and cool underneath. People are the same; that is why we should not judge others.

Values are like this too: They can look good and yet be cheap; they can look life-enhancing and yet be destructive. When at Baptism we "renounce Satan and all his empty promises," we are committing ourselves to wisdom in contradiction to the slogans and fads of our culture.

The wisdom of the Church comes from its fidelity to the past and its openness to the future. We measure the present by the past and validate the past by expanding it into the present. The rule of Christian wisdom is to be "like the master of a household who brings out of his treasure what is new and what is old."

Reflecting on This Week's Gospels

Seventeenth Week of the Year

> *Pray daily: God our Father and protector, without you nothing is holy, nothing has value. Guide us to everlasting life by helping us to use wisely the blessings you have given to the world. We ask this through Christ our Lord. Amen.*

Monday: Matthew 13:31-35. "The kingdom of heaven is like yeast that a woman took and mixed in with three measures of flour until all of it was leavened." How are the teachings of Jesus transforming your heart?

Tuesday: Matthew 13:35-43. "The one who sows the good seed is the Son of Man; the field is the world, and the good seed are the children of the kingdom; the weeds are the children of the evil one." What words, images, actions around you plant "weeds" in your heart?

Wednesday: Matthew 13:44-46. "The kingdom of heaven is like treasure hidden in a field, which someone found and hid; then in his joy he goes and sells all...and buys that field." What have you traded off for the sake of knowing God better?

Thursday: Matthew 13:47-53. "Again, the kingdom of heaven is like a net that was thrown into the sea and caught fish of every kind." In the Church, are you more conscious of the "good" fish or the "bad" fish? What effect does your particular bias have on you?

Friday: Matthew 13:54-58. Jesus returned to Nazareth and taught the people in the synagogue. They were astonished and said, "Where did this man get this wisdom and these deeds of power?" Do you admire Christ's wisdom? Why?

Saturday: Matthew 14:1-12. "The king was grieved, yet out of regard for his oaths and for the guests...he sent and had John beheaded in the prison." When do you feel conflict between your desire to please others and your desire to please God?

Living This Week's Gospels

As Christian: Identify one area of your life which seems to have no relation to God. Ask how you can make Jesus an active part of it.

As Disciple: Look at your daily schedule and ask how everything you do is—or can be—directed toward your final goal, God.

As Prophet: Pick one action of your daily life and make it a visible expression of your life's true goal.

As Priest: Ask what keeps you from participating in the "spiritual" things offered in your parish (Scripture study, adult religious education, prayer). Is it lack of appreciation for the spiritual? Is there something you need to "sell" in order to buy "the treasure in the field"?

As King: Ask yourself how the Church in its changing rules and policies is bringing out of its treasure both the new and the old? Does anything seem to you to be inconsistent, incompatible with the real values of the past? Does anything seem to you to be an enslavement to the past, a fear of what is new? How can you peacefully, without anger or aggressiveness, work to improve the situation?

Eighteenth Sunday of the Year

Eucharist: Lesson of Love

Isaiah 55:1-3; Romans 8:35, 37-39; Matthew 14:13-21

What kind of God is Jesus? What kind of person? What kind of savior? What kind of leader and head of the Church?

The answer to all of these questions is "nurturing, nourishing": a God, Savior, leader who builds us up, who enhances our lives, who feeds us in our need and makes us grow.

And what Jesus feeds us is love—which is another way of saying he feeds us with himself. Jesus is the kind of God, the kind of Savior, leader whose basic desire is to give us himself that we might live and grow into the fullness of life. This desire tells us something about Jesus, about God, about love and about ourselves.

What love is, in its most life-giving form, is the desire, the free choice, to invest what we are in what another can become. This is what God is: that Being who for some reason—or rather, for no reason except his own free desire—chooses to invest what he is in what we can become. This choice is not the effect of some cause, not something won from him or produced in him by anything we are. It is something God chooses to do because of what he is. That is why John can define or describe God to us so simply: "God is love" (1 John 4:8).

We can be like God by choosing to invest what we are in what others can become. The more we help others to come into the fullness of life and the more this becomes the one driving desire of our lives, our single goal and aim in everything we do, the more our love for others becomes like God's, like the love Jesus showed us on earth.

This kind of love is free; no one has to win it from us; no one has to deserve it; there are no conditions whatsoever attached to it. We offer it to everyone, just as God offers his love to us. People do not even have to respond to our love; we still choose to invest ourselves in them, to give ourselves to them and for them in the measure they allow us, doing whatever we can to enhance their lives and help them grow into life in its fullness. We say with God, "[E]veryone who thirsts, / come to the waters; and you that have no money, / come, buy and eat! Come, buy wine and milk / without money and without price."

Love is a paradox. It is always given freely and we can receive it without cost, but we cannot profit from it without cost. We do not grow from being loved until we begin to give love. At first we might only be required to love ourselves—and that can cost a lot: cost courage, cost faith, cost trust, cost forgiveness, cost risk and cost accepting our vulnerability. It costs what freedom costs, which is the cost of being like God. But as we continue to grow through being loved, we must turn outward to give ourselves to others, to become "bread of life" for others, to give "our flesh"—our physical words, actions, gestures, all our visible forms of self-expression— "for the life of the world."

When we receive Jesus in Eucharist, we receive him as food. But when we digest this food, we do not transform it into ourselves; we are transformed into it. As we assimilate Christ, we are assimilated into him; we become his Body, we take on his mind and heart, uniting ourselves to his love. Eucharist tells us the form this love takes. It takes the same form in us that it took in Jesus. His love reveals itself in us by the gift we make of ourselves to the world. When the host is offered to us as "the Body of Christ," and we open our hand to receive it and say, "Amen," we are saying yes not only to *receiving* Christ's Body but to *being* his Body. We are saying, in effect, "Amen, yes, I believe that this is the Body of Christ, and that this is the Body I am called to be. I receive him to become him, to be Eucharist for others, giving my flesh for the life of the world."

Reflecting on This Week's Gospels

Eighteenth Week of the Year

Pray daily: God our Father, gifts without measure flow from your goodness to bring us your peace. Our life is your gift. Guide our life's journey, for only your love makes us whole. Keep us strong in your love. We ask this through Christ our Lord. Amen.

Monday: Matthew 14:22-36. Peter said to him, "Lord, if it is you, command me to come to you on the water." When did you most recently take the risk of responding to something you thought might be an inspiration from God? How did you feel afterwards?

Tuesday: Matthew 15:1-2, 10-14. Jesus said, "[I]t is not what goes into the mouth that defiles a person, but...what comes out of the mouth that defiles." Are you as careful about what comes out of your mouth as you are about what goes into it?

Wednesday: Matthew 15:21-28. Jesus said, "It is not fair to take the children's food and throw it to the dogs." Has Jesus ever refused to give himself to you? Have you ever refused to give yourself to someone you did not think was worth it?

Thursday: Matthew 16:13-23. "From that time on, Jesus began to show his disciples that he must go to Jerusalem and undergo great suffering at the hands of the elders and chief priests and scribes, and be killed, and on the third day be raised." When do you accept pain, trouble or sacrifices for others? What is your attitude toward this?

Friday: Matthew 16:24-28. "[W]hat will it profit them if they gain the whole world but forfeit their life? Or what will they give in return for their life?" Do you see the Eucharist as nourishing your life? For what are you willing to trade or give up Eucharist?

Saturday: Matthew 17:14-20. "For truly I tell you, if you have faith the size of a mustard seed, you will say to this mountain, 'Move from here to there,' and it will move; and nothing will be impossible for you." Have you given up on anybody? How much have you prayed for that person?

Living This Week's Gospels

As Christian: Ask what could separate you from the love of Christ. Do something about it.

As Disciple: Take as much time each day as you take for your coffee just to sit down and let Jesus feed you with his words.

As Prophet: Target one person each day for whom you will do something freely, with no conditions before or after, just to give the kind of love God gives to you.

As Priest: Name something that you have to share, no matter how small or insignificant, and share it with someone, asking God to multiply its effect. You can share your faith, your gifts of ministry or your material resources.

As King: Identify something in your environment—at home, at work, in your circle of friends, in your city—that you have come to accept as hopeless. Ask if there is one thing, no matter how small, that you can do to make the situation better. Draw strength from what Saint Paul wrote: "No, in all these things we are more than conquerors through him who loved us" (Romans 8:37).

Great Sorrow, Unceasing Anguish

1 Kings 19:9a, 11-13a; Romans 9:1-5; Matthew 14:22-33

Saint Paul felt "great sorrow and unceasing anguish" because his fellow Jews had not as a people accepted Christ as Messiah. Elijah wanted to die because God's enemies controlled Israel. Jesus left his disciples feeling alone and powerless in a small boat battered by waves and wind. Why?

On the wall in a Nazi concentration camp an unknown prisoner wrote:

> I believe in the sun, even when it isn't shining.
> I believe in love, even when there's no one there.
> And I believe in God, even when he is silent.

Elijah had just triumphed over all the false prophets of Baal, calling down fire from heaven. After that God sent wind and rain, ending the drought in Israel. But in spite of these signs and wonders, his enemy Jezebel retained her power and was threatening Elijah's life. That is when discouragement hit him. He complained to God, "I've had enough; take away my life, for I am no better than my ancestors."

God's answer was to reveal himself to Elijah, not in the power of the wind "splitting mountains and breaking rocks," or of the earthquake or the fire, but in a "tiny whispering sound;" or, as it is also translated, in "a sound of sheer silence"—stone silence.

Scholars compare this event with God's giving Moses the Ten Commandments on Mount Sinai, shaking the mountain and wrapping it in fire and smoke. But, in spite of this, the people lost faith and worshiped the golden calf. After that God showed his innermost self to Moses, his true divine glory, which could only be translated into words as "a God merciful and gracious, slow to anger, and abounding in steadfast love and faithfulness" (Exodus 34:6).

John's Gospel picks up this description of God and declares Jesus Christ the embodiment of it; "The law was indeed given through Moses; grace and truth [one translation says "enduring love"] came through Jesus Christ" (1:17). Jesus was the ultimate, the most perfect revelation of God's true personality, of his glory, on earth. Jesus revealed that glory most fully in the hour of his crucifixion and resurrection, the hour of his greatest vulnerability and love (see John 17:1).

At Jesus' death there were also signs of power: "At that moment the curtain of the temple was torn in two, from top to bottom. The earth shook, and the rocks were split.... Now when the centurion and those with him, who were keeping watch over Jesus, saw the earthquake and what took place, they were terrified and said, 'Truly this man was God's Son!'" (see Matthew 27:51-54). But the true revelation of God in Jesus was his acceptance of the Father's silence during the crucifixion and the gentleness, the "steadfast love" Jesus showed after his Resurrection, when he appeared to his disciples saying, "Peace be with you" (Luke 24:36). Believers recognized that it was through powerlessness, vulnerability and love that God revealed in Jesus the full divine glory.

God reveals himself to us, too, in the "stone silence" of his apparent absence from the world. When there are no external signs of God's power and the emotional comfort of interior consolations is gone, then we discover his most authentic, most reliable, most strengthening presence in our hearts. It is then that we experience the depth and the reality of purest faith, purest hope and purest love.

God, in his deepest nature is love, not power; forgiveness, not retaliation; a God who is patient to the point of appearing powerless, who appeals to freedom rather than using force. Jesus on the cross reveals him as he truly is.

Reflecting on This Week's Gospels

Nineteenth Week of the Year

> ***Pray daily:*** *Father, we come, reborn in the Spirit, to celebrate our oneness with you in Jesus Christ. Touch our hearts; help them grow. Touch our lives; make them signs of your enduring love. We ask this through Christ our Lord. Amen.*

Monday: Matthew 17:22-27. Jesus said, "'The Son of Man is going to be betrayed into human hands, and they will kill him, and on the third day he will be raised.' And they were greatly distressed." Do you see it as defeat or victory when someone suffers injustice, oppression or violation and yet loves back?

Tuesday: Matthew 18:1-5, 10, 12-14. "Truly I tell you, unless you change and become like children, you will never enter the kingdom of heaven." Are you willing to be as powerless and vulnerable as a child? What do children get through love that you cannot obtain through power?

Wednesday: Matthew 18:15-20. "If another member of the church sins against you, go and point out the fault when the two of you are alone." Have you ever done this? With what results? Why is this so risky to do?

Thursday: Matthew 18:21—19:1. Peter asked, "Lord, if another member of the church sins against me, how often should I forgive? As many as seven times?" Jesus answered, "Not seven times, but, I tell you, seventy-seven times." How much will you take before getting violent in word or act?

Friday: Matthew 19:3-12. Some Pharisees tested him, saying, "Is it lawful for a man to divorce his wife for any cause?" If they had asked instead about "killing for any cause," how do you think Jesus would have answered? Why?

Saturday: Matthew 19:13-15. Jesus said, "Let the little children come to me, and do not stop them; for it is to such

as these that the kingdom of heaven belongs." What
is special about children that makes them eligible for
the Kingdom?

Living This Week's Gospels

As Christian: Choose one thing you are trying to change
by power; use Jesus' method of love instead.

As Disciple: Read one of the four Gospels completely. See
if you can identify a value for which Jesus says we should be
willing to kill.

As Prophet: Ask how you most frequently use violence against
others (for example, in words) and decide how you can change
that into a way that witnesses to God's "enduring love."

As Priest: Think of one thing which recurs in your
life that you could accept as a way of offering yourself in
union with the Lamb of God, a way of working against sin
in the world by enduring evil with love. Offer yourself for
this during Mass.

As King: Count the ways you or those you are associated
with (at home, at work, as an American) try to force people
by intimidation or threats to do what is right. Take one
concrete step toward changing this so that you can work
through persuasion (conversion) and respectful love instead.

Twentieth Sunday of the Year

The Church Kata-holos

Isaiah 56:1, 6-7; Romans 11:13-15, 29-32; Matthew 15:21-28

Matthew's theme in his Gospel is that Jesus is the promised Son of David, the Messiah. But Jesus is called this only three times in direct address (9:27; 15:22; 20:30), twice by blind men and once by this Canaanite woman, who should not have known this Jewish title.

Jesus ignores her. When she falls at his feet and asks for help, he responds, "It is not fair to take the children's food and throw it to the dogs." This does not sound like Jesus. His mother would have been ashamed of him! But Jesus was not being rude. He knew this woman; she was not the wilting type. Undaunted, she answers, "Yes, Lord, yet even the dogs eat the crumbs that fall from their masters' table." Jesus says, "Woman, great is your faith!" and then cures her daughter.

What Jesus did here was to deliberately lead the woman into making an act of faith. Essentially, she acknowledged the truth of God's revelation to Israel by accepting that the Jews are the "children," the chosen family of God. This does not mean she felt inferior! She probably would have insisted to the whole world (Jesus included): "A Canaanite is better than a Jew any day!" But she acknowledged that for some reason God had chosen them. This was her act of faith.

She did not convert to Judaism. At that time religion and nationality were identified. To accept the Jewish faith meant to accept Jewish culture and life-style. There was no distinction between religious expression and cultural expression, between religious identity and ethnic identity. And there would not be until the Church became catholic.

The passage to catholicism is described in the Acts of the Apostles. When the Church decided to give the Greek Christians their own leaders (Acts 6:1-7) and to accept converts from paganism without requiring them to become

Jews first or to follow the Jewish cultural-religious laws (see Acts 10:1—11:18 and 15:1-29), the Church broke the identification of Christianity with a single culture or cultural pattern of expression. This is what opened the door for Christ's Church to spread "throughout the whole" (*kata-holos*), which is what *catholic* means. The Catholic Church is the Church whose teaching and belief are the same throughout the whole world, but whose expression of this belief is embodied differently in the diverse cultural forms of every race, nationality and ethnic group.

There is no such thing, therefore, as a "Roman Catholic Church." There is the Roman (or Latin) rite of the Catholic Church—which is just one of eighteen rites recognized as equal in every way. The Church we belong to is the Armenian-Bulgarian-Chaldean-Coptic-Ethiopian-Georgian-Greek-Italo/Albanian-Latin-Malabar-Malankar-Maronite-Melkite-Romanian-Russian-Serbian-Syrian-Ukrainian Catholic Church. Each of these rites has its own rules, government, liturgy and culturally influenced ways of expressing the faith we all hold in common. And all are equal.

The Catholic Church is not tied down to any one mentality. Catholics can express their devotion silently or by dancing in the aisles; choose bishops by appointment or by majority vote; require priests to be married or celibate; give women public roles in liturgy or reserve these to men. All these choices are cultural, not religious. To be catholic is to refuse to identify religion with a single culture.

At the same time, since religion has to be expressed and all human expression is determined by human culture, being Catholic also means accepting one's own rite and following its rules until they change. One can change rites, just as one can change countries, but everyone has to belong to some culture and accept its rules or just leave the human race. The same is true of any religion incarnated as Church.

Reflecting on This Week's Gospels

Twentieth Week of the Year

> *Pray daily:* Lord, you came to draw everything in
> heaven and on earth into unity under your headship.
> Open my mind and my heart to accept diversity in
> the Church so that you can use me to bring about
> the unity you desire. Amen.

Monday: Matthew 19:16-22. Jesus said to him, "If you
wish to be perfect, go, sell your possessions, and give the
money to the poor, and you will have treasure in heaven;
then come, follow me." Do you identify religion with
observing commandments and customs or with following
the words and example of Jesus?

Tuesday: Matthew 19:23-30. Peter said to Jesus, "Look,
we have left everything and followed you. What then will
we have?" What have you renounced to follow Jesus? Is
giving up sin enough to make you a follower of Jesus?

Wednesday: Matthew 20:1-16. "So the last will be first,
and the first will be last." What practical effect do these
words have on your life? How do you respond to them
in action?

Thursday: Matthew 22:1-14. "But when the king came
in to see the guests, he noticed a man there who was not
wearing a wedding robe...." If you accept the invitation
to the wedding feast and show up, but do not have deep
respect and appreciation for what is going on, where
does this leave you?

Friday: Matthew 22:34-40. A scholar of the law tested
Jesus by asking, "Teacher, which commandment in the law
is the greatest?" What commandment looms largest in your
own consciousness?

Saturday: Matthew 23:1-12. "The scribes and the Pharisees
sit on Moses' seat; therefore, do whatever they teach you and

follow it; but do not do as they do." In what ways do you go beyond "cultural Catholicism"? Beyond the example of the clergy, the hierarchy and your peer group?

Living This Week's Gospels

As Christian: Identify the title of Jesus which says the most to you: Savior, Teacher, Friend, Model, Leader, Priest, Victim, Lord or any other.

As Disciple: Write down five things that are rule or policy for Catholics in the Latin rite but which do not have to be this way in the whole Catholic Church. Can you name five things that other Catholic rites do which differ from Latin rite practice?

As Prophet: Choose a concrete, visible way to express the relationship you have with Jesus, using the title you identified under "Christian" above.

As Priest: In some specific way this week share the "children's food" with someone who does not have what is available to Catholics: the saints, the Mass, a Catholic conference or retreat, the writings of the mystics, a good pastoral letter from a bishop or the pope, or this book!

As King: To break down the parochial narrowness that makes us tend to identify the Catholic Church with our own rite, go with a friend to experience the Mass in the church of some other Catholic rite.

Twenty-First Sunday of the Year

Is the Pope Catholic?

Isaiah 22:19-23; Romans 11:33-36; Matthew 16:13-20

The guiding principle of Christian spirituality is to understand Jesus as "fully human, fully divine." This is the rule preachers, theologians and other individuals must navigate by to remain on course amid the diverse currents and shifting winds of changing cultures. And the "rule of the rule" is "never '*either-or*'; always '*both-and*'."

The Church teaches that Jesus made Peter the head of the universal Church. Because both Peter and Paul died as witnesses to the faith in Rome, the Church recognizes the bishop of Rome as heir to that office. But every bishop is true head of the Church in his own diocese, holding authority directly from Christ, not as a delegate or branch manager for the pope. Although the pope as bishop of Rome has supreme teaching authority in the Church, every bishop is the chief teacher in his diocese. Just as the whole Church remains united through union with the bishop of Rome, every diocese remains united as a faith community through union with its bishop. If we see ourselves as faced with the choice of following either the pope or our local bishop, we are in trouble. We are on track when we try to follow *both* the bishop *and* the pope. In practical terms, this means that if we ignore papal teaching and focus exclusively on our local bishop's preoccupations, we are not Catholic. On the other hand, if we look to the bishop of Rome for leadership and ignore what our own bishop is pointing to on the local scene, we are not Catholic either. And most of us tend to do one or the other: We take sides by choosing what to read and hear.

What do we do when there are differences of opinion in the Church, as there are about birth control? Suppose our bishop does not agree with a particular direction in which the pope is leading the Church (which we may see as "right," or "left," "forward" or "backward")? What if our bishop disagrees with a policy the pope supports, for example, the exclusion of married men from the ordained priesthood? As loyal Catholics should we line up behind our pope or behind our bishop?

To keep on track we must accept fully the divine authority of both pope and bishop while at the same time fully accepting their human limitations. The Gospel shows us in one and the same scene Jesus giving to Peter the "keys of the kingdom," supreme authority in the Church, and Peter immediately teaching error and trying to lead the Church down a path contrary to the way of God. Jesus has to say to him, "Get behind me, Satan! You are a stumbling block to me; for you are setting your mind not on divine things but on human things."

We reconcile apparent contradictions by precision. We preserve our belief in the divine presence of God teaching through pope and bishop by asking very precisely, "Is he speaking here and now under the conditions required for divine guidance?" We believe, for example, that the pope is infallible when he uses his full authority as pope. But when he is not formally defining a doctrine as the revealed truth of God, the pope himself would warn us not to take his teaching as infallible. To accept ordinary papal teaching as totally divine, as if there could be no mix of human error in it, would be making ourselves more Catholic than the pope. The same is true of directions and policies, whether of popes or bishops. To be authentically Catholic we must give full value both to the divine guidance God promised to our teachers and to the human limitations under which they, like us, continue to act and to do their best.

This is the glory of the Church: we don't get angry or rebellious or lose our faith in God or in the Church because a particular pope or bishop leans—as we do—to the right or left, or seems to be going too fast or too slow. We accept the human in our Church's teaching and government without ever denying the divine. We respect the divine in the human and accept the human in the divine. And we glory in the mix!

Reflecting on This Week's Readings

Twenty-First Week of the Year

> *Pray daily: Father, help us to seek the values that will bring us lasting joy in this changing world. In our desire for what you promise, make us one in mind and heart. We ask this through Christ our Lord. Amen.*

Monday: Matthew 23:13-22. Jesus said, "Woe to you, blind guides, who say, 'Whoever swears by the sanctuary is bound by nothing, but whoever swears by the gold of the sanctuary is bound by the oath.'" What effect do the big buildings, rich art works, pomp and ceremony in the Church have on you? Are you judging reality by its wrappings?

Tuesday: Matthew 23:23-26. "Woe to you, scribes and Pharisees, hypocrites. For you tithe mint, dill, and cummin, and have neglected the weightier matters of the law: justice and mercy and faith." Which commandments do you think of most often? How often do you confess sins of not showing mercy, of not making judgments according to the mind of Christ about the needs of those around you?

Wednesday: Matthew 23:27-32. "Woe to you, scribes and Pharisees, hypocrites! For you are like whitewashed tombs, which on the outside look beautiful, but inside they are full of the bones of the dead and of all kinds of filth." Do you judge values by appearances—importance by dress, dignity by titles, acceptability by signs of success? When and with whom do you do this? What is the result?

Thursday: Matthew 24:42-51. "Who then is the faithful and wise slave, whom his master has put in charge of his household, to give the other slaves their allowance of food at the proper time?" What is it that inspires you to trust Church leaders (laity and clergy)? What makes you feel trust in business and professional people? In politicians?

Friday: Matthew 25:1-13. "Then the kingdom of heaven will be like this. Ten bridesmaids took their lamps and went to meet the bridegroom." When you go to various Church services, what are you looking for? Are you consciously seeking an encounter with Jesus?

Saturday: Matthew 25:14-30. The king in today's parable said, "[T]o all those who have, more will be given, and they will have an abundance; but from those who have nothing, even what they have will be taken away." How can you lose your spiritual gifts by not using your human gifts and talents?

Living This Week's Gospels

As Christian: Ask yourself what external thing in your religion you like most: building, decoration, music, statue, devotional practice or something else? How does this particular thing affect your relationship to Christ?

As Disciple: Read an encyclical of the pope or a pastoral letter from your bishop.

As Prophet: Begin asking what each Church title, dress or gesture expresses and whether what each one expresses is real.

As Priest: Identify three "ritualistic" forms of self-expression in your personal life—words or gestures you frequently use—and ask if you mean and do what you express.

As King: Ask what one thing you can do here and now to bring the Church's external expression a little more into conformity with its interior truth, values and reality.

Twenty-Second Sunday of the Year

"Do not conform..."

Jeremiah 20:7-9; Romans 12:1-2; Matthew 16:21-27

Through Baptism we offered our bodies "as a living sacrifice, holy and acceptable to God...." This means that wherever our live bodies are, we are sacrificed, offered, given to doing God's work in every thought, word and action. We are not our own; we have been purchased at the price of Christ's blood. Our bodies are temples of the Holy Spirit within us. Therefore, Saint Paul says we are committed to "glorify God" in our bodies (1 Corinthians 6:19-20).

To do this we obviously need to be "transformed by the renewing" of our minds. If we conform to this world's values, we cannot "discern what is the will of God—what is good and acceptable and perfect." We have to choose between thinking like Christ or thinking like ordinary, good Americans. If we choose Christ, we will no longer fit in with American society anymore or with any other human culture.

Jeremiah warns us that God will seduce us if we listen to him. "O LORD, you have enticed me, and I was enticed." (The Jerusalem Bible says "seduced" here.) Jeremiah spoke the truth God showed him, and as a result everyone laughed at him or turned positively hostile. This bothered Jeremiah so much that he decided never to mention God again. But he could not stop. God's words overpowered him. They became like a fire in his heart. He had to speak out, no matter what it cost.

Jesus is our model in this as in everything else. He was not just won over, seduced by the word of God; he was the Word of God made flesh who came to seduce us, to overpower us (if we let ourselves be overpowered) with the clarity of his truth, with the attraction of his love. Jesus came to ask us to make the total gift of ourselves: to surrender our bodies to him as "living sacrifices," to be taken and offered at every moment for the life of the world, to be used simply as the continuing expression of his love and truth so that the healing, transforming power of his life within us might transform everyone whose life we touch.

If we offer ourselves, we will be offered. Jesus was offered as the Lamb of God to take away the sins of the world. And, we will be offered in the middle of our working day, on the job, in our homes, in our social life, in the hubbub of our daily activities to "take away the sin" of the world—that is, to challenge the distorted attitudes which breed and are bred by sin; to question our culture's false priorities, priorities which we ourselves, our friends and our associates have so far accepted.

If we open ourselves to God's words and to the Word of God made flesh in Jesus Christ, we will be seduced. Our minds will be overpowered by truth, our hearts by love and his life, his Spirit within us, will become "a burning fire" which we cannot hold in. We will speak out—and like the Lamb of God with whom we were identified at Baptism, with whom we are offered up in every Eucharist, to whom we are united in every Communion—we will suffer for it. We will lose money and opportunities, jobs and friends. At times we will feel that we are losing life itself. But if we accept losing ourselves and everything life holds out to us, for the sake of the Bridegroom, we will find ourselves and in Jesus will "have life to the full."

This is our mission as Church: to hold up to the world an ending worthy of its beginning, to offer people something—Someone—worth losing themselves for: to witness to a truth worth proclaiming at the cost of our lives; a life worth everything we can sacrifice to live it: Good News seducing, overpowering the heart.

Reflecting on This Week's Gospels

Twenty-Second Week of the Year

> *Pray daily: Lord, God of power and might, nothing is good that is against your will, and all is of value that comes from your hand. Place in our hearts a desire to please you and fill our minds with insight into love. We ask this through Christ our Lord. Amen.*

Monday: Luke 4:16-30. Jesus quoted the prophet Isaiah, "The Spirit of the Lord is upon me, / because he has anointed me...." What were you anointed at Baptism to do? What in the ritual expressed this?

Tuesday: Luke 4:31-37. Jesus was teaching on the sabbath. "They were astounded at his teaching, because he spoke with authority." Do the assumptions and values of our culture carry as much weight with you as Christ's example and principles? What in your life shows this?

Wednesday: Luke 4:38-44. Jesus said, "I must proclaim the good news of the kingdom of God to the other cities also; for I was sent for this purpose." Do you see yourself as sent into business and family and social life to proclaim the Good News? What makes this obvious?

Thursday: Luke 5:1-11. Jesus said to Simon, "Put out into the deep water and let down your nets for a catch." How often do you put out into deep water with people you talk to? Can you bring people closer to God through superficial relationships?

Friday: Luke 5:33-39. Jesus said, "But new wine must be put into fresh wineskins." Can you judge what is good, acceptable and perfect in God's eyes if you simply reflect the goals of our culture? What is the basic goal or aim in life that most influences your decisions? How does it affect your judgment?

Saturday: Luke 6:1-5. Some Pharisees asked, "Why are you doing what is not lawful on the sabbath?" Jesus answered, "The Son of Man is lord of the sabbath." What cultural assumptions and priorities are you afraid to challenge?

Living This Week's Gospels

As Christian: List three things obedience to the culture can do for you—for example, "I can make more money." Then see if you can identify something Jesus said about each of those three things.

As Disciple: Search the Gospels until you can find something Jesus said about being rich, feeling secure, being accepted and being a success.

As Prophet: Identify one attitude or value that is generally accepted in your social or professional circle but that you think Jesus challenges. Begin to act visibly against it.

As Priest: Every morning consciously offer your body "as a living sacrifice to God," the same way the bread and wine are offered at Mass. What words or gesture would express this for you?

As King: Seriously examine what authority you accept in your social or professional life, in family life or politics. Look for one thing you could do that would make Jesus Lord in a more practical way over the decisions and activities of your life.

Twenty-Third Sunday of the Year

Speaking the Truth in Love

Ezekiel 33:7-9; Romans 13:8-10; Matthew 18:15-20

According to Saint Paul, the only thing we owe to anyone is love. This is a rule of life which frees us from false demands, and thereby asks more of us than any person could through social pressure.

To let ourselves be dominated, manipulated or intimidated by others is the easy way out, even when we tell ourselves that we are acting out of love. Love never acts through or responds to an abusive use of force, whether physical or emotional.

Love must be based on truth because in God (therefore in reality) love, truth and goodness are all one; reality follows the same rule. That is why God tells us through Ezekiel that love requires us to tell people when they are doing wrong. But we constantly give ourselves excuses not to do this.

How many people tell their pastor if they think he is doing something wrong? How many priests write their bishops every time they think he is taking a wrong direction? How many bishops are honest with the pope? Ezekiel would say to us, "If you told your pastor, your bishop or the pope what you think about his decisions, and if he pays no attention to you, God will not hold you responsible. But if you see mistakes they are making and say nothing, you will be held responsible for all the damage that is done to your parish, to your diocese, to the Church." The same principle holds with family and friends, business associates and politicians. We are not responsible for what another person does, but we are responsible for lovingly telling others the truth as we see it. And if we do not speak out when we should, we, too, are responsible for all the evil that is done.

Jesus adds something to this principle. "When you tell

others what you think they are doing wrong," he says, "do not go in with power. Go in defenseless, vulnerable." The process he teaches for resolving differences is the exact opposite of what we usually do.

Usually, when we disagree with what someone is doing, we first talk about it to others. We criticize; we complain; in effect, we gather a lynch mob. We try to make sure that if it ever comes to a confrontation we have a lot of support at our backs. Then we try to get others to talk to the person or we appeal to higher authorities, saying, "Don't use my name!"

Jesus tells us that our first step should be to go to the person, one on one, and say what we think. This way we have no power; we are vulnerable. This makes us more likely to question rather than to accuse, to speak softly instead of yelling, to seek agreement rather than capitulation. This procedure is less threatening and more effective. But we find it a scary thing to do, especially if the person we are talking to seems to have more power than we do: power to take action against us, to make us look stupid with quick words, to make us look bad by pointing out our own faults.

There is no human power greater than truth spoken in love, but this power does not protect us from retaliation. It is the only power Jesus chose to use to save the world; when Pilate asked, "Are you a king?", Jesus answered, "You say that I am a king. For this I was born, and for this I came into the world, to *testify to the truth*. Everyone who belongs to the truth listens to my voice" (John 18:37). Then Pilate ordered Jesus to be crucified.

Jesus does not promise we will not suffer for speaking the truth. But he says, "If you seek to save your life on this earth, you will lose it. How do you profit if you gain the whole world and lose your own soul, your self, your person?" We are not on earth to save our lives—or our jobs or our relationships with others if we have to suppress the truth to keep them—but rather to "testify to the truth." The identity we are creating for ourselves, the person we will be for all eternity, is determined by that.

Reflecting on This Week's Gospels

Twenty-Third Week of the Year

> ***Pray daily****: God our Father, you redeem us and make us your children in Christ. Look upon us and give us true freedom. We ask this through Christ our Lord. Amen.*

Monday: Luke 6:6-11. Jesus said to them, "I ask you, is it lawful to do good or to do harm on the sabbath, to save life or to destroy it?" Are you afraid to ask challenging questions in response to false values or promises?

Tuesday: Luke 6:12-19. Jesus spent the night in prayer to God. When day came, he called his disciples to himself, and from them he chose the Twelve, whom he also named apostles. Were you chosen and sent to spread the truth, the words of Jesus, just as explicitly as the apostles were? When? How do you do it?

Wednesday: Luke 6:20-26. "Blessed are you when people hate you, and when they exclude you, revile you, and defame you on account of the Son of Man." How often does fear of public opinion keep you from expressing what you know is true?

Thursday: Luke 6:27-38. Jesus said, "Do not judge, and you will not be judged; do not condemn, and you will not be condemned." If you hear something bad about someone, can you avoid judging unless you go to the person as a friend to get the other side of the story?

Friday: Luke 6:39-42. Jesus said, "Why do you see the speck in your neighbor's eye, but do not notice the log in your own eye?" How often does talking honestly to others about faults you think you see in them lead you to discover things in your own attitudes that need correcting? Is this good for you? Does it help you appreciate others more?

Saturday: Luke 6:43-49. Jesus said, "[F]or it is out of the abundance of the heart that the mouth speaks." If you are afraid to say to others what you really believe and think, are you really in touch with your own self? How can fear of losing relationships with others cause you to lose relationship with your own self?

Living This Week's Gospels

As Christian: Ask what you fear more than losing your relationship with Jesus. How can you act against this fear?

As Disciple: The first time this week you find yourself feeling critical of someone, try to find where in the Gospel Jesus says something about what that person is doing.

As Prophet: Think back on what you said or did when you felt critical. Is there a better way you could have handled it or can handle it the next time?

As Priest: Ask how, without giving offense, you can communicate to a person toward whom you felt critical the attitude of Jesus you found in the Gospel. Do it in a loving, nurturing way.

As King: Ask what three things you would like your pastor or bishop to do for the Church. Tell him this by word or letter. Or do this with someone at work or in government— or simply with a friend who could be making a greater impact on the world.

Forgiveness Is a Mission

Sirach 27:30—28:9; Romans 14:7-9; Matthew 18:21-35

Forgiveness is an individual act. But it is also a communal mission, in which we all share as members of the Church, as the continuation of Christ's human presence on earth.

With Saint Paul we are "ambassadors of Christ." God, he wrote, has "reconciled us to himself through Christ, and has given us the ministry of reconciliation; ...entrusting the message of reconciliation to us" (see 2 Corinthians 5:17-21).

What is this ministry of reconciliation? Besides being the proclamation of God's forgiveness to individual persons, it is also the work of bringing individuals and ethnic groups, different races and nations, into unity of mind and heart with each other. It is the work of peace.

The peace of Christ is what Paul described as the goal of Christ's coming to earth: Jesus came to bring everything in heaven and on earth together into unity in himself, to reconcile everything to himself by making peace through the blood of his cross (see Ephesians 1:10, Colossians 1:20). The peace of Christ is that loving union of all people with each other and with God that can only be realized in the communion of the Holy Spirit. It is made visible when all the members of the Church are united with God and with one another in the act of receiving the Eucharist at Mass.

Receiving Communion is a commitment, a dedication, to working for peace. The Church emphasizes this by inviting us to offer a Sign of Peace to the Body of Christ present around us before we receive the Body of Christ in Communion. The Sign of Peace expresses more than friendship, even more than reconciliation with those around us. We make this gesture in the act of asking Jesus to grant us the peace and unity of his kingdom. It is a gesture which says we are opening ourselves to the grace of God at work on earth, bringing acceptance, unity and harmony to the whole human race. It is a promise to accept Christ's peace for ourselves and to extend that peace to others—not just to those present in church, but to the whole world.

Peace is not an accomplished fact but a process. The "peace of Christ" is the presence of the Spirit in our hearts, working to perfect our reconciliation with God and with one another. The peace of Christ is the "ministry of reconciliation" to which every member of the Church is dedicated by Baptism. When Jesus says, "Peace I leave with you; my peace I give to you" (John 14:27), he is giving us a gift. But it is a gift like life, a gift to be used in action.

In *The Scent of Jasmine*, Sister Patricia McCarthy, C.N.D., writes: "Every gift from God carries its own responsibility. God's gifts are free but they draw us into the experience of love and the need for response. With [the sacraments], we are drawn into the process of forgiveness. And forgiveness is a process, not a feeling. To enter into this process is to enter into continual conversion. Forgiveness requires faith, effort and determination. We acknowledge our need for forgiveness, we believe God forgives us, and we accept the obligation to forgive others. Throughout our lives we live this cycle of forgiveness as a never-ending process."

Jesus tells us that the man who would not forgive was "handed over to the torturers." As long as we cling to anger in our hearts and look for revenge—against individuals, groups or nations—we choose the torture which our own hearts inflict on us. We prefer the torture that racial and ethnic divisions bring to society. We can cling to torture— or we can work for peace.

Reflecting on This Week's Gospels

Twenty-Fourth Week of the Year

> *Pray daily: Father in heaven, creator of all, look down upon your people in our moments of need, for you alone are the source of our peace. We ask this through Christ our Lord. Amen.*

Monday: Luke 7:1-10. The centurion sent friends to tell Jesus, "Lord, do not trouble yourself, for I am not worthy to have you come under my roof." How awed should you be that Jesus comes to you in Communion any day you desire?

Tuesday: Luke 7:11-17. "As [Jesus] approached the gate of the town, a man who had died was being carried out. He was his mother's only son, and she was a widow." We do not know how the man died. If he had been executed for rape and murder, would Jesus have raised him? Would you?

Wednesday: Luke 7:31-35. "Nevertheless, wisdom is vindicated by all her children." Do you really believe that everything Jesus teaches is true wisdom—even when it shocks you? Do you believe it is always wise to forgive?

Thursday: Luke 7:36-50. Jesus said to Simon [the Pharisee], "Do you see this woman? ...[H]er sins, which were many, have been forgiven; hence she has shown great love. But the one to whom little is forgiven, loves little." How much has God's forgiveness won your love and trust? Will your forgiveness bring love to life in others? With whom will you begin?

Friday: Luke 8:1-3. Jesus journeyed from one town to another, preaching and proclaiming the Good News. Accompanying him were the apostles and several women who had been cured of evil spirits and infirmities, including Mary Magdalene from whom seven demons had been cast out. What would disqualify someone from being a coworker with Jesus?

Saturday: Luke 8:4-15. Jesus said, "But as for [the seed that fell on] good soil, these are the ones who, when they hear the word, hold it fast in an honest and good heart, and bear fruit with patient endurance." Do you ever read or hear something that gives you good desires, but then do nothing about it? Why?

Living This Week's Gospels

As Christian: Choose one attitude you have toward one person or group and ask Christ to let you see what his attitude is. Ask yourself which attitude promotes life and which diminishes it.

As Disciple: Make one list of sins or faults you find easy to forgive and another list of the ones you find hard to forgive. What do the faults within each list have in common? What is the difference between the faults in one list and those in the other? What does this tell you about yourself?

As Prophet: Make some friendly gesture which shows acceptance of someone with whom you ordinarily have no relationship.

As Priest: Think of someone who has hurt you; do something loving for that person.

As King: Do one positive thing, however small, to help heal the resentments or prejudices that cause division where you live or work.

Every Moment Counts

Isaiah 55:6-9; Philippians 1:20c-24, 27a; Matthew 20:1-16a

Jesus tells of an owner who came into the marketplace at any and every hour of the day and found men standing around idle. Why were there no women? One answer is that in the structure of that society, women probably did not hire themselves out as day laborers the way men did. Women did work in the fields, but more in the context of working as a family.

Even though more and more women work outside the home and even though men are doing more work within households, women are still much more likely to perceive the deeper needs of family members and friends. They are taught to be more relationship-oriented and less likely to bury themselves in work to compensate for rough spots in relationships. If human society is to reach its potential, it can do so only by recognizing the gifts of all its members, including the ability to see which relationships are withering for lack of attention and support.

Isn't it true that women are almost always the first to think of calling someone who is sick? To remember anniversaries? Aren't women frequently the ones first involved—and who involve men—in issues that politicians tend to overlook.

Could we ask, just as speculation, without falling into simplistic stereotypes, whether men are more likely to identify their "work" as what they are paid to do? Are women more inclined to see building relationships among people and maintaining a pleasant and supportive environment—on the job and at home—as the constant, ongoing "work" of every human being?

If these generalizations have any truth, God is more like a woman than a man. When Jesus was criticized for healing on the sabbath, he said: "My Father is still working, and I also am working!" (John 5:17). Jesus was at work twenty-four hours a day, every day, because his work was doing the will of the Father at every moment: loving people back to life at every moment, responding with redemptive, life-giving love to each moment's need and opportunity.

And this is our work, whether we are at home or on the job, whether we are praying in church, watching TV or eating in a restaurant. Wherever we are and whatever we are doing, we are the Body of Christ; we are his embodied presence, consecrated and sent to continue his work in that place, at that time, under those particular circumstances, as prophets, priests and stewards of his kingship.

The focus Jesus had, which he invites us to adopt, is not on what we do but on what we are. We do not get our identity from what we do on the job; rather, what we do on the job or anywhere else should be the expression of what we are. Whatever Jesus did or said, at any moment of his life, he was revealing God. Everything we do and say, the way we dress, the expression on our face, our body language, the atmosphere of our homes, all this should reveal the presence of God in our hearts. This is our work: to be the constant, prophetic expression of God's truth; the constant expression, as priests, of God's healing, ministering love for others; the constant expression, as Christ's coworkers and stewards, of God's constant concern to reform and renew the structures of society. Our work, at every moment, is to extend the reign of God.

Reflecting on This Week's Gospels

Twenty-Fifth Week of the Year

Pray daily: Father, guide us, as you guide creation, according to your law of constant love. May we love one another at every moment and grow to that perfection of love which you hold out to us as the

*goal of every Christian life. We ask this through
Christ our Lord. Amen.*

Monday: Luke 8:16-18. "No one after lighting a lamp
hides it under a jar, or puts it under a bed, but puts it on a
lampstand, so that those who enter may see the light."
Is the light of truth and love within you visible at all
times, in everything you do?

Tuesday: Luke 8:19-21. Jesus said to them in reply, "My
mother and my brothers are those who hear the word of
God and do it." Do you look upon the work of God as your
family business?

Wednesday: Luke 9:1-6. Jesus summoned the apostles
and gave them power over all demons and to cure diseases,
sending them to proclaim the kingdom of God and to heal
the sick. Are you conscious of having power from God to
proclaim divine truth and to heal woundedness? Do you use
it constantly?

Thursday: Luke 9:7-9. Herod Antipas heard about all that
was happening and he was greatly perplexed because some
people were saying that John had been raised from the dead.
What in your life and action makes it evident that Jesus is
risen and living in you?

Friday: Luke 9:18-22. Jesus said, "The Son of Man must
undergo great suffering, and be rejected by the elders, chief
priests, and scribes, and be killed, and on the third day be
raised." Are you always aware that your real work in life is
to be given and sacrificed for others?

Saturday: Luke 9:43-45. "And all were astounded at
the greatness of God.... [e]veryone was amazed at all he
was doing." Are you aware in everything you do that the
goodness and greatness of God should shine out in you?

Living This Week's Gospels

As Christian: Ask when in your day you are least aware of Christ's presence in you? Find some physical, visible way to remind yourself of him.

As Disciple: Think about the goal of being offered for others as Christ's Body in everything you do. Is this an example of how God's thoughts and ways are higher than our thoughts and ways?

As Prophet: Ask what truth or teaching of Jesus seems to be most ignored where you live. What can you do to bear witness to it?

As Priest: Do one thing this week which expresses your belief that power to bring healing to the woundedness of others is within you.

As King: Who in your acquaintance seems to be "standing around idle" without a sense of purpose? Who has a gift that is not being used? Think of a way that person's gift could be put to use and suggest it.

The Law of Life

Ezekiel 18:25-28; Philippians 2:1-11; Matthew 21:28-32

Jesus tells us of a son who says to his father, "Yes, sir!" when told to work in the vineyard but does not go. The son does not want to appear disobedient, because he sees that as bad or "sinful." But he sees no sin in letting the work itself go undone. Another son does not care about obeying, but when he thinks about the work he realizes it has to get done and he does it. Which thinks more like his father?

Do we obey laws just because they are laws or because what they tell us to do is good? Does God insist on obedience because he is on a divine power trip or because God wants us to have everything that is best for us?

Jesus showed us how unconcerned God is about clinging to power and prestige; God the Son emptied himself, taking the form of a slave, being born in human likeness. Christ came not to be served but to serve. Jesus insists that we should obey God the Father because Jesus realizes how much damage we will do to ourselves and others if we fail to obey.

Sometimes we justify a sin by saying, "It doesn't hurt anybody." The truth is, we just don't *know* how much harm we are doing. The only reason God gives us laws is to tell us what does, in fact, hurt people, whether we know it or not. If we don't take God's word for it, we will learn the hard way and the world will suffer from our actions.

Some things are wrong, not because they do harm every time, but because they are dangerous. Would you say that an engineer who ignored the safety regulations in a nuclear power plant was not guilty so long as the plant did not blow up? Or is it wrong just to take a chance on causing terrible devastation? Is it OK to abuse drugs a little, as long as you and your friends do not get addicted? Or is it wrong to take a chance on leading yourself or another into a drug-devastated life? Is it OK to drive drunk so long as you don't actually hit anyone?

As an adolescent I thought the argument against seeking sexual arousal outside of marriage was pretty weak. Making out did not mean you were going to go all the way. And even if a couple did lose control, everyone knew how to keep from getting pregnant. Now that there are over a million abortions a year in our country, and after seeing how many well-informed high school and college students get pregnant in spite of their control and their precautions, not even to mention the AIDS factor, I put as much faith in "safe sex" as I do in "safe drugs" or "safe drunk driving." I now see what I suppose God—and even the adults—knew all along: that every step into sexual arousal outside of marriage is gambling with the life of an unborn child.

So much of our moral teaching has focused on sex that we may forget that the real focus is life. Ezekiel equates sin with death: whoever sins, dies. Therefore, whoever causes death sins. "Death" here means any diminishment of the quality of human life on earth. Sin is sin because it keeps us or others from that fullness of life which Jesus came to give. How much would change in our behavior, moral teaching and confessions if we asked about our every act, "What does this contribute, or take away from, the fullness of life on earth?"

Catholics of my generation were taught that taking pleasure in watching sexually arousing movies is sinful. What about taking pleasure in movies that satisfy our lust for revenge through violence? Is the thrill of watching the "good guy" finally beat the "bad guy" to a pulp any less sinful than the thrill of watching two naked bodies engage in sex? What about movies in which we take vicarious pleasure in watching people drink too much (attractively, of course), spend too much money on their pleasure or focus their lives solely on their own gratification? In short, are things wrong because they are forbidden or because they are destructive?

Reflecting on This Week's Gospels

Twenty-Sixth Week of the Year

Pray daily: Father, you show your wisdom and love through the laws which reveal your heart to us. Help us to believe in your law and obey it, that we might have "life to the full." We ask this through Christ our Lord. Amen.

Monday: Luke 9:46-50. "An argument arose among [the disciples] as to which one of them was the greatest." How would this be settled in a movie? Where you work? By our government? How does Jesus settle it?

Tuesday: Luke 9:51-56. When a Samaritan village would not welcome Jesus, the disciples asked, "Lord, do you want us to command fire to come down from heaven and consume them?" Where does this reaction come from? What nourishes it? How did Jesus answer them? Why?

Wednesday: Luke 9:57-62. "To another [Jesus] said, 'Follow me.' But he said, 'Lord, first let me go and bury my father.'" Why should every command or invitation of Jesus be obeyed, even at great sacrifice?

Thursday: Luke 10:1-12. Jesus said to them, "The harvest is plentiful, but the laborers are few; therefore ask the Lord of the harvest to send out laborers into his harvest." At Baptism and Confirmation, God sent you to work in his vineyard. You said yes. Did you go?

Friday: Luke 10:13-16. Jesus said: "Woe to you, Chorazin! Woe to you, Bethsaida! For if the deeds of power done in you had been done in Tyre and Sidon, they would have repented long ago, sitting in sackcloth and ashes." If a nation (family, individual) does not follow Christ's teaching, does God punish by sending evil on them? Or is Christ's way simply the only way to a happy life on earth? If it is, what should you do for your country, family or yourself?

Saturday: Luke 10:17-24. "...Do not rejoice at this, that the spirits submit to you, but rejoice that your names are written in heaven." Jesus rejoices not in dominating others, but in achieving a loving relationship with others. Do you try more to manage people or to relate to them?

Living This Week's Gospels

As Christian: Tell Jesus explicitly in prayer that you believe he is the Way, the Truth and the Life. Write out your prayer.

As Disciple: Identify one attitude, value or practice you take for granted, but that seems to diminish the quality of life. Find something Jesus teaches about this.

As Prophet: Change one thing in your life which is not forbidden by any law but which you think contradicts the teaching or example of Jesus.

As Priest: Ask what attitude, value or practice in your environment causes pain to others. Do something to bring comfort or healing to that pain.

As King: Ask again what attitude, value or practice in your environment causes pain to others or diminishes their lives. Then ask what you can do to change the environment and make it more life-giving. What can you do to remove the cause of the evil?

Twenty-Seventh Sunday of the Year

The People of God

Isaiah 5:1-7; Philippians 4:6-9; Matthew 21:33-43

Did God reject Israel and replace the Jews with another chosen people? No! In the parable of the unfaithful tenants, it is not the vineyard (Israel) that the owner rejects, only those who were in charge of it. It is significant that when Jesus tells this story he is speaking to the "chief priests and the elders" and the Pharisees (see verses 23 and 45).

The chosen people were not rejected; they simply came under a new government: that of Jesus, the promised "Son of David" and "King of the Jews" who was destined to "reign over the house of Jacob forever." Jesus gave religious leadership to the twelve apostles, all Jews, who succeeded Jacob's twelve sons from whom the twelve tribes of Israel descended. The apostles then opened up membership in the new chosen people to the Gentiles without requiring them to take on the ethnic customs of the Jews. Membership became a catholic (universal) religious reality rather than a religious reality identified with race.

God did not reject the Jews or replace the chosen people with anyone. Any gentiles who accepted the Good News also became Jews in the full religious meaning of that word, and heirs to all the religious history of Israel and all the promises God made to his people.

All Christians are Jews—not in the ethnic or racial meaning of the word because all distinctions based on race were abolished—according to the religious meaning of the word. Membership in the chosen people was never just a matter of accepting the Scriptures in faith or of conscientiously keeping God's law as one privately understood it. There was never any such thing as a "private Judaism." To be a member of the chosen people meant you became a member of an organized people, following their laws and customs.

Jesus made a point of showing that he was not changing this. He chose twelve apostles to show a continuation with the twelve tribes of the new Israel. When Judas betrayed Jesus, the remaining apostles filled his place so that the number twelve would be complete. The Church neither replaced nor broke off from Israel. The Church is simply the continuation of Israel under a new government, enriched and transformed by the teaching and grace of Jesus Christ. Those who became members of the Church in the time of the apostles knew that they were accepting not only the teaching and grace of Jesus but also entering "a chosen race, a royal priesthood, a holy nation, God's own people" (1 Peter 2:9), organized according to religious rather than civil laws.

We can no more reject "organized religion" and be Christian than we can reject all government and be citizens of any nation. Christianity is not simply a philosophy, a doctrine or a movement; it is membership in the People of God governed by Jesus the anointed king through his apostles and their successors. There was only one chosen people and there is only one Church, with varying degrees of membership.

For more Scriptural background on this, see Genesis 35:22; Matthew 2:2 and Chapter 27; 19:28; 21:23, 45; Luke 1:33; Acts 1:15-26 and Chapter 15; Galatians 3:28-29; 1 Peter 2:9; and Revelation 7:5-8; 21:10-14.

Reflecting on This Week's Gospels

Twenty-Seventh Week of the Year

Pray daily: Almighty and eternal God, Father of the world to come, your goodness is beyond what our spirit can touch and your strength is more than the mind can grasp. Lead us to seek beyond our reach and give us the courage to stand before your truth. We ask this through Christ our Lord. Amen.

Monday: Luke 10:25-37. A man was robbed while traveling. A priest and a Levite—a church worker—passed him by. "But a Samaritan traveler while traveling came near him; and when he saw him, he was moved with pity. He went to him and bandaged his wounds.... Which of these three...was a neighbor to the man who fell into the hands of the robbers?" How much of your compassion for others is based on racial or social bonding? In the Scriptures, to "have mercy" means to come to the aid of another person out of a sense of relationship.

Tuesday: Luke 10:38-42. "Martha, Martha, you are worried and distracted by many things; there is need of only one thing." What do you consider the most necessary item on your daily agenda? Would Jesus agree?

Wednesday: Luke 11:1-4. One of Jesus' disciples said to him, "Lord, teach us to pray, as John taught his disciples." Who taught you to pray? Who might teach you to pray better at your present stage of growth?

Thursday: Luke 11:5-13. "So I say to you, Ask, and it will be given you; search, and you will find; knock, and the door will be opened for you." What do you ask for? What do you seek? Where do you knock? When?

Friday: Luke 11:15-26. Jesus said that every kingdom divided against itself will fall. What divides Christians? What brings them together?

Saturday: Luke 11:27-28. A woman from the crowd called out, "Blessed is the womb that bore you and the breasts that nursed you." Jesus replied, "Blessed rather are those who hear the word of God and obey it!" Do you think it is enough to practice your religion by doing what you were taught? Is it essential that you personally reflect on God's word until you understand how to live it? When do you do this?

Living This Week's Gospels

As Christian: Ask yourself what would change in your relationship (interaction) with Jesus if you gave up your relationship (interaction) with the Church.

As Disciple: In two columns list the advantages and disadvantages of belonging to an organized religion.

As Prophet: Make a list of the things you do because you are a Catholic which make you different from other Christians.

As Priest: Make a list of the things you do as a Catholic that give you something in common with other Christians and a sense of being one with them.

As King: Read the last thing written by your bishop, the successor of the apostles in charge of your local Church, and ask what you can do to put into practice what he is teaching.

Twenty-Eighth Sunday of the Year

Our Glory Is God's

Isaiah 25:6-10a; Philippians 4:12-14, 19-20; Matthew 22:1-14

God saves. Isaiah's message is that God will destroy death and wipe away the tears from all faces, and we will say, "This is our God, to whom we looked to save us. Let us rejoice and be glad that He has!"

The name *Jesus* means "God saves." In Jesus the power of God acted through his human nature: through both the strength of his human powers and the weakness of his human vulnerability. That tells us something: From its very beginning the salvation of the human race was a divine-human reality. Even though God accomplishes it by divine power, that power acts in some dependence on human action.

Jesus describes God's saving action as an invitation to a wedding feast. There would be no feast if God didn't provide it; we could not if God didn't invite us. Also, God is so totally in control that nothing can stop the feast from taking place or keep us from getting there if we want to come. But we are free to say no. God invites and makes possible, but he does not force. God respects our human freedom.

Once again, we see that everything authentically Christian is fully human and fully divine. As human beings we are not inert blobs, waiting for God to drag us to safety. Even when Jesus healed people who were completely paralyzed, he said, "Rise and walk!" He did not carry them; he empowered them. When Jesus saved people, he saved their human dignity as well.

Some Christians think that any credit given to human nature is glory taken away from God; that celebrating the lives of the saints, for example, turns our focus away from God and deprives God of glory. In reality, every time we acknowledge the goodness and capability of human nature, we give glory to God as its Creator. And every time we

celebrate any human victory over sin and evil—the saints
are outstanding examples of this—we give glory to Jesus
as the Redeemer of human nature.

If no credit is to be given to human beings acting by
grace, then "the grace of our Lord Jesus Christ" has no
power to redeem what is human, and Jesus' death on the
cross was in vain. If we say with Martin Luther that the
redeemed soul, the soul in grace, is "like a dunghill
covered with snow," we seem to be humbling ourselves
by saying nothing human is ever good or worthy of praise,
but in fact we are saying that the blood of Christ has no
power to take away sin; but only to cover it up. (That is
where the fundamentalist expression "covered by the
blood" comes form: it is an acceptance of Luther's
doctrine of "extrinsic salvation.")

Saint Irenaeus, a Father of the Church and a disciple
of Saint Polycarp, himself a disciple of Saint John the
Evangelist, became bishop of Lyon shortly after his
ordination to the priesthood in A.D. 177. Irenaeus wrote,
"Life in man is the glory of God; the life of man is the
vision of God." The splendor of Christ's redemptive act
shines out in people who are alive with the gift of divine
life. Jesus is glorified in his disciples.

Our confidence, however, is not based upon what we
as human beings can do. We look to God for everything:
for light, strength and love, and even for the grace to pray
for these and to accept them when they are given. God is
our Father; God cares for us the way a parent cares for
a tiny child. Jesus is our Savior; he does not simply offer
advice and encouragement; he empowers, he saves. He
teaches us to call on him and trust in him for everything
we need. If we ask, we will receive. If we receive, we will
know from experience that Saint Paul's words are true:
"God will fully satisfy every need of yours according to
his riches in glory in Christ Jesus."

Reflecting on This Week's Gospels

Twenty-Eighth Week of the Year

Pray daily: Father in heaven, the hand of your loving-kindness powerfully yet gently guides all the moments of our day. Go before us in our pilgrimage of life, anticipate our needs and prevent our falling. We ask this through Christ our Lord. Amen.

Monday: Luke 11:29-32. Jesus said, "The people of Nineveh will rise up at the judgment with this generation and condemn it, because they repented at the proclamation of Jonah, and see, something greater than Jonah is here." What does Jesus do that is greater than to call us to conversion?

Tuesday: Luke 11:37-41. Jesus said, "Now you Pharisees clean the outside of the cup and of the dish, but inside you are full of greed and wickedness. You fools! Did not the one who made the outside make the inside also?" Does Jesus forgive you simply on the outside or does he make you interiorly clean? What is the difference?

Wednesday: Luke 11:42-46. "But woe to you Pharisees! For you tithe...and neglect justice and the love of God; it is these you ought to have practiced, without neglecting the others." What do you emphasize more: good behavior or good thoughts and desires? Which is more important?

Thursday: Luke 11:47-54. "Woe to you lawyers! For you have taken away the key of knowledge; you did not enter yourselves, and you hindered those who were entering." Which of your actions help others to know and love God? Which hinder others?

Friday: Luke 12:1-7. Jesus said: "I tell you, my friends, do not fear those who kill the body.... [E]ven the hairs of your head are all counted. Do not be afraid; you are of more value than many sparrows." When you are afraid, do you remember God's love for you? Do you believe then that you are as precious to God as a child is to its parents?

Saturday: Luke 12:8-12. "When they bring you before the synagogues, the rulers, and the authorities, do not worry about how you are to defend yourselves or what you are to say; for the Holy Spirit will teach you at that very hour what you ought to say." What do you fear as being beyond your strength? Do Jesus' words here apply to that also?

Living This Week's Gospels

As Christian: Ask which of your daily actions you do without consciously involving Jesus or asking his help. How can you change this?

As Disciple: Use your human mind to look for something in Scripture which will enlighten your life and give you guidance. God's words are "a feast of rich food and choice wines." How will you eat and drink?

As Prophet: Use your free will to make one decision this week that clearly shows you are accepting Jesus' invitation to come to the wedding banquet.

As Priest: Consider yourself sent to invite others to the wedding banquet. Whom can you invite? How?

As King: To show you believe in God's power, attempt to change one thing in your environment (home, work, social) which fosters sin or diminishes the quality of life.

Twenty-Ninth Sunday of the Year

Whose Image Are We?

Isaiah 45:1, 4-6; 1 Thessalonians 1:1-5b; Matthew 22:15-21

The point of this story is that Jesus does not answer the question—an insincere one anyway. He does not give us here a neat answer about how we are to divide our loyalties between God and the government.

The First Commandment forbids dividing our loyalty between God and anything or anyone else. There is nothing which "belongs to Caesar" rather than to God. There is no action in life in which we can serve the government as if God were not involved. Any action which we cannot perform for God, as a service to God, we should not perform at all. "Hear, O Israel: The LORD is our God, the LORD alone. You shall love the LORD, your God with all your heart, and with all your soul, and with all your might" (Deuteronomy 6:4-5).

The Pharisees and the followers of King Herod were not asking whether it is moral to pay taxes to a government which is going to use them for immoral purposes. That is our modern question, but it was not theirs; Jesus' answer does not address that question. In this context Jesus' opponents are probably looking at money merely as something that benefits one's self, not as something to be used for social purposes. If so, they saw taxes just as money taken away from them, money which they could have used for their own security or enjoyment.

And so when Jesus asks, "Whose image is this on the coin?" and they answer, "The emperor's," he tells them, "Give therefore to the emperor the things that are the emperor's...." In effect, Jesus says that money is not that important and the things government is concerned about are not that important either. If money comes from the state, give it back to the state. Who cares?

We must remember that terms like *social action* and

social justice did not yet exist. The Jews had no say in how their taxes would be spent. They did not vote for their Roman rulers or have any say about how government might serve the people. Governments served the purposes of the ruler or the ruling class; those purposes, although they might have been more or less enlightened, did not look beyond the values of life in this world. For Christians, insofar as our own good is concerned, anything limited to this life alone is ultimately trivial. People who feel blessed to be poor, powerless and persecuted, as Jesus teaches in the Beatitudes, are hardly going to be excited about anything government can provide.

Poverty and oppression cannot harm those who follow the teaching of Jesus, because he gives "life to the full" in spite of these. But indifference to the poverty and oppression of others can harm Christians because there is no fulfillment in life except in union with God; and there is no union of mind and heart with God unless we share in God's passion for justice and mercy on earth. Injustice and indifference to the poor destroy God's image in us.

What Jesus asked about that coin he also asks about us: Whose image is this? What image do we bear? What image do we want to bear? God's or Caesar's? If we are dedicated first and foremost to being "loyal Americans," then our answer to Jesus' question is, "Caesar's!" If for all practical purposes we accept the goals of the state—that is, of human society—as ultimate, we say with those who first sent Jesus to the cross in our name, "We have no king but Caesar!"

We do not have to formally renounce our faith or declare the government superior to God in order to do this. We just have to put the goals of the state—our peace, prosperity, our liberty and the pursuit of our own happiness on this earth— ahead of the prosperity and even the lives of others. If, for example, we give to any government the authority to command us to kill other people for the sake of preserving our "national security," or any other earthly value, we have to ask very seriously about ourselves, "Whose image is this?"

Reflecting on This Week's Gospels

Twenty-Ninth Week of the Year

Pray daily: Lord our God, Father of all, guard us under the shadow of your wings and remove the blindness and fear that would separate us from your way. We ask this through Christ our Lord. Amen.

Monday: Luke 12:13-21. Someone said to Jesus, "Teacher, tell my brother to divide the family inheritance with me." He replied, "Friend, who set me to be a judge or arbitrator over you?" Do you pray mostly for health and material benefits or for help to know and love God more deeply?

Tuesday: Luke 12:35-38. Jesus said, "Blessed are those slaves whom the master finds alert when he comes." Are you specifically conscious of working for Jesus in every action of your life? How could you be?

Wednesday: Luke 12:39-48. Jesus said, "Who then is the faithful and prudent manager whom his master will put in charge...?" What has Jesus put you in charge of? What does it mean to be faithful? Prudent?

Thursday: Luke 12:49-53. "Do you think that I have come to bring peace to the earth? No, I tell you, but rather division!" What does Jesus mean by *peace* here? From whom does he divide us? Whose choice is that?

Friday: Luke 12:54-59. Jesus said, "And why do you not judge for yourselves what is right? Thus, when you go with your accuser before a magistrate, on the way make an effort to settle the case." How often do you accept what is legal as being moral? Do God and government have the same standards of morality? What is the basic difference between them?

Saturday: Luke 13:1-9. Some people told Jesus about the Galileans whose blood Pilate had mingled with the blood of their sacrifices. Jesus said to them, "Do you think that because these Galileans suffered in this way they were worse sinners than all other Galileans? No, I tell you; but unless you repent, you will all perish as they did." Are the state's enemies God's enemies? Does God kill God's enemies? If we kill ours, are we preventing or perpetuating violence?

Living This Week's Gospels

As Christian: Ask yourself what you expect the state to save you from. Does the state use means that Jesus refused to use? How can you refuse to cooperate with these?

As Disciple: List the three main means our government uses to accomplish its goals. Find something in the gospels Jesus says about each.

As Prophet: Say one time this week—by word or deed— that something the law allows is immoral. In the same way, challenge some illegal practice which people tend to accept by expressing (in word or action) your belief that this practice is also immoral.

As Priest: Do or say something to show you accept our country's enemies (or those who commit crimes) as children of God, as brothers and sisters by grace, as temples of the Holy Spirit.

As King: To show it is God you obey in everything, choose one law you find it difficult to observe—perhaps the speed limit—and follow it conscientiously as an act of loyalty to Christ.

Thirtieth Sunday of the Year

Religion Pure and Simple

Exodus 22:20-26; 1 Thessalonians 1:5c-10; Matthew 22:34-40

What are parishes all about, anyway? Why do you gather in church on Sunday morning with other people when you could be relaxing at home? Why do you contribute money to your parish's work when you could be spending it on yourself or on other causes? Every dollar you spend, every minute of your time you spend on anything, is a vote. When you spend time and money on your religion, what are you voting for?

Some might say, "It's an insurance premium for life after death; call it 'future life insurance.'" Others might say, "I just need this to get me through the week. It helps me cope with the things I deal with in my life—things like stress, temptations, loneliness and fear. Call it my 'moral and psychological fitness program.'" Others might say, "I need to get refocused. All week long I'm bombarded by secondary stuff. Every time the phone rings, the door opens or a commercial comes on, my attention is drawn to needs that are not fundamental, to values that are not my basic values, to objectives and goals that are not the real purpose of my existence. I just need to get back in touch with the real meaning of life, with the authentic truth that makes life meaningful and good. Religion is my 'existential compass.' I just need to look at it sometimes."

Others might just say, "Religion is the strongest force there is for preserving law and order and morality in this world. I support it the way I support good education and good government. It is something I need and society needs to keep life civilized on earth."

Although religion is all of these things, none of them is religion as Jesus taught it. For Jesus, most simply, religion meant loving God with all one's heart, soul and mind.

And since love seeks union, the more authentic our religion is, the more we will be like God in mind, will and heart, and the more we will love every member of the human race—not only as we love ourselves but as Jesus loves each person.

Today's reading from Exodus measures true love of neighbor by the stance we take toward aliens, widows, orphans and the poor—in other words, by the love and compassion we show to those we easily marginalize; those with whom we have no natural bonds through family or social grouping; those whom society tends to consider unimportant; those with whom, by cultural standards, relationship is not rewarding. This is to love as God loves.

The goal of religion—of Christ's religion—is to change and keep changing us, until we love God with all our heart, soul and mind, and love every other member of the human race as God loves.

After his visit to the tombs of Archbishop Romero and of the nuns, laywomen and Jesuits who were martyred in El Salvador, Archbishop Rembert Weakland said: "What set these people apart is that they stood for a kind of religion— a religious belief—that influences lives. Religion, for them, was not a case of obeying rules but of influencing lives—and that is very threatening to those who want to keep order. But if religion doesn't influence lives, why bother with it?" (Paul Wilkes, *The Education of an Archbishop*, Orbis Books, 1992).

If our religion simply makes us moral people or what our culture recognizes as "good Christians," we will not influence anybody as Jesus did (that is, bear witness, which is what the word *martyr* means). For that we have to accept those whom society does not accept, to help others in ways society would call exaggerated. In short, we have to be imitators of Christ, the Lamb of God, and put our bodies on the line daily, just as he offered his body to take away the sins of the world.

Reflecting on This Week's Gospels

Thirtieth Week of the Year

> *Pray daily: Praised be you, God and Father of our Lord Jesus Christ. There is no power for good that does not come from your covenant, and no promise to hope in that your love has not offered. Strengthen our faith to accept your covenant and give us the love to carry out your command. We ask this through Christ our Lord. Amen.*

Monday: Luke 13:10-17. When Jesus saw the woman who had been sick for eighteen years, he called to her and said, "Woman, you are set free from your ailment." Do you know anyone who is sick or wounded in any way? What can you do to help?

Tuesday: Luke 13:18-21. Jesus said, "[The kingdom of God] is like yeast that a woman took and mixed in with three measures of flour until all of it was leavened." What effect do you have on those around you? How do you leaven (lift up) their attitudes, values, spirits?

Wednesday: Luke 13:22-30. Jesus said, "Strive to enter through the narrow door." Why is a straight line the narrowest concept that exists? (Ask a mathematician.) What is the difference between "keeping in bounds" (broad or narrow) and directing every choice toward Jesus as imitators of Christ? Which is the "narrower" way?

Thursday: Luke 13:31-35. "Jerusalem, Jerusalem, the city that kills the prophets and stones those who are sent to it! How often have I desired to gather your children together as a hen gathers her brood under her wings, and you were not willing!" Why are people threatened by a religion that asks more than law observance? What more are you giving than obedience to God's laws?

Friday: Luke 14:1-6. Jesus said, "If one of you has a child or an ox that has fallen into a well, will you not immediately pull it out on a sabbath day?" Do you ever use your religion as an excuse for not helping people? For example, do you ever say, "The Church doesn't say I have to do this" when you feel you should do something?

Saturday: Luke 14:1, 7-11. Jesus said, "For all who exalt themselves will be humbled, and those who humble themselves will be exalted." In how many different ways could love call you to "humble" yourself?

Living This Week's Gospels

As Christian: Do one thing daily that expresses unambiguously that your whole religion, your entire life, is focused on growing in relationship with Jesus Christ. Daily Mass? Prayer time? A way of loving and serving others?

As Disciple: Read one Gospel through (or one chapter, if time is short), making a list of every reason you find for loving God.

As Prophet: Ask what actions or visible characteristics of your life-style have the most influence on others. How can you make sure that your actions bear witness to the values Jesus lived and taught?

As Priest: Offer yourself consciously with Jesus as Lamb of God before Communion, thinking about what this means in practice for your life. How can you "take away" the effects of sin in your world?

As King: Ask what influence your parish is having on your neighborhood or city. What can you do to make religion in your parish a love of God and others that has an impact on society?

Thirty-First Sunday of the Year

Jesus on Discipleship

Malachi 1:14b—2:2, 8-10; 1 Thessalonians 2:7b-9, 13;
Matthew 23:1-12

O ne key to understanding Jesus in the Gospels is to
realize that he teaches through examples, usually
leaving us to figure out the general principle behind
his examples.

One advantage to this method is that there is less danger
anyone will turn a specific example into a rule; Jesus worked
hard to keep his religion from being turned into a set of laws.
Instead of presenting rules, he gives concrete examples of
how we should act and lets us figure out the general
principles behind them.

Another advantage is that this method forces us
to think. If Jesus had laid down rules, we might just keep
them without thinking about them. But if we have only a few
examples of how we might act in particular circumstances,
then we have to figure out for ourselves the guiding principle
behind them. When we do this, we are beginning to think
like Jesus.

The best way to misunderstand this gospel passage is to
see it as a set of rules: "Christians should not use the titles
rabbi, teacher or *father*—or sit in the front seats in church
or the head table at banquets." Indeed, there are people who
actually do this: Every Catholic priest in the Bible Belt has
met some fundamentalist who very deliberately calls him
"Mister" because "The Bible says not to call any man
father." They usually are not consistent, since they use the
title for their own fathers—whom Jesus was actually talking
about since there were no Catholic priests around in his day,
and no one called priests "Father" until about nine hundred
years later. These same fundamentalists call their ministers
"Doctor"—another word for "teacher"—and rarely have a

problem about sitting at the head table during an awards banquet. But they still claim a gospel rule as the reason for not giving this particular title to priests.

It makes no difference whether a priest is called "Father" or not. But to see this gospel passage as a set of rules keeps the fundamentalists and everyone else from understanding Jesus' teaching here. He obviously meant, "Don't think that what the word *father* means to you—with all the obedience, reverence and loyalty it involves—applies only to your biological father. Your Father is God; God's will comes even before the desires of your own parents."

How many people would not think of becoming Catholics—even if they were drawn to it—because they "just couldn't do that" to their parents? How many Catholics have refused to think about a vocation to priesthood or religious life because their parents were opposed? And, most frequently of all, how many Christians, of all religions, have accepted and gone along with the standards of this world in their social life, choices of career or life-style because they just could not break with the values and life-style of their parents? These are the ones who are calling a human being "father" in exactly the way that Jesus rejects.

The underlying lesson of this passage is that, according to Jesus, discipleship means more than obeying a set of rules. We are not disciples of Jesus Christ unless we ponder his words, reflect on the example of his life, think about the examples he gives of ways that we should act, unless we try to arrive at the general principles, attitudes and values behind everything Jesus said and did. An authentic disciple of Jesus Christ must be a thinker—not necessarily an intellectual, but a thinker: someone who ponders what Jesus taught.

The alternative to studying and pondering the teaching of Jesus is to accept him, not as the Light of the world, our constant model and lifelong Teacher, but as the designer of another system of rules and practices to live by, called "the Christian religion." But then, once we have learned the system, we do not need the Teacher anymore. Those who focus on the system and follow it are disciples of the Pharisees. The disciples of Jesus must focus on his heart.

Reflecting on This Week's Gospels

Thirty-First Week of the Year

Pray daily: Lord, in giving us God as our Father you taught us not to love our fathers and mothers less, but to love them for what they are: our guides to learning how to love as sons and daughters of God. Help me to model for everyone the same love for God and for others that you modeled for us. Amen.

Monday: Luke 14:12-14. Jesus said, "When you give a luncheon or a dinner, do not invite your friends...or your relatives or rich neighbors.... [I]nvite the poor." Do you use your love for friends and family as a guide to the love you should have for all?

Tuesday: Luke 14:15-24. Jesus said, "Someone gave a great dinner and invited many.... But they all alike began to make excuses." Is God inviting you to more than you are accepting? What is your excuse?

Wednesday: Luke 14:25-33. "Whoever comes to me and does not hate father and mother, wife and children, brothers and sisters, yes, and even life itself, cannot be my disciple." Does Jesus mean these words literally? What does he mean? How does it apply to you?

Thursday: Luke 15:1-10. The Pharisees and scribes began to complain, saying, "This fellow welcomes sinners and eats with them." What kind of social distinctions did Jesus respect? Whom would you not invite to your table? Whom do you invite?

Friday: Luke 16:1-8. "[T]he children of this age are more shrewd in dealing with their own generation than are the children of light." Are there any principles of good business that you could profitably apply to the way you live out your religion? What do you do to make your business work? Would that help make your religion work?

Saturday: Luke 16:9-15. "No slave can serve two masters; for a slave will either hate the one and love the other, or be devoted to the one and despise the other. You cannot serve God and wealth." How many of your choices are influenced by the desire to make money? How many are influenced by the desire to help people? Do you experience any conflict between these in your work?

Living This Week's Gospels

As Christian: Put the numeral *1* somewhere where you will see it all day. Use it to remind you to serve God first in everything you do.

As Disciple: Figure out how much time during each day or week you are receiving input which reinforces the attitudes and values of our society. How much of the time are you hearing or being reminded of the attitudes and values Jesus taught?

As Prophet: Break free of the pattern our culture imposes on your life; change something in your daily schedule to allow time for reflection and prayer over the words of Jesus.

As Priest: Each day choose one person you deal with and ask, "How would I act if this person were my brother or sister?"

As King: Deliberately spend some of your money this week to help make this a better world to live in.

Jesus on Expectation

Wisdom 6:12-16; 1 Thessalonians 4:13-18; Matthew 25:1-13

When we really want something we look forward to it, we prepare for it. We make sure we do everything necessary to make it happen. Think of the care you have put into studying for an exam, packing for a trip, dressing for a special occasion or arranging a party for someone you love.

High school teachers notice that once graduation is near the seniors begin to get concerned about their grades. They start studying more because their minds are on graduation, college or future jobs. They have been working toward graduation for four years, but it did not motivate them before because they were not actually looking forward to it. But once the preparations make it real to them, they realize it is something they really want.

As long as we do not look forward to something, we do not appreciate it very much. And we do not prepare for it. Usually we do what appeals to us at the moment, not thinking ahead. Then when we have lost the opportunity to do something great, we feel stupid. The only explanation we can give is the one a truck driver gave from a hospital bed after he took his hands off the wheel to slap a wasp in his truck's cab: "It just seemed more important at the time!"

Saint Thomas Aquinas described wisdom as the habit of looking at everything in the light of our last end. The wise or sensible person is the one who evaluates everything—every option, every decision and choice—in the light of what life is all about: the final goal of life, the ultimate purpose of existence. And this goal, of course, is ecstatic union with God and with the rest of the human race in love forever in heaven.

At the moment of death, described in this Gospel as the moment when the bridegroom arrives to celebrate the wedding, this final goal, this ultimate purpose of our lives will be very important to us. But right now we think about it very little. Like graduation, heaven is a very abstract concept while it remains a remote possibility. And it will remain remote as long as we are not actually preparing for it. But most of us do not make much preparation for heaven. We tend to think there will be time to think about that later on. Then suddenly we find ourselves at the end of our lives, having made little or no effort to "know, love and serve God" perfectly, and all the things we have wasted our time on seem of no importance at all. And the only explanation we can give for placing business, pleasure or the development of body and mind ahead of development of our spiritual lives will be, "It just seemed more important at the time."

I think I have been guilty, as I am sure other priests have been, of understating the demands of the Kingdom of God. None of us wants to put a guilt trip on anyone or make religion into a burden. Therefore we make suggestions—I do, anyway—such as, "Wouldn't it be nice to read Scripture every day?" or "It would be really helpful to go to Mass daily if you can." I am beginning to think I am guilty of misrepresenting the love of Jesus Christ.

A man passionately in love does not suggest to his beloved that it would "be nice" for them to marry, or to pour out their souls to each other in conversation or to give themselves totally in love to each other as husband and wife. And Jesus Christ is not casual about wanting to share his mind and heart with us through his word, and wanting to give us his Body and Blood daily in the Eucharist. He did not offer himself casually on the cross for us, hoping that occasionally—weekly or perhaps even more frequently—we might remember his act of love and let its meaning sink in a little more deeply. He gave himself passionately for us and he wants us to long for him passionately, and express our love for him passionately at every moment of our lives. This is what it means to "keep oil in our lamps": to long for Jesus as the Bride longs for the Bridegroom.

Reflecting on This Week's Gospels

Thirty-Second Week of the Year

Pray daily: Lord, keep me aware that you are coming to bring me into the fullness of life and joy. Show me how, day by day, in concrete ways, I can make things ready for your coming. Keep me constantly aware that I am waiting and preparing for you. Amen.

Monday: Luke 17:1-6. "The apostles said to the Lord, 'Increase our faith!'" How often do you say this? Faith in what? If Jesus wanted to increase your faith, what would he suggest you do?

Tuesday: Luke 17:7-10. Jesus said, "...[W]hen you have done all that you were ordered to do, say, 'We are worthless slaves; we have done only what we ought to have done!'" What do you do that goes beyond religious obligation?

Wednesday: Luke 17:11-19. Jesus asked, "Were not ten made clean? But the other nine, where are they?" Only one man cured of leprosy expressed the gratitude he felt. How important is it to express to God what you believe, desire and choose? How often do you express gratitude?

Thursday: Luke 17:20-25. Then Jesus said to his disciples, "The days are coming when you will long to see one of the days of the Son of Man, and you will not see it." What do you really think Jesus is offering you? How seriously do you take his invitations and warnings?

Friday: Luke 17:26-37. "They were eating and drinking, marrying and being given in marriage, until the day Noah entered the ark, and the flood came and destroyed all of them." What do you take most seriously in life? What in your actions reveals this?

Saturday: Luke 18:1-8. "And yet, when the Son of Man comes, will he find faith on earth?" By *faith* does Jesus just mean people who go to church and recite the profession of faith sincerely? What does it mean to really believe in Jesus Christ and his teachings?

Living This Week's Gospels

As Christian: Sit down and imagine what your life would be like without money. Without your family. Without the work you do. Without alcohol. Without Jesus. What do your reactions tell you?

As Disciple: In a rough way, calculate how many hours you have spent learning how to fit into life in this world and how many you have spent learning how to fit into life in the next world. What if, when you die, religion is still not something you enjoy?

As Prophet: Decide on some action that would be a very concrete way to "provide oil" for the light of faith, hope and love within you. Then do it.

As Priest: Think of some people you know who are apparently not doing much to provide oil for their lamps. Could you suggest a way you might help one another to seek this oil together?

As King: At Baptism we received a lighted candle and were told to keep it burning brightly until Christ comes. What in your environment tends to blow it out or weaken its light? What can you do to change that?

Thirty-Third Sunday of the Year

Jesus on Responsibility

Proverbs 31:10-13, 19-20, 30-31; 1 Thessalonians 5:1-6;
Matthew 25:14-30

The whole point of this Gospel is that Jesus expects us to do something for the salvation of the world. What he expects of us is determined by the particular gifts and talents we have. In other words, we are "responsible"—that is, we will be required to "answer"—for the way we use what we have in order to help others know and serve God.

This may be shockingly new to us! Many of us are accustomed to think that all we are obliged to do as Christians is avoid sin and fulfill whatever other duties the Church has seen fit to make a rule about. For example, most Catholics would assume they are not obliged to go to Mass more than once a week since the law of the Church requires Mass only on Sunday. They would be shocked to hear that for some people, to go to Mass only on Sunday might be a serious failure in responsibility.

Suppose you were the only person in the world on close enough terms with the presidents of two hostile countries to be able to persuade one or both of them to pull back from the brink of war. Do you think you would have a responsibility —that you would be obliged in conscience—to make whatever sacrifice might be needed to prevent the war? And if you said, "I am too busy right now" or "I just don't have the money to spend on a trip like that," and war did break out, would not every soldier and civilian killed in the war have the right to rise up from the grave and say to you, "This is your fault. My blood is on your hands"? If you could have prevented the war—or even had a good chance of being able to prevent it—and did not try, would that not be a serious lack of responsibility?

Is it farfetched to say that we Catholics, who know

God and who know that Jesus Christ is offering himself every day on the altar for the salvation of the world, have a serious responsibility to go to him and pray seriously for peace? If you are more than just a nominal Christian or a Catholic, if you are an active Catholic, a Christian blessed with a strong faith and instructed about what the Mass really is, do you not have a greater responsibility to pray for peace than someone who is lukewarm or spiritually ignorant? And if we Catholics, who *could* pray in union with Jesus in the Mass, do not pray, and do no prevent wars by prayer, does not every man and woman, every invalid, aged person and child who is going to be bombed and burned to death in war have the right to rise up from the grave and say to us Catholics, "My blood is on your hands. If you had filled the churches and prayed for peace, I would not have died!"?

The threat of war is only one example. We live in cities where lives are being ruined by drug abuse; where lives are destroyed by murders every year; where there are terrible pockets of poverty and thousands of people who suffer from the even greater poverty of not knowing God, who are "unchurched." We live in cities where there is still racial division, even without segregation; where there are old people not being visited, living in loneliness day after day. We live in a country in which thirty-seven percent of the girls and twenty percent of the boys now under eighteen either have been or will be sexually abused before their eighteenth birthday; a country in which two women a day die violently at the hands of their husbands. Since World War II our country has been militarily involved in more than one hundred countries; during that same time more than a quarter of a million people have died in wars. Does this not call for some kind of response—for some kind of fervent, extreme response—from those who believe in God?

We all need to take stock of the gifts we have received from God: gifts of faith, gifts that can be used for Christian witness and ministry, the gift of knowing how to pray. And we need to ask what is required of us, what our responsibilities are in our times. If we take the gospel seriously, we have no choice about this.

Reflecting on This Week's Gospels

Thirty-Third Week of the Year

> *Pray daily: Lord, you have entrusted to me the treasure of your grace, your truth, your love for the world, your mission. Do not let me squander my life by letting my gifts go unused. Inspire me, act in me to bring about the peace and unity of your Kingdom on earth. Amen.*

Monday: Luke 18:35-43. A blind man was sitting by the roadside near Jericho, begging. After they told him that Jesus of Nazareth was passing by, he shouted, "Jesus, Son of David, have mercy on me!" How are you crying out to Jesus? Are you helping others by it?

Tuesday: Luke 19:1-10. "[Zaccheus] was trying to see who Jesus was, but on account of the crowd he could not, because he was short in stature." What keeps you from seeing Jesus? What extraordinary things have you done to turn that obstacle into a blessing?

Wednesday: Luke 19:11-28. "I tell you, to all those who have, more will be given; but from those who have nothing, even what they have will be taken away." What gifts do you have to use in God's service? If you think you have none, how can you discover what they are?

Thursday: Luke 19:41-44. As Jesus drew near, he saw Jerusalem and wept over it, saying, "If you, even you, had only recognized on this day the things that make for peace! But now they are hidden from your eyes." Is Jesus weeping over you?

Friday: Luke 19:45-48. Jesus entered the Temple area and proceeded to drive out those who were selling things, saying, "It is written, 'My house shall be a house of prayer'; / but you have made it a den of robbers." What are you choosing to do that reveals your body as a house of prayer and temple of the Holy Spirit?

Saturday: Luke 20:27-40. "Those who belong to this age marry and are given in marriage; but those who are considered worthy of a place in that age and in the resurrection from the dead neither marry nor are given in marriage. Indeed they cannot die anymore...." What is important in a Christian marriage? What is unimportant? What difference does being married or not married make?

Living This Week's Gospels

As Christian: At Baptism you "offered your body as a living sacrifice to God." At the Offertory of the Mass, tell God again that wherever your body is, you will be sacrificed to doing God's will and work.

As Disciple: Read Romans 12:6-8 and 1 Corinthians 12:7-12. Write down what you perceive to be your gifts.

As Prophet: Pick out your greatest talent, what you most have to offer at work or for your family and friends. Ask how you can use that gift explicitly and consciously to promote the reign of God.

As Priest: Identify one gift God has given you and use it consciously to minister to someone each day this week.

As King: What is it that you and you alone can do for the reign of God because of your particular talents, your job, the special time and place where you are, the particular challenges you face or solutions you see? Assume your responsibility and act with faith, hope and love.

Christ the King

Ezekiel 34:11-12, 15-17; 1 Corinthians 15:20-26, 28;
Matthew 25:31-46

This Gospel invites us to think ahead to the day when we will be present before Jesus in his glory, seated on his royal throne. When we see him, not just as Savior or Teacher but also as King, how will we feel?

We celebrate this feast in order to prepare for that day: to recognize now that Jesus is King of the universe and our King, to reflect seriously on how we can acknowledge his kingship in our lives.

Kings ask service. We recognize Jesus as King by devoting ourselves to what he wants to accomplish on earth. As members of a parish, we accept Jesus as King by participating actively and consciously in the shared mission he has entrusted to us. And how do we do this?

In a down-to-earth manner, Jesus says that the way to acknowledge him as King is through our use of material things (such as feeding the hungry, clothing the naked) and through our use of time (visiting the sick and imprisoned). And from the parable of the talents in last week's Gospel we can add the gifts we have received from God, beginning with the gift of our faith. In a word, we acknowledge his kingship over us by employing in his service everything we have received from him: our lives, our gifts, our possessions. All is his because everything comes from him and is given us to be used to continue his mission on earth.

This is something to ponder seriously. Our God became flesh. God did not show his love for us just "spiritually." Jesus offered his body and his blood. He came to earth and lived a very poor and human life. He spoke to us; he revealed his heart to us through physical, human actions: through choices about how to use material things, about what to do with his body, how to spend his time, how to use his own gifts and power in the concrete circumstances of his own time and place, responding physically to the people he met and to the situations in which he found himself.

And that is what he asks us to do: to recognize him as King, not just in thoughts and words but also in actions. He tells us in today's Gospel that we do not acknowledge his kingship in our lives unless we do it through physical gestures, by putting our time at his disposal, using our gifts and talents to continue his mission, giving him priority over our material possessions.

I once spoke to a fund-raisers' convention about the spirituality of fund-raising. I told the man who invited me that it was a little out of character for me since I have an emotional block against asking people to give money. He said, "Do you have a block against asking them to read Scripture? To pray? To fast?" "No," I said, "because those things benefit their souls." "Well," he answered, "the three traditional acts of devotion in the Scriptures are prayer, fasting and almsgiving. All three help us to grow in grace. Why do you omit almsgiving? Jesus didn't."

Although I still have the same emotional block, at least my theology is now clear! The fact is, we probably reveal our priorities, our values, our selfishness or our love, our faith or our lack of faith more often and more consistently through our use of money and material things than in any other way. The Church constantly urges people to *pray* (daily Mass!) and to *fast* at particular times or for special purposes. In today's Gospel Jesus urges us to give radical expression, through our use of money and possessions, to our faith in him as King. Do we really believe that everything we own comes from him and belongs to him? If so, how radically, how concretely, will we express this? This Gospel invites us to be concrete: to sit down and take inventory of all we have, deciding how we will use it to acknowledge Christ as King.

Reflecting on This Week's Gospels

Thirty-Fourth Week of the Year

Pray daily: Almighty and merciful God, you break the power of evil and make all things new in your Son Jesus Christ, the King of the universe. May every creature in heaven and on earth serve your majesty and praise you without end through Christ our Lord. Amen.

Monday: Luke 21:1-4. When Jesus noticed a poor widow putting in two small coins, he said, "Truly I tell you, this poor widow has put in more than all of them." Would Jesus say that everything you own is used in some way for the service of God?

Tuesday: Luke 21:5-11. While some people were speaking about how the temple was adorned with costly stones and votive offerings, Jesus said, "As for these things that you see, the days will come when not one stone will be left upon another; all will be thrown down." How can you use your money to do good that will last forever?

Wednesday: Luke 21:12-19. "You will be hated by all because of my name. But not a hair of your head will perish." What do you fear most? If you are loyal to Christ as King, can anything that happens on earth truly harm or destroy you?

Thursday: Luke 21:20-28. "Now when these things begin to take place, stand up and raise your heads, because your redemption is drawing near." Every time you read of crimes and catastrophes, what can you do to remind yourself that Jesus is Lord and that he has in fact triumphed over all evil?

Friday: Luke 21:29-33. "Heaven and earth will pass away, but my words will not pass away." What in your life shows that you believe this? How much attention do you give to God's words compared to other people's words? How much time do you spend reading or hearing the Scriptures?

Saturday: Luke 21:34-36. "Be on guard so that your hearts are not weighed down with dissipation and drunkenness and the worries of this life, and that day catch you unexpectedly." More than anything else, what distracts you from the reality of God, from your life's real purpose or from preparing to meet Jesus Christ at death?

Living This Week's Gospels

As Christian: Write up a formal contract, deeding over to Christ as King all your time, possessions, skills and abilities. See how you feel about signing it.

As Disciple: Read the Preface for the Feast of Christ the King and reflect on it.

As Prophet: Develop the habit of bowing your head every time you hear the name of Jesus spoken, whether it is spoken with reverence or not.

As Priest: Kings are responsible for their subjects. In the name of Christ, minister with kindness to someone around you who needs it.

As King: Formally accept responsibility from Jesus for working to make everything in the world conform to his law of love. Then decide what you are actually able to work on here and now.

Note: You will need to check the Liturgical Calendar on page x to find out what week of the year follows Trinity Sunday this year. Once you know which week it is, you can find the weekday Gospel reflections after that week's Sunday Gospel reflection. For example, if the week following Trinity Sunday is the Ninth Week of the Year, then locate the Ninth Sunday of the Year and the weekday reflections for the Ninth Week will follow.

SOLEMNITIES OF THE LORD

During the
Season of the Year

Trinity Sunday (Sunday After Pentecost)

"That Everyone Who Believes..."

Exodus 34:4b-6, 8-9; 2 Corinthians 13:11-13; John 3:16-18

God sent his Son, not "that we might have life," but "so that *everyone who believes*" might have eternal life. Even while rescuing us, God respects us. In the act of redeeming human nature wounded by sin, he uses the human nature he created. Jesus came "that everyone who believes" "might not die but might have eternal life."

John wrote, "And this is eternal life, that they may know you, the only true God, and Jesus Christ whom you have sent" (John 17:3). Eternal life is knowing and believing in the God whom Jesus preached: the God who revealed himself to Moses as "merciful and gracious, slow to anger, and abounding in steadfast love and faithfulness" (Exodus 34:6).

When John wrote the Good News of Jesus Christ, he picked up these two theme words which appear together repeatedly in the Hebrew Scriptures: *hesed*, which we translate as "steadfast love," "kindness" or "grace"; and *emet*, which we translate as "faithfulness," "fidelity" or "truth." The 1970 edition of the New American Bible translated them together as "enduring love" (see John 1:17). Eternal life, according to John, is to know God as the God of "enduring love." Jesus came that "everyone who believes" in this God of kindness and faithfulness, this God of enduring love, might have eternal life. The key is: "everyone who believes."

God did not "send the Son into the world to condemn the world." This doesn't mean that Jesus does not denounce sin. There would be no greater condemnation of the world than for God to write off human nature as hopeless and therefore accept any human behavior as the best that can be expected from poor, miserable creatures like us. On the contrary, Jesus revealed God as a God of mercy and compassion so that we might extend mercy and compassion to one another. Jesus showed us God's love lifted up to the height of self-giving on the cross; Jesus commanded us to "love one another as I have loved you" (John 15:12). He came "that everyone who believes" may have eternal life in love.

To love as Jesus loves is hard for us because we think everything about us is so important. And, in truth, we are more important than we can even dream of, but no particular thing about us is important enough to fight over. Jesus showed us God's love carried to the depths of humility when he "did not regard equality with God / as something to be exploited, / but emptied himself, / taking the form of a slave" (Philippians 2:6). Jesus accepted the reality of human nature. He took flesh, and was born in nakedness and poverty, in human vulnerability, to unite us with himself. And everyone who believes must do the same.

Jesus came down to us, he met us where we were—in our woundedness, in our need. He did not let our rejection of him or our sins against him keep him from coming to us, from offering us the hand of friendship. But he *requires us to believe*—to recognize, to decide, to accept the love he offers us—and to offer it to one another. "This is eternal life": to know God's self-abasing love revealed in Jesus Christ *and to believe* that in his emptying of himself for us and in our emptying of ourselves for one another, we come to life in its fullness.

Truth revealed took flesh in Jesus Christ. Truth received must take flesh in all those who believe. "Everyone who believes" is commissioned to bear prophetic witness to the grace of our Lord Jesus Christ by embodying in human words and actions the divine life of God's Son, the life present in his Body on earth. "Everyone who believes" is consecrated a priest to mediate the love of God to others, to take on the priestly office of expressing constantly the life-giving, nurturing love of the Father, to be the channel through which the Father continues to give life to the world.

Finally, "everyone who believes" is sent as a *steward of Christ's kingship* to bring everything in heaven and on earth together into unity in the "fellowship of the Holy Spirit"—

so that "they all may be one.. so that the world may believe" and "everyone who believes may have eternal life."

Note: You will need to check the Liturgical Calendar on page x to find out what week of the year follows Trinity Sunday this year. Once you know which week it is, you can find the weekday reflections after the article on that week's Sunday Gospel. For example, if the week following Trinity Sunday is the Ninth Week of the Year, then locate the Ninth Sunday of the Year and the weekday reflections for the Ninth Week will follow.

Body and Blood of Christ (Corpus Christi)

Flesh That Gives Life

Deuteronomy 8:2-3, 14b-16a; 1 Corinthians 10:16-17;
John 6:51-58

When Jesus took bread and wine at the Last Supper, preparing to say the words which would transform them into his Body and Blood and establish the sacrament of Eucharist forever, he knew he was bringing to fulfillment a thousand-year promise. In the desert, centuries before, God had fed his people with a strange food that rained down from heaven. The people called it *manna*, which means, "What is this?" (see Exodus 16:15). This was the preview of an even more mysterious food from heaven, which Jesus was now preparing to give: his flesh for the life of the world.

The Eucharist is a clear sign of an incomprehensible reality. The mystery it speaks is beyond our understanding, but the blessing it promises is obvious to the smallest child. The greatest genius could not explain the Eucharist, but only a fool would fail to make use of it. Even while our wondering hearts repeat, "What is this?," we are able to "taste and see that the LORD is good" (Psalm 34:8).

We need not understand the Eucharist fully to receive it, but we must receive Eucharist to appreciate it. The Eucharist is given to be experienced. Those who receive it frequently will recognize it for what it is: Jesus' flesh for the life of the world:

Eucharist is available to all who believe;

Eucharist is experience for all who receive.

The promise implicit in the manna was made explicit by Jesus when he said, "I am the living bread that came down from heaven. Whoever eats of this bread will live forever; and the bread that I will give for the life of the world is my flesh." The meaning is clear: Jesus is food. His body is food that gives life. And the life his body nourishes in us will continue forever. "Just as the living Father sent me, and I live because of the Father, so whoever eats me will live because of me." The Eucharist is the living Body of Jesus given to us as food: his flesh for the life of the world.

Jesus added: "Those who eat my flesh and drink my blood abide in me, and I in them." Eucharist is interpenetration. It is union. It is closeness. It is sharing in the thoughts of Jesus Christ, in his desires, in his passion to be one with us, to be united to us. It is an embrace of love. In Eucharist Jesus gives us his body, his flesh, to penetrate our being, to expand our hearts, to fill us with his life and make us one with him. In Eucharist Christ says to us, "Open your inmost self to me, receive me, take me into your body, be one with me, surrender to my passion, let down your defenses, abandon yourself to unrestrained union with me, give yourself to me as I am giving to you, receive my body, be my body, eat my flesh and be my flesh—my flesh for the life of the world!"

We receive Eucharist in the context of celebrating the passion of Jesus Christ: the passion in which he delivered himself to torture and death for us that we might have life in an ecstasy of joy with him, with the Father, the Spirit and with all who have given themselves to be Christ and be "in Christ" forever. But our ecstasy comes from his agony; our possession of God from his surrender to men. In the Eucharist we celebrate life through death, conquest through surrender, total fulfillment through total abandonment. Before we receive Jesus in Communion, we are invited to unite ourselves with Jesus, "the Lamb of God," offered for the sins of the world; to offer ourselves with him and in him "so that sins might be forgiven;" to offer ourselves in love to friends and enemies alike; to offer ourselves in vulnerability and defenselessness that all divisions might be overcome; to die as many grains of wheat to become one bread; to unite ourselves to him in his act of love on the cross and to give our flesh with his: one body, one flesh, for the life of the world.

Note: *You will need to check the Liturgical Calendar on page x to find out what week of the year follows the Feast of the Body and Blood of Christ this year. Once you know which week it is, you can find the weekday reflections after the article on that week's Sunday Gospel. For example, if the week following the Feast of the Body and Blood of Christ is the Ninth Week of the Year, then locate the Ninth Sunday of the Year and the weekday reflections for the Ninth Week will follow.*

Friday of Second Sunday After Pentecost
Sacred Heart of Jesus

Deuteronomy 7:6-11; 1 John 4:7-16; Matthew 11:25-30

"All things have been handed over to me by my Father; and no one knows the Son except the Father, and no one knows the Father except the Son and anyone to whom the Son chooses to reveal him." To know the Father as the Son does, how deeply, how intimately united to the Son must we be?

OTHER SOLEMNITIES and FEASTS

Which Replace Sunday

February 2 • Presentation of the Lord

Presenting Jesus, Gifts, Us

Malachi 3:1-4; Hebrews 2:14-18; Luke 2:22-40

As Jesus was presented in the Temple, we present
ourselves every time we celebrate Mass together.
At the Presentation of the Gifts, when the bread
and wine are brought up and placed on the altar, we are
brought up. We are placing ourselves on the altar.

In some Protestant churches, especially during
revivals, the preacher invites people to come forward after
the preaching and accept Jesus as their Savior or give
themselves to Jesus. It is a moment of choice in response to
the word of God. And it is an adult choice: All who come up
are declaring their faith personally and choosing as adults to
live in relationship with Jesus Christ.

In the custom of the altar call the Protestants have
kept, in a modified way, that moment of the Mass that we
call the Offertory, which begins when the bread and wine
are brought up and placed on the altar. Like the Catholic
Offertory, the Protestant altar call takes place after the
Scripture readings and preaching. And, like the Offertory,
it expresses a personal, adult response. But there are
some differences.

In the Catholic celebration, it is taken for granted that
everyone who is participating in the eucharistic celebration
has already been consecrated and made one with Jesus Christ
by Baptism—and is, in fact, a priest, offering Jesus to the
Father and offering himself or herself in Christ for the life of
the world. Just to remind ourselves of this, we have restored
an ancient custom: During one phase of the *Rite of Christian
Initiation of Adults,* we ask all those who are preparing for
Baptism to leave Mass before the Preparation of the Gifts.
This is to make the point that in order really to participate in
what takes place in the Liturgy of the Eucharist, one has to

be—not just in intention but in fact—a "priest in the Priest," made one with Jesus by Baptism.

That is why we don't invite just a few people, those who have not yet done so, to come up and accept Jesus. The whole congregation has already accepted Jesus in Baptism. What we do is invite all present to reaffirm their Baptism, to recommit themselves by sending up the bread and the wine as symbols of themselves to be placed on the altar and changed into the Body and Blood of Christ. As we do this we express our participation in everything that will be expressed in the offering of the bread and wine during the rest of the eucharistic sacrifice. "Pray, brothers and sisters in Christ, that our sacrifice will be acceptable...." And the people answer, "May the Lord accept the sacrifice at your hands"—the sacrifice we make of ourselves in union with Jesus Christ. We offer ourselves with him and in him, as his real Body on earth.

The offering we make of ourselves by placing ourselves on the altar under the form of bread and wine has a very precise meaning. It is not just an act of accepting Jesus in general as our Savior, or of giving ourselves to Jesus in some vague way. In the Offertory we join ourselves to Jesus precisely and explicitly to be offered with him as Lamb of God. By identifying ourselves with Jesus offered in the Mass, we identify ourselves with everything he did and expressed on the cross.

We die to ourselves and to sin to live in Christ. We go down into the grave with Christ as we went down into the waters of Baptism and we rise with him, leaving all our sins behind, to live a new life on earth. In Paul's words (see Romans 12:1-2), we offer our bodies as a living sacrifice to God. This means that wherever our bodies are, we are sacrificed, offered, committed to doing whatever Christ wants to do through us. We live now, no longer for ourselves, but that Christ may live through us. We live for his mission.

June 24 • Birth of John the Baptist

Luke 1:57-66, 80

"Fear came over all their neighbors, and all these things were talked about throughout the entire hill country of Judea." How, as a community, do we nurture in each other awe at God's working in each person and in the Church?

June 29 • Peter and Paul, Apostles

Matthew 16:13-19

He said to them, "But who do you say that I am?" What do your actions say Jesus is for you?

August 6 • Transfiguration of the Lord

Matthew 17:1-9

"...from the cloud a voice said, 'This is my Son, the Beloved; with him I am well pleased; listen to him!'" If you had seen this vision and heard these words, would you be doing anything more to "listen" and learn from Jesus? What?

August 15 • Assumption of the Blessed Virgin

The Triumph of Human Vulnerability

Revelation 11:19a, 12:1-6a, 10ab; 1 Corinthians 15:20-27;
Luke 1:39-56

All three readings for the Feast of the Assumption
celebrate God's victory over sin and death, over all
that is evil and life-diminishing for the human race.
And all three emphasize the role that human nature, in all its
weakness, plays in this victory.

A woman "crying out in the pangs of childbirth" is the
image of total helplessness and awesome power. On the one
hand, nothing can stop the birthing process; she must
surrender to it, cooperate with it or die. On the other hand,
through the weakness of her flesh, through the surrender of
her body to the inevitable, she is going to accomplish the
greatest thing any human person can do: She is going to
bring a human being to life. This is an exercise of power
unsurpassed in human existence.

This is the image God chose to express the reality of the
Church on earth. On the one hand, we are as helpless and
vulnerable as a woman in labor, undergoing pain, suffering
from the resistance of our own flesh and from the opposition
of the world around us as we labor to "bring Christ to full
stature" (see Ephesians 4:13). On the other hand, we are
actually bringing about God's presence in human flesh on
earth and establishing the reign of God in human affairs.

The Assumption—the taking up of Mary's body
into heaven that exempted her from the disintegration of the
grave—is a sign and preview of the triumph of fragile human
flesh over all that threatens our existence on earth. It is
God's assurance to us that these bodies of ours, so vulnerable
to sickness, injury and death, will share in the resurrection
of Jesus. Jesus rose as the "first fruits" of a human race
delivered from the power of sin and death. His resurrection

is a sign that God has given to him all "sovereignty, authority and power," that the reign of God will be realized. Mary's assumption is a sign that the human race will share—in body as well as in soul—in his victory and his heavenly glory, just as we have shared in the weakness and humiliation he accepted on earth.

The human race came under the power of sin and death when a man and a woman, Adam and Eve, freely chose to sin. Jesus broke this power by freely choosing as God to become a member of this sinful race and by freely surrendering himself to death. But he chose to become human only through the free surrender of a woman who agreed to give him flesh—and who, standing under the cross, accepted with him to endure the birth pangs again as her heart was torn open with his flesh and the human race reborn. Mary had to be under the cross. And she had to be there, not just as a spectator, but actively offering her Son to the Father for the life of the world. She had to join him in his act of priesthood and offer him as he offered himself, just as all of us do at Mass. She had to take part.

The Assumption, by proclaiming the share human beings have in the Resurrection of Jesus, also proclaims the share human beings have in the redeeming work, the sacrifice of Jesus. Like Mary, all of us who have "offered our bodies as a living sacrifice to God" in Baptism have agreed to give flesh to Jesus on earth. We have consented to become his Body so that he may continue in us his human presence in the world, and through our actions continue his ministry. Like Mary, we are called to embrace his way of redeeming the world through vulnerability, through human powerlessness, through sacrifice and the offering of ourselves for others in love—especially for those who violate our rights, oppress us and kill us. Like Mary, we have agreed to give our bodies, our "flesh for the life of the world," so that in us Jesus may continue to live and act, to give himself up to death in love, to redeem the world.

Mary triumphed through surrender. In celebrating her Assumption we celebrate the triumph of fragile humanity, of vulnerable human flesh, over all the death-dealing power of this world and over all those who claim the authority to direct the course of human affairs in disassociation from God. With Mary we celebrate freedom from all fear of death. We proclaim the greatness of the Lord, for he who is mighty has done great things, even through the lowliness of his servant. Holy is his name!

September 14 • Exaltation of the Cross

John 3:13-17

"Indeed, God did not send the Son into the world to condemn the world, but in order that the world might be saved through him." How can you respond to people who annoy you in a way that saves and does not condemn?

We Are All Saints

Revelation 7:2-4, 9-14; 1 John 3:1-3; Matthew 5:1-12a

The word *saint* comes from the Latin word for "holy" (*sanctus*), but it doesn't mean what we may take it to mean. We think that a "holy" person is a virtuous person, someone who seldom if ever sins. But the real meaning of *holy* is "consecrated, set aside, separated from the ordinary."

God is the "holy of holies," the absolutely Holy One, because God is by nature separate, apart, different from everyone and everything—while at the same time close to and most intimately involved with everyone and everything. God is in a category all his own—or more accurately, God is not in any category; God just is. There is God and, on a completely different level, there is everything else.

The Jews were holy because God chose them and set them apart to be his special people: "For I am the LORD who brought you up from the land of Egypt, to be your God; you shall be holy, for I am holy" (Leviticus 11:45). The sabbath observance was a reminder of this: "You shall keep my sabbaths, for this is a sign between me and you throughout your generations, given in order that you may know that I, the LORD, sanctify you" (Exodus 31:13).

Because the Church is the continuation of the chosen people, Saint Peter calls us "a chosen race, a royal priesthood, a holy nation" (see 1 Peter 2:9). We are holy as a Church, however, not only because God has set us apart for special relationship, but also because this relationship is a sharing in God's own divine life by grace. God has joined us to the divine self by making us members of the Body of Christ, "the high priest, holy, blameless, undefiled, separated from sinners, and exalted above the heavens" (see Hebrews 7:26). By Baptism we have "become Christ." And so we are holy—different, set apart, consecrated—as he is holy.

Jesus came down to earth to be one of us, like us in every way except sin. Jesus,

> though he was in the form of God,
>> did not regard equality with God
>> as something to be exploited,
> but emptied himself,
>> taking the form of a slave,
>> being born in human likeness.
> And being found in human form,
>> he humbled himself,
>> and became obedient to the point of death—
>> even death on a cross.
> Therefore, God also highly exalted him
>> and gave him the name
>> that is above every name,
> so that at the name of Jesus
>> every knee should bend,
>> in heaven and on earth and under the earth,
> and every tongue should confess
>> that Jesus Christ is Lord
>> to the glory of God the Father (Philippians 2:6-11).

We proclaim in the *Gloria* of the Mass, "For you alone are the Holy One, you alone are the Lord, you alone are the Most High, Jesus Christ...." But now God has made us holy in Christ. By Baptism we were "separated" from this world; we died to it in Christ and we came back into it as his risen Body to continue what he came to do—or, better, to let him continue it in us. Saint Peter constantly calls the members of the Church "the holy ones" and urges, "as he who called you is holy, be holy yourselves in all your conduct; for it is written, 'You shall be holy, for I am holy'"(1 Peter 1:15).

That is what we are. We have been set apart and consecrated through union with Jesus Christ to do his work in the world. That is why we must live his life in the world; live it as he lived it. Those whom we celebrate as "saints" are simply those who have shown us in every age—in every walk of life, and under every set of circumstances—how to do this.

In the Beatitudes Jesus gives us a thumbnail sketch
of the mindset we need to live as Christ. The only way to
understand the Beatitudes is to see them as the attitudes and
values of those who are holy—set apart and consecrated to
be different from what is considered normal on earth. For
people who take life on earth at face value, it is definitely
not a blessing to be poor, sorrowing or persecuted. The meek
don't inherit the earth; they lose it to the strong and ruthless.
And those who go to work every day hungering and thirsting
above all for uprightness, seeking purely the kingdom of
God, will probably not have their pockets filled at the end
of the day.

But they are being filled—with all the fullness of God.
They are receiving what they have been set apart to receive,
because they are giving what they have been set apart to
give. And it is one and the same thing: the life of God, life
in abundance, life to the full. That is what Jesus came into
this world to give.

November 2 • Commemoration of
the Faithful Departed (All Souls)

John 6:37-40
"This is indeed the will of my Father, that all who see the
Son and believe in him may have eternal life; and I will raise
them up on the last day." Does God desire your salvation
more than you do? Does Jesus? How do you know this?

November 9 • Dedication of the Lateran Basilica

John 2:13-22
"Making a whip of cords [Jesus] drove all of them out of
the Temple, both the sheep and the cattle... [He said] 'Take
these things out of here! Stop making my father's house a
marketplace!'" How much respect do you have for church
buildings as such? Why? How do you personally show
respect when you are in church?

FEASTS and SAINTS' DAYS

January 25 • Conversion of Paul, Apostle

Mark 16:15-18

"And these signs will accompany those who believe: by using my name they will cast out demons;...and if they drink any deadly thing, it will not hurt them." Have I seen people who live by Christ's teachings exposed to our culture's corrupting influences without being harmed by them?

February 22 • Chair of Peter, Apostle

Matthew 16:13-19

When Jesus went into the region of Caesarea Philippi, he asked his disciples, "Who do people say that the Son of Man is? ...Who do you say that I am?" How would you answer that question? What is Jesus for you? God? Friend? Teacher? Leader? Spouse? How do you usually relate to Jesus?

March 19 • Joseph, Husband of Mary

Matthew 1:16, 18-21, 24a

"Now the birth of Jesus the Messiah took place in this way. When his mother Mary had been engaged to Joseph, but before they lived together, she was found to be with child from the Holy Spirit." Joseph agreed to have no sexual relations with Mary, his true wife, for as long as he lived. It was his contribution to saving the world. Do you think it was worth it? How are the sacrifices in your life the price you pay for helping to save the world? Is it worth what it costs you?

March 25 • The Annunciation of the Lord

Luke 1:26-38

"And now, you will conceive in your womb and bear a son, and you will name him Jesus." Do you believe you are called as truly as Mary was to conceive thoughts in your head through the seed of Christ's word, and bear fruit by giving them flesh in action? How do you open yourself to his words?

April 25 • Mark, Evangelist

Mark 16:15-20

"And they went out and proclaimed the good news everywhere, while the Lord worked with them and confirmed the message by the signs that accompanied it." Is this a description of your life? How are you exercising priesthood?

May 3 • Philip and James, Apostles

John 14:6-14

"Very truly I tell you, the one who believes in me will also do the works that I do and, in fact, will do greater works than these, because I am going to the Father." What are the "works of Jesus" that you do as his priest?

May 14 • Matthias, Apostle

John 15:9-17

"I have called you friends, because I made known to you everything I have heard from my Father." How do you recognize someone's friends? Is it obvious you are Christ's friend?

May 31 • Visitation

Luke 1:39-56

Elizabeth said to Mary, "And blessed is she who believed that there would be a fulfillment of what was spoken to her by the Lord." What divine promises to you do you find hard to believe? See Matthew 21:22 and John 15:16.

June 11 • Barnabas, Apostle

Matthew 10:7-13

"As you go, proclaim the good news, 'The kingdom of heaven has come near.' Cure the sick, raise the dead, cleanse the lepers, cast out demons." Which of these actions is an example of acting as prophet? As priest? As king?

July 3 • Thomas, Apostle

John 20:24-29

Then Jesus said to Thomas, "Put your finger here and see my hands. Reach out your hand and put it in my side. Do not doubt but believe." In how many ways has Jesus met you more than halfway when you had little faith?

July 22 • Mary Magdalene

John 20:1-2, 11-18

"Jesus said to her, 'Mary!' She turned and said to him in Hebrew, 'Rabbouni,' (which means Teacher)." What name does Jesus use when he talks to you? What name do you use when you talk to him? Why?

July 29 • Martha

Luke 10:38-42

"Martha, Martha, you are worried and distracted by many things; there is need of only one thing. Mary has chosen the better part, which will not be taken away from her." What worries distract you from God? How could these unite you to God?

August 10 • Lawrence, Deacon and Martyr

John 12:24-26

Jesus said, "Those who love their life lose it, and those who hate their life in this world will keep it for eternal life." What are you willing to do to other people in order to preserve your life? Your livelihood? Your standard of living?

August 24 • Bartholomew, Apostle

John 1:45-51

"Nathanael said to [Philip], 'Can anything good come out of Nazareth?' Philip said to him, 'Come and see.'" What external signs did Jesus use to show people he was important? What did he not use?

September 8 • Birth of Mary

Matthew 1:1-16, 18-23

"When his mother Mary had been engaged to Joseph, but before they lived together, she was found to be with child...." How many people in Nazareth judged Mary for being pregnant before marriage without asking her any questions? What would they have learned if they had?

September 15 • Our Lady of Sorrows

Luke 2:33-35

"Then Simeon blessed them and said to his mother Mary, 'This child is destined for the falling and the rising of many in Israel, and to be a sign that will be opposed....'" How much opposition would you experience if, every time you heard anyone criticized, you spoke about the Christian call to forgive and to love?

September 21 • Matthew, Apostle and Evangelist

Matthew 9:9-13

"As Jesus was walking along, he saw a man called Matthew sitting at the tax booth; and he said to him, 'Follow me.' And he got up and followed him." In everything you do, are you most aware of yourself as being a disciple and follower of Jesus?

September 29 • Michael, Gabriel and Raphael, Archangels

John 1:47-51

"Nathanael replied, 'Rabbi, you are the Son of God. You are the King of Israel!'" Do you really believe that everything Jesus teaches is a way to greater happiness and fulfillment, even on this earth? What follows from this?

October 2 • Guardian Angels

Matthew 18:1-5, 10

Jesus said, "Whoever becomes humble like this child is the greatest in the kingdom of heaven." Do you believe you will be happier by becoming humble (having no more prestige than a little child) or by becoming important? Why?

October 18 • Luke, Evangelist

Luke 10:1-9

Jesus said, "Whatever house you enter, first say, 'Peace to this house!'" In your dealings with other people is peace with mutual understanding and affection your first priority? What do you focus on first?

October 28 • Simon and Jude, Apostles

Luke 6:12-16

"And when day came, [Jesus] called his disciples and chose twelve of them, whom he also named apostles." *Disciple* means "learner." *Apostle* means "one who is sent." Which are you? What visible actions in your life show you are each of these?

November 30 • Andrew, Apostle

Matthew 4:18-22

"Immediately they left the boat and their father, and followed him." How is following Jesus different from just keeping God's law? What are you willing to leave to follow him more closely?

December 12 • Our Lady of Guadalupe

Luke 1:38-47

Elizabeth cried out, "Blessed are you among women, and blessed is the fruit of your womb." How are you blessed? How does your life bear divine fruit?